P9-CLZ-941

# Chapter 1 GET READY!

Shaking with excitement, a lone angler sat on the boat's deck and forced himself to calm down. Surrounding his boat in the crystalline water swam the cause of his excitement, hundreds of big tarpon. Composure regained, he stood up and presented his fly to one of the giants. The tarpon obliged, and the biggest fish of his life was on the end of his leader.

Florida rightly owns a heady reputation as a fly fishing destination. The glamour species (bonefish, permit, and tarpon) get a lot of press, but there are oh, so many other opportunities for saltwater fly rodders. Redfish probably keep more guides working than any other species. They hit flies readily and exceed thirty pounds in some areas. Seatrout populations in many parts of the state have unfortunately hit an all time low, but they can still be caught and they also like flies. With the net ban now in effect, watch for a strong comeback from these fish! Snook make an exceptional fly rod target, and commonly reach double digit weights. Cobia, black drum, ladyfish, jack crevalle, Spanish mackerel, bluefish, sharks, and even flounder, all take well presented flies.

Offshore aficionados find plenty of fly fishing opportunities, too. Exciting fisheries for blackfin and yellowfin tuna exist in the Keys and elsewhere. Kingfish and wahoo, pelagic species of sharks, sailfish, and of course the always cooperative dolphin are all taken regularly by knowledgeable fly rodders.

A fishing trip to Florida, like a fishing trip to anywhere, requires planning in order to maximize the chances for success. Unlike fishing trips to wilderness or overseas destinations, Florida anglers can readily find and purchase overlooked tackle needs. Information on fish and fishing spots is easily obtained. Fine fly shops sprout like mushrooms across Florida's urban landscapes.

This chapter takes a look at various aspects of planning a trip to Florida, or within Florida for those who are Florida residents. Topics covered in this section include tackle and accessories; boats and boating; finding and hiring guides; and hazards and safety concerns for Florida's saltwater angler.

## What Tackle?

### RODS

Rod choice for any fishing depends on what flies you like using and what you hope to catch. Someone casting small glass minnow patterns for seatrout in a Panhandle creek wouldn't need the same gear as a potential tarpon tamer on a Homosassa flat. You must also consider your own skills as a caster and a fish fighter.

For day-in, day-out fishing for redfish, snook, bonefish, and seatrout the best choice for most folks would be a nine foot, eight- or nine-weight rod. This stick has plenty of power to push large flies into the wind, be they streamers or surface baits like poppers or hair bugs. Unfortunately it overpowers most of the seatrout we find here nowadays, but it has the strength to stop a tarpon up to fifty pounds (or larger, in skilled hands).

Good casters might increase their sport by dropping to a seven-weight, or even a six-weight, depending on fly size and the anticipated fish. Remember though that in Florida's saltwater, a fish much larger than anticipated could show up at any time.

I won't recommend specific brands or manufacturers, but almost any rod costing more than $150.00 perform well. Before running off to purchase the latest high-tech wonder from the trendy rod companies, remember those famous words of Lefty Kreh - "most rods cast a lot better than the people using them."

Having gone through all of the above, should a different rod besides the basic 7-8-9-weight be needed for any specific type of fishing or fish, that point will be made in the specific section that deals with that particular fishery.

## REELS

The "old standby" for years for saltwater use was the Pfleuger Medalist 1498. It has adequate line capacity, will not immediately self-destruct in saltwater, has a rudimentary drag system, balances well on an eight-or nine-weight rod, and is inexpensive enough (about fifty dollars) to be considered a starter reel. All types of saltwater critters have been caught with the Pfleuger, and plenty of them still give good service. Other legendary saltwater fly reels include the venerable Fin-Nor and the classic Seamaster.

The past few years have seen the market for saltwater fly reels has simply explode. Valentine, Ross, Scientific Anglers, Lamson, Orvis, and STH all manufacture reels in the $150-250 price

*A selection of fly reels suitable for saltwater use. From left:: Pflueger Medalist 1498, the Valentine reel, Scientific Anglers System 2, and the Fin-Nor.*

range. These reels are quality pieces of equipment with good drag systems, and provide as much reel as most anglers ever need.

For the person who wants the best, get out the wallet and take a look at reels like the Fin-Nor, the Billy Pate, or the Abel. There are several manufacturers of premium fly reels, all of whom ask plenty for their products. These reels are made for those who take pleasure in owning the finest, and will last for several lifetimes with a modicum of care. Regardless of the reel you get, make sure it balances properly with the rod!

## LINES
*"Oh, what a tangled web we weave..."* -Sir Walter Scott, <u>The Lay of the Last Minstrel</u>

The number of specialty fly line types on the market rapidly approaches mind-boggling proportions. Most anglers fishing Florida need to purchase a weight-forward, floating line first. A saltwater or bass bug taper works well for general use.

While some manufacturers want you to believe that without a bonefish taper you can't catch a bonefish, the fish don't care what type of taper you use. If you spend the majority of your fishing time bonefishing, the bonefish tapers work wonderfully. An angler throwing hairbugs at seatrout near St. Augustine in November will likely find that these bonefish tapers simply become too stiff in the cooler temperatures to work well.

Not all Florida fly fishing occurs in shallow water. Certain circumstances require lines other than floating types. Surf casting comes to mind. When casting streamers from a beach an intermediate sinking line often performs better than a floating line. The line sinks beneath the wave action, giving the angler a better feel for where the location of the fly and what it is doing.

Another example? Sight fishing for tarpon in the Keys, or along the west coast. The fish often travel in water 10 or 12 feet deep. They might never see a fly cast on a floating line, but an intermediate sinking type pulls the fly down to their level.

Yet another example would be fishing in canals or at power plant outflows during the winter. The fish sometimes huddle together in incredibly tight masses right down on the bottom. A sink-tip or even a high density shooting head gets the fly down to the fish. They usually eat it! A floating line keeps the fly near the surface and is completely useless in either of these situations.

The moral of this tale clearly is that a fly fisher who intends to be prepared for all contingencies will have floating, slow sinking, and fast sinking lines available, and will not hesitate to change lines when the situation dictates.

Regardless of the line you choose, fill the reel as full as possible by adding backing underneath the fly line. For saltwater, backing is important for fighting the fish. A fly line is only about 90 feet long, and most sizeable saltwater fish pull that much line off in just a few seconds. Attach the backing, usually 20 pound test Dacron for an eight- or a nine-weight, at the rear of the fly line. Then a big fish can continue its run without coming up abruptly against the end of the line.

The strongest way to attach backing to fly line entails whipping a loop in the end of the line. Tie a Bimini twist in the backing. Simply loop the two together. A correctly looped connection resembles a square knot. This connection further has the advantage of making line changes on a single spool relatively easy. Just unloop one line off and loop on the next!

How much backing do you need? As much as you can fit on the reel. The line should just brush the pillars with all the line wound onto the reel.

For smaller fish on lighter tackle, 20 pound Dacron is standard. For bonefish you need 150 to 200 yards of this. If you've got enough for bones, you'll be able to handle most anything that comes along that you would tackle with a 7-, 8-, or 9-weight rod.

For big tarpon, or sailfish or other offshore species, you need more and heavier backing. Two hundred fifty to 300 yards of 30 pound dacron is standard for tarpon, and offshore more is better. Special reels are available for offshore fly fishing which will hold 500 or even 600 yards of 30 pound Dacron. These reels are enormous and expensive, but if you hook a big yellowfin tuna without one you'll be out of the game within seconds.

One other word about backing- the new braided, high tensile strength lines offered by several manufacturers may make Dacron obsolete, at least as backing for big game fish. Thirty pound braid has the diameter of eight pound mono, so any given spool can hold two to three times as many yards of the braid as Dacron- an obvious advantage when a 150 pound yellowfin tuna heads for the African coast. The braided line has almost no stretch, either. Doug Hannon told me he rolls tarpon over at 100 yards when using this braid. I've heard from other anglers that the small diameter and low stretch of this material can cause severe cuts if you touch it carelessly while it's under tension. Be forewarned.

## LEADER SYSTEMS

We all know that the most important link between any fisherman and the fish he seeks is the hook. In most saltwater fly fishing a sharp hook seldom fails. Typically, the critical link between the fish and the fly fisherman is the leader. You will find the leader involved in most fly tackle system failures. Let's examine different types of leader systems for saltwater applications.

The first item of business is the line-to-leader connection. Presented here are three different ways of making this connection. Be advised others exist.

Use the nail knot for the fastest line-to-leader connection. The monofilament leader material digs into the finish of the fly line and holds it securely. Covering the knot with a tapered layer of Pliobond allows it to slip easily through the guides. This method is entirely adequate for the lighter rod weights (lower than about seven weight), but when using heavier tackle sufficient pressure on the knot can cause the finish of the fly line to peel off of the core, leading to system failure and a lost fish.

Orvis manufactures a hollow braided line-to-leader connector which works on the Chinese finger puzzle principle. The end of the fly line is shoved into the hollow connector for two or three

*Leaders or leader sections can be pre-tied, then placed in labelled ziplock bags. The bags can be stored in a fly vest packet and the sections tied on when needed.*

# FLYRODDING FLORIDA SALT-

## *How and Where to Catch Saltwater Fish on Flies in the Sunshine State*

## by Captain John A. Kumiski

*ARGONAUT PUBLISHING COMPANY*
*MAITLAND, FLORIDA*

DISCARD

Front cover art by **Bill Elliott**.
Front cover design by **Barry Kent**.

Fla.
799.16
Kum

# Flyrodding Florida Salt-
How and Where to Catch Saltwater Fish on Flies
in the Sunshine State

BY **CAPTAIN JOHN A. KUMISKI**

Published by:
> **Argonaut Publishing Company**
> **P.O. Box 940153**
> **Maitland, FL 32794-0153 U.S.A.**

All rights reserved. No part of this book may be reproduced or transmitted in any form or means, electronic or mechanical, including photocopying, recording, or by any information storage and retrieval system without written permission of the author, except for the inclusion of brief quotations in a review.

Copyright ©1995 by John A. Kumiski
First printing 1995
Printed in the United States of America

**Publisher's Cataloging in Publication Data**
Kumiski, John A., 1952-
   Flyrodding Florida salt: how to find and catch saltwater fish
on flies in the Sunshine State / by John A. Kumiski.
   p. cm.
   Includes bibliographical references and index.
   Preassigned LCCN: 95-79622
   ISBN 0-9635118-1-5

3. Florida — Saltwater
Fly fishing — Guidebooks

   1. Saltwater fly fishing--Florida--Guidebooks. 2. Florida--
Guidebooks. I. Title.

SH483.K86 1995                799.1'6614
                                     QBI95-20152

## TABLE OF CONTENTS- Section One, How-to

Introduction
## CHAPTER 1- GET READY!
Rods, 10
Reels, 11
Lines,12
Leader Systems, 14
Accessories, 20
Knots, 20
Waders and Wading Gear, 30
Boats, 31
Guides, 35
Hazards and Safety,37
## CHAPTER 2- ANGLING TECHNIQUES
Searching for and Finding Fish, 42
Sight-fishing, 44
Blind-casting, 49
Teasers and Teasing, 50
Wading, 52
Chumming, 57
Fighting Fish, 60
Handling Fish, 64
## CHAPTER 3- THE FISHES, 65-103
An alphabetized discussion of all of the popular fly rod
gamefish, including habits, habitats, and tricks used to take
them, starting with barracuda and ending with tuna.
**Fish/Tackle/Fly Quick Reference Chart**, 104


## Section Two, Where-to
Introduction, 105
EAST COAST
-Jacksonville, 106
-St. Augustine, 111
-Daytona/New Smyrna, 115
-Titusville, 121
-Cocoa/Melbourne, 126
-Sebastian, 131
-Stuart, 136
-Palm Beach/Ft. Lauderdale, 141
-Miami, 145
-Flamingo, 150

## Section Two, Where-to, continued
THE KEYS
-Upper Keys, 154
-Middle Keys, 158
-Lower Keys, 163
WEST COAST
-10,000 Islands, 168
-Naples, 172
-Sanibel/Captiva Islands, 176
-Boca Grande, 180
-Sarasota, 185
-Tampa/St. Pete, 189
-Homosassa, 195
-Cedar Key, 201
-St. Marks, 205
-St. Joseph Bay, 210
-Panama City, 214
-Destin/ Ft. Walton Beach, 219
-Pensacola, 224

## Section 3- Flies for Florida Salt
-Fly Selection, 229
-Tying the Flies, 233
-Tying a Double Mono Loop Weedguard, 235
-Clouser Deep Minnow- Bob Clouser, 236
-Hair Bugs, 237
-Bolstad Foam Flies- Sheldon Bolstad, 240
-Surfin' Wooley- John Bottko, 241
-Fuzzy Crab- John Kumiski, 243
-Rattlin' Minnow- Tom Jindra, 244
-Seaducer- Homer Rhodes, 247
-Lefty's Deceiver- Lefty Kreh, 249
-Rabbit Strip Flies, 251
-The Snapping Shrimp- Chico Fernandez, 253
-The Braided Cuda Fly, 255
-Cockroach Tarpon Streamer, 257

**Last Word**, 259

APPENDIX
Commercial Fly Tiers, 260
Fly Tackle Manufacturers and Suppliers, 262
Fly Fishing and Conservation Groups, 267

**Index**

**Resource Catalog**, 282

# WARNING-DISCLAIMER

This book is designed to provide information in regard to the subject matter covered. It is not, and was never intended to be, a substitute for good judgement or common sense. The reader ventures into or onto the water at his or her own risk.

Every effort has been made to make this book as complete and as accurate as possible. However, there may be mistakes both typographical and in content. Therefore, this book should be used only as a general guide and not as the ultimate source of boating or fly fishing information.

The purpose of this book is to educate and entertain. The author and Argonaut Publishing Company shall have neither liability nor responsibility to any person with any loss or damage caused, or alleged to be caused, directly or indirectly by the information contained in this book.

# ACKNOWLEDGEMENTS

This book would never have happened without the cooperation and help of literally dozens of people. My wife Susan was a
tremendous help, encouraging me, making many suggestions for
improvements, and herding the boys while I wrote. My great friend
Ken Shannon once again provided excellent proofreading and
editing suggestions, and helped underwrite the project.

Many anglers, writers, artists, and manufacturers also
helped by supplying artwork, photographs, and/or technical information. Artist extraordinaire Bill Elliott provided the cover art and
supplied many photos. The incredibly talented Barry Kent designed
the front cover. Bob Huttemeyer, Walt Jennings, and Captain Mike
Holliday also supplied photos. Mike Fine´ at Stren Fishing Lines
supplied most of the line art, and Pete Barrett at the Fisherman
Library Corporation allowed my use of the drawings of the Hufnagle
knot from my Saltwater Fly Fishing book. Bert Green at Universal
Map Enterprises, 1120 E. Colonial Drive, Orlando, FL, graciously
granted permission to use the map of Florida appearing on p. 106.

Thanks must also go to Rick and Bob Czesnakowicz at
Progressive Communications Incorporated in Apopka, Florida
for their help and tremendous service in preparing the photographs
for the text. Your assistance is deeply appreciated, gentlemen!

Suggestions for improvements came from some of the best
known and most respected names in saltwater fly fishing: Ed
Jaworowski, Lefty Kreh, Boyd Pfeiffer, and Lou Tabory.

But the folks who really made the book were the interviewees,
mostly guides but others who are simply extremely knowledgeable
saltwater fly fishers. They are Captains: Lee Baker, Frank Bolin, Joy
Dunlap, Jim Dupre, J.R. Fairbanks, Gregg Gentile, Todd Geroy,
Bob Gray, Pete Greenan, John Guinta, Paul Hawkins, Steve Huff,
Steve Kantner, Tommy Locke, Mike Locklear, Joe McNichols, Bill
Miller, Phil O'Bannon, Flip Pallot, Terry Parsons, Nat Ragland, Ron
Rebeck, Mike Rehr, Rodney Smith, Ben Taylor, Mike Ware, Jim
Weber, and Jose Wejebe. Other interviewees are: Paul Darby,
Warren Hinrichs, and John Underwood.

I am grateful and deeply indebted to each and every one of
you, for without your cooperation and information this project would
never have reached fruition.

# INTRODUCTION

Dear Reader,

You've picked up this book because you need information about fly fishing in Florida's saltwater. You need to know what tackle to use. You need to know how to rig that tackle. You need to know what techniques work, and which ones do not. You need to know some fly patterns that are effective, and how to tie them. You need to know, probably more than anything else, where to go to find Florida's great saltwater gamefish.

This book contains all that information, and MORE!

In 1982 I found myself in exactly the predicament described above. I had just moved to Florida from Massachusetts, and knew nothing about fly fishing in saltwater, especially Florida's saltwater. There was no guidebook available to help me figure things out. Fortunately I met many great anglers, some of whom took a liking to me and showed me the ropes. In only five years or so I started to get the hang of things.

This book is designed to help shorten that learning curve!

The book is divided into three sections and has an appendix. The first section has three chapters. The first dicusses tackle, the second techniques, and the third has sketches of most of the species you are likely to encounter while fishing in Florida salt.

The second section contains the results of interviews with dozens of top flyfishing guides from all sections of the Florida coast. In these interviews they share information on access, types of fishing available, best times of the year, favorite spots and flies, and a great deal of little known how-to information.

The third section discusses fly selection and contains detailed descriptions on tying locally important fly patterns. What you will find are some of the classic saltwater patterns like the deceiver and the seaducer, and some more more modern patterns like John Bottko's Surfin' Wooly, or Sheldon Bolstad's Foam Diver, or my own Fuzzy Crab.

Lastly, the appendix is a resource probably worth the price of the book in itself. Florida fly tiers (phone numbers and addresses included), suppliers of fly fishing tackle and fly tying equipment, a listing of Federation of Fly Fishers affiliated clubs in Florida, and of course an index are all included here.

The Florida coastline is about 1500 miles long. No one individual could possibly know it all, and no single book could possibly cover every inch of it. So I haven't tried. What I have done is to pinpoint easily available, and sometimes not well known, fly fishing opportunities from all over the Sunshine State. I want anyone to be able to visit any area in Florida with or without a boat, fly tackle in hand, and find an hour, or a day, or a week of quality fishing.

Try the book on for size, and let me know how it helps you. I welcome your corrections, comments, criticism, and of course praise, too! I love good news, especially when I helped make it happen! I'm available at (407) 834-2954, or P.O. Box 940153, Maitland, FL 32794-0153.

Good luck fly fishing in Florida's great saltwater!

Your new fishing buddy,

Captain John A. Kumiski

inches and then cemented into place with superglue. Pulling on the looped end of the connector causes the braid to dig tightly onto the finish of the fly line. Again, this is fine for the lighter rod weights.

The strongest but most time-consuming method of attaching line to leader involves making a loop-to-loop system. One way to do this is to make a loop in the end of the fly line by stripping off about a quarter inch of the coating of the line and doubling it back on itself. Then, use fly tying or rod wrapping thread in a bobbin and wrap the loop the same way you'd wrap a rod, leaving the end of the loop open. Cement the finished wrap with superglue and the coat it with Pliobond. You can then easily connect the looped end of the leader butt to the fly line.

For those who prefer, several brands of both knotless and knotted tapered leaders for saltwater are on the market. Climax offers some, as does Umpqua. If you don't want to make your own, try these ready-made leaders.

Also, a new leader material has recently been introduced, called fluorocarbon leader material. The fluorocarbon has an index of refraction close to that of water, making it more difficult to see while in the water. It's also more dense than water, so it sinks readily. The manufacturers claim it has better knot strength and more abrasion resistance than nylon, and my own tests verify the latter claim. Need I say it costs much more than nylon? Several companies offer fluorocarbon leader material, and it's certainly worth giving a try.

For those who prefer tying their own, the basic leader design is the tapered leader without a shock tippet. This works fine for nonabrasive species of fish, such as bonefish, permit, redfish, and seatrout. The basic formula for the tapered leader is 60-20-20, that is, 60 percent butt, 20 percent taper, and 20 percent class tippet. It's important to realize that this is only a starting point. Experiment with this until you get the desired result.

So, a typical ten foot bonefish leader for a seven through nine weight system consists of six feet of 30 pound test, a foot of 20, a foot of 15, and two feet of 10, with all the sections joined by blood or double surgeon's knots. Remember that leader length is a compromise and must be adjusted to suit conditions. Longer leaders spook fewer fish but cause more problems when casting, particularly with large or wind-resistant flies. Again, experimentation produces the best results.

If we wanted a leader for permit with a ten or eleven weight system we would increase the butt section to 40 pound test. The

*When a tarpon goes tailwalking, you'll want your leader system to hold!*

larger diameter of the fly line would call for a larger diameter monofilament in the butt of the leader. Then our taper section would consist of a foot of 20, a foot of 17, and lastly two feet of 14 pound for the tippet. Bigger fish, bigger flies, bigger system.

What about fish with abrasive mouths? A shock tippet at the business end of the system becomes a necessity. Use 30 pound shock for snook, ladyfish, and baby tarpon, 100 pound shock for large tarpon, and single strand wire for sharks, bluefish, or barracuda. Every addition requires changes in the basic leader system.

When adding a 30 pound mono shock tippet, it should be 10 to 12 inches long. For those interested in IGFA regulations for record, the shock tippet must be less than 12 inches long including the knots. Yoy can attach the class tippet to the shock by a variety of methods. Again, for those interested in records, the class tippet must be at least 16 inches long excluding the knots.

The standby for years used to attach shock to class tippets has been the Albright special. You can use other knots, including the double surgeon's knot and the Hufnagle. All of these knots permanently (we hope, anyway!) attach the shock leader to the class tippet.

Another method which can be used in place of a permanent attachment is a loop to loop system. Pre-tie shock tippets to the flies and keep them all on a leader stretcher. Use a double surgeon's loop to tie a loop in the end of the shock tippet opposite from the fly. Use a Bimini twist to put a short doubled line in the end of the class tippet and tie a loop in it, using a double surgeon's loop. Then just loop the shock tippet to the class tippet.

Although this is a good system and makes changing flies a snap, it isn't IGFA standard. If you don't care about records this won't bother you, but you can't carry a leader stretcher very easily while you wade. So you may want still another method.

Tie a short doubled line in the class tippet by using a Bimini twist, then attach the doubled class tippet to the shock using a Hufnagle knot. You'll find these a pain in the neck to tie while up to your butt in water, so tie up several the night before going fishing, carefully coil them, and put them in a labelled ziplock bag. When a shock tippet gets too short from changing flies, cut off the class tippet, take out a new one with the shock already attached, and tie it to the leader with a double surgeon's knot. Tie the fly back on, and you're back in business.

Finally, some anglers prefer simplicity. Tie the shock directly to the class tippet by using either an Albright special or a double surgeon's knot. Try all of these methods and simply use the one that works best for you.

When using a wire trace for toothy critters, attach the wire

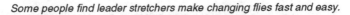

*Some people find leader stretchers make changing flies fast and easy.*

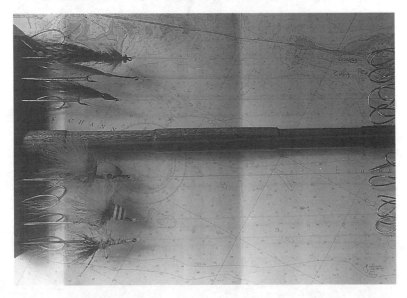

(#2 or #3 single strand) to the fly with a haywire twist. Attach the other end of the wire, which should be three or four inches long, to a short piece of 30 pound mono with an Albright special. You then join the shock tippet to the class tippet by whatever means you like.

One thing to keep in mind is that adding any of this stuff to the far end of the leader usually makes casting more difficult. You may need to shorten your leader until it becomes comfortable again.

Finally, the big game leaders used for big tarpon or billfish add a whole new dimension. Lines for tarpon typically are from ten to twelve weight, and for offshore work from twelve to fifteen weight. Leader butts usually consist of about four feet of 40 or 50 pound mono. Both ends of the butt section have loops formed by a double surgeon's loop. One end is looped to the fly line, the other to a specially prepared 16 pound (or 12 pound, or 20 pound) class tippet, to which is tied the shock.

One may wonder how a 150 pound tarpon could possibly be landed with a 16 pound test tippet. I once watched a demonstration by Captains Nat Ragland and Lee Baker where they attached a ten pound mushroom anchor to a 16 pound class tippet rigged as though they were tarpon fishing. The leader was attached to the fly line, which ran onto a reel mounted on a thirteen weight fly rod. In other words, a normal thirteen weight tarpon fishing rig was used.

Several grown men in succession, myself included, stood

*A tarpon box holds up to three dozen pre-rigged flies and leaders without tangling.*

on a table and tried using the rod to lift the anchor off of the floor. With all our strength we could barely move the anchor, and in fact it was the rod that finally broke, not the tippet. It was very enlightening. All saltwater fly fishers should try it sometime.

Anyhow, prepare the 16 pound class tippet by doubling the line at each end with a Bimini twist. Remember, IGFA rules state there must be at least 16 inches between the knots for record consideration. At one end, make a loop with a double surgeon's knot. Loop this end to the leader butt. At the far end, attach the 12 inch long 100 pound shock tippet with either the Albright or the Hufnagle, whichever you prefer.

Typically, tarpon leaders are made up ahead of time with the flies already tied on. The shocks are kept straight and the leaders organized in a leader stretching box that will hold as many as three dozen flies and leaders without making any tangles.

All the above presupposes the use of a floating or an intermediate fly line. What about going deep by using a sink-tip line or a high density shooting head?

In deep water the splash of the line as it hits the water doesn't spook the fish. Since you want to get the fly down, use a short leader. A long leader allows the fly to ride up well above the level of the line. Short in this situation means only two or maybe three feet, nothing more.

You sacrifice delicacy of presentation here but with the fish deep this won't be important. Although some folks just use a section of 20 or 30 pound mono looped to the end of the fly line, I suggest you make sure that the tippet's breaking strength is less than that of your backing. Your system's weakest component will then be the leader. If something breaks, it will be the tippet. You won't lose the expensive fly line.

Some last words on leader construction- fluorescent sections can be tied into the leader during its construction to give increased visibility to it while casting. This comes in handy when fishing against mangrove shorelines or other dark backgrounds.

Use the same type of leader material throughout your leader. If you use a stiff mono then a limp mono, and go back to a stiff section, the leader will not turn over properly. To help the loop make it the whole way to the fly, keep the sections made from the same material.

Remember to lubricate your knots before you pull them up (use saliva), pull them up slowly, and if they don't look right, break and re-tie them. If you don't, you can be sure a big fish will.

## ACCESSORIES

Fly fishing seems to attract folks who love gadgets. Manufactuers respond by offering scads of them. This section only discusses those items considered essential, leaving convenience items out of the picture.

You need a good pair of fishing pliers, preferably with a wire cutter. Manley pliers have long been popular with Florida anglers. Abel and API market exquisite tools designed to last a lifetime. My own preference is the Leatherman tool. Since we're fishing the salt, stainless steel simply works better.

You absolutely must have and use a good hook file. The best hook sharpening devices for saltwater hooks are carbon steel files, about four inches long. Unfortunately, these rust like crazy so prepare to purchase several every year.

Delay the inevitable by making a holster for your file. Get a piece of corrugated cardboard and wrap it around your file. Cut it to size, then place it in a small polyethylene bag like those flies come in. Soak the cardboard with three-in-one oil, silicone spray, WD-40, or some combination of these. Wrap duct tape around the bag, and your holster is complete. Keep the file in its holster when not sharpening hooks and it will last much longer.

A stripping basket comes in very handy for surf fishing or wading in weedy places. When I wanted to know more about these I called John Bottko, owner of the Salty Feather Fly Shop in Jacksonville, since he fishes the surf a lot. John said that he finds carrying a small stripping basket just as inconvenient as carrying a big ones, so get the biggest one you can find. He also said that a Rubbermaid laundry basket works as well as any commercially available basket if the bottom had a LOT of holes drilled in it. I followed his advice, hanging my basket off my waist with an old belt.

When I wade out too far, wave action in my basket tangles the line. Commercially made baskets have projections which stick up from the bottom, designed to hold the line in place. Lefty Kreh told me it's easy to hot glue projections made from weed wacker string into the bottom of a laundry basket. If you find line tangling in your stripping basket bothering you, give this a try.

### KNOTS

Every fly fisher will have a love-hate relationship with knots. He'll love some and hate others, some of whose use unfortunately cannot be avoided.

Saltwater fly fishers should know how to tie the following knots: Bimini twist; double surgeon's knot; Albright special; Hufnagle knot; improved clinch knot; Uni-knot (Duncan loop); and the haywire twist. Tarpon and offshore fishers should be able to snell a hook, too. Illustrated instructions for all of these knots follow, along with notes for their most appropriate uses.

### Improved Clinch Knot

Use this easy to tie knot to use when tying a fly directly to a class tippet (no shock tippet).

1. Pass tag end of line through the eye of the hook. Double back and make five turns around the running line. Thread the tag end through the first loop above the eye of the hook, then through the big loop as shown.

2. Wet the knot, then pull the running line to tighten the coils. Take care that the coils are in a spiral, not overlapping each other. Pull the knot up TIGHTLY, then trim tag end close to the knot.

### Uni-Knot

This knot, known by some as the Duncan loop, can be used for a variety of applications. Vic Dunaway, expert angler, former editor of "Florida Sportsman" magazine and author of numerous books on fishing, has developed a system in which the Uni-knot can be varied to meet most knot-tying needs in salt water fishing. See Vic Dunaway's Complete Book of Bait, Rigs, and Tackle for details.

Use this knot to make a looped connection between the fly and the shock leader. The loop allows the fly to swing freely, giving it much more freedom of movement and better action, especially when a heavy shock leader is used.

1. Run the line through the eye of the hook at least six inches and fold back to make two parallel lines. Bring the end of the line back in a circle towards the eye of the hook.

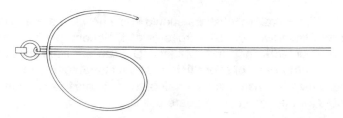

2. Make four to six turns with the tag end around the double line and through the circle. The number of turns you make depends on the diameter of the monofilament. Four turns are sufficient for 30 pound test, but lighter lines require more turns. Hold the double line at the point where it passes through the lure eye, wet the knot, and pull on the tag to snug up the turns.

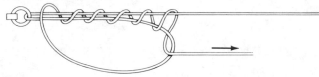

3. Slide the coils to the position that you desire. Take the pliers and pull firmly on the tag end. The knot will lock into place and the loop will allow your fly natural free movement in the water.

*Bimini Twist*

Use this to put a doubled line at the end of the backing so the fly line can be attached. Also use it in tying the big game leaders used for tarpon and billfish. When tied correctly, this knot maintains one-hundred percent of the line's breaking strength. Actually tying it is much easier than explaining it!

1. Pull off a little more than twice the amount of line you want for your doubled line. Bring the tag end back to the running line and hold them together. Rotate the end of the loop at least 20 times (I use 21), twisting the two sections together.

2. At this point place the loop over a foot and the arms of the loop around the knees. The tag end is in the right hand for right-handers- lefties please reverse all hand references- and the running line is in the left. Pressure can now be placed on the column of twists by spreading the knees apart. See drawing below.

3. Spread the knees to force the twists tightly together. Hold the running line in the left hand with tension just slightly off the vertical position. With the right hand, pull the tag end to a position at right angles to the twists. Keeping tension on the loop with the knees, gradually ease tension on the tag end so it will roll over the column of twists starting at the top of the twists.

4. Spread legs apart slowly to maintain pressure on the loop. Steer the tag end into a tight spiral coil as it continues to roll over the twisted line.

5. When the spiral of the tag end has rolled over the entire column of twists, keep knee pressure up while moving left hand down to grasp the knot. Place your index finger in the crotch of line where the loop joins the knot to prevent its slipping. Tie a half-hitch around the right leg of the loop to lock the knot into place and pull it up tight. Although the knot proper is now tied, the half-hitch holding the whole thing together is itself not secure and needs to be locked into place.

6. Release the knee pressure, but keep the loop stretched out tight. Use the tag end to make a half-hitch around both legs of the loop. A simple way to hold the knot together is to make a series of five more half-hitches around the doubled line and then just trim the tag.

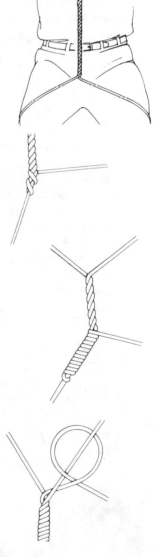

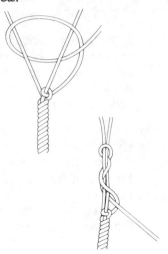

7. A better method is to keep the first half-hitch loose. Make two more turns with the tag around both legs of the loop, winding inside the bend of line formed by the loose half-hitch. Wet the knot, then pull slowly on the tag end, forcing the three loops to gather in a spiral.

8. When the loops are pulled tightly into place, trim the tag about 1/4 inch from the knot.

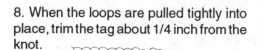

Believe it or (k)not, the Bimini twist is actually an easy knot to tie. It's explaining it that is difficult. Practice it at home before you go on your trip, and it will be a snap to tie when you need it.

*Double Surgeon's End Loop*
Use this knot to create a loop on the line end of the butt section of the leader. If the fly line has a loop whipped onto the end, the two can then be easily joined by looping them together.

1. Form a loop in the end of the line. Treating this loop as if it were a single strand, tie a simple overhand knot in it, but don't pull it tight. A loop will form in the line.

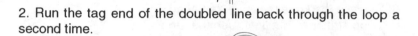

2. Run the tag end of the doubled line back through the loop a second time.

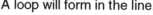

3. Pull the knot up tight. The line will now have a loop in the end. Trim off the tag end.

### Haywire Twist

Use this only when using single strand wire for leaders, for example, when fishing for sharks, barracuda, or bluefish. Haywire twist the wire to the hook at one end, and Albright a section of 30 pound monofilament to the other end.

1. Run the end of the wire through the eye of the hook, then wrap both strands around each other five times. It's easier to do this if you hold the loop of wire at the hook eye with a pair of pliers.

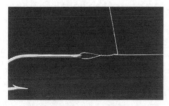 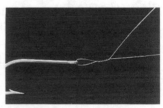

2. Take the tag end and wrap it around the running strand four times.

3. The twist is now completed, but the tag needs to be removed. Using cutters on the tag will leave a sharp end. Bend the tag back and forth where it's wrapped around the running strand. Metal fatigue will snap it off without leaving a dangerously sharp point.

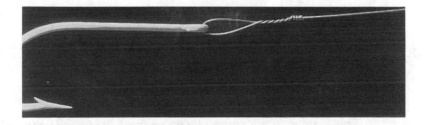

### The Albright Special

Use this knot to tie a heavy shock tippet to a class tippet, or to attach single strand wire to monofilament.

1. Double back about three inches of the heavy line, making a loop. Insert about 10 inches of the lighter line through the loop in the heavy line.

2. Grip the light line and both leader strands with your left thumb and forefinger (for right-handers). Use your right hand to wrap the light line back over both leader strands and itself.

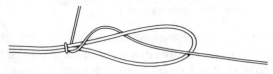

3. After making a dozen turns, insert the tag end of the light line back through the loop in the leader.

4. Pull gently on all ends of all lines, sliding the knot to the end of the leader loop. You want the lighter line to coil tightly around the leader. Pull both standing lines as tightly as possible, then clip the off the tag end.

It's easy to make mistakes tying this knot. If you do, break it and start over. You'll hate yourself if you lose a big fish to carelessness.

*The Hufnagle knot*

This is used in the same places as the Albright (with the exception of attaching wire). It's for folks who don't like the Albright.

1. First put a short section of doubled line in the class tippet with a Bimini twist.

Then take the shock tippet and tie an overhand knot in it near one end. Do not pull it up tight.

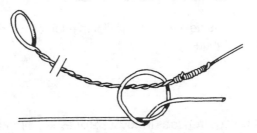

2. Slide the doubled class tippet through the loop in the overhand knot, but don't shove the Bimini twist through. Tighten the overhand knot down, then tug on the end of the doubled line until it jams against the overhand knot.

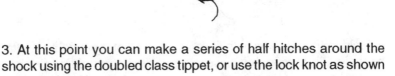

3. At this point you can make a series of half hitches around the shock using the doubled class tippet, or use the lock knot as shown in the illustrations below.

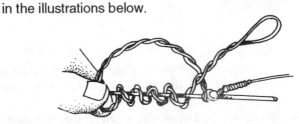

4. Trim the tag ends afterwards.

### Double Surgeon's Knot

This is a good knot to use when building tapered leaders, or to attach shock tippets to class tippets quickly.

1. Lay the two lines next to and parallel to each other, overlapping them six to eight inches.

2. Treating the two strands as if they were one, tie a simple overhand knot, pulling the entire shorter strand through the loop.

3. Leaving the loop of the overhand knot open, pull the shorter end of both the line and leader through the loop a second time.

4. Hold both ends and both lines and pull all of them tight simultaneously. Clip tags end off close to the line to help avoid tangles and snagging.

### Snelling a Fly to a Shock Tippet

Some guides prefer to snell the heavy shock leaders used in tarpon or offshore fishing to the fly. This way the fly always lies in line with the leader- it can't foul.

Although the drawings below show the leader threaded through the eye of a turned-down-eye hook, tarpon and offshore flies are tied on ringed eye hooks, and the leader should NEVER be threaded through the eye. Rather, the leader should lie underneath the eye of the hook. Other than that the drawings are correct. This is another knot that is much easier to tie than to explain how to tie.

1. Lay the tippet under the eye of the hook with about an inch of line extending past the bend (see sketch next page). Make a large loop, which should hang down under the hook.

2. Holding both lines against the hook shank, wind five tight coils around the hook shank and both lines. Start at the eye of the hook and wrap toward the bend.

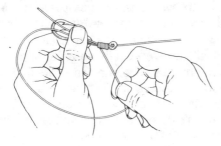

3. Hold coil tightly in place while pulling on the leader until you've pulled the loop out through the coils. Make sure the leader is running along the bottom of the shank, and passing under the eye.

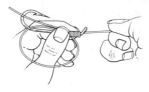

4. When the coils are neatly snugged, use pliers to pull on the tag end, clinching the snell down. Then clip off the tag end tightly against the snell.

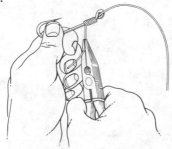

## WADERS AND WADING GEAR

Winter in Florida often comes with windy weather. Fly casting from a boat in 20 knot winds challenges even the finest casters, and most of us simply don't want to deal with it. Simply use the most elegant solution to this problem, one that trout fisherman up north have used practically forever- get in the water and wade.

Even during the summer months, many anglers find wading an effective way to fish. It's usually cooler than fishing from a boat, and allows the angler to approach the fish more closely. The aesthetics of being in the fish's own element while stalking them adds to the pleasure of fly fishing for many people.

During the summer months waders are hardly necessary (you'd sweat to death in no time) but specialized footwear makes wading more pleasant. Orvis markets the Tropical Wading Bootie, the finest wading shoe made for wading Florida flats. A thick sole provides support and protection from oysters, crabs, sea urchins, and other hazards natural and man-made to the foot. The high, tight fitting boot top keeps sand, shells and other debris out of the boot as well as resisting the incredible suction effect the soft marly bottoms have on shoes. In other words, they stay where they belong- on your feet.

During the winter in the northern half of the state waders are a must. I happily used chest high nylon boot foot waders from Red Ball for many years, but when my last pair blew out I broke down and got neoprene stocking foot waders. They outperform the nylon waders by a huge margin and anyone who wades a lot will probably find the investment more than worthwhile. Wear wading booties over the neoprenes and you have waders that are light, dry, warm, and comfortable.

Be sure any boots you wear over stocking foot waders have plastic and not felt soles. The fertile muck in which so many of the state's lush seagrass beds grow sticks to the felt in huge clods and before you know it the boots each weigh 15 or 20 pounds. Plastic soles resist this agglomeration and make wading mucky flats much easier and more enjoyable.

## Boats

boat (bot), *n.* 1 a hole in the water into which one pours money

The boat. What a piece of equipment it is! Here in Florida many anglers take their boats VERY seriously. It's not at all unusual while on the water here to see state-of-the-art flats skiffs, only 18 feet long, which retail for well over $25,000 for a boat/motor/trailer package, especially during tarpon season. Something about those tarpon brings out the true fanaticism in anglers!

Undeniably these boats, the Silver King, the Maverick, the Hewes, the Action Craft, and all of the other, newer boats that have appeared on the scene in the past few years, are incredibly fine fishing machines which are a joy to own and use. Speaking strictly from the standpoint of the fish, though, for many applications the boat is simply not all that important. Fish don't really care what kind of boat you are in! What features does a good saltwater fly fishing boat need? What makes it easy to fish from?

Generalizations are difficult due to the wide variety of fishing done here, but any boat used for any type of fishing will need a good rod storage area to protect expensive rods and reels. A casting area free from protrusions of any type saves many headaches, heartaches, and sometimes broken tackle.

Of course, for some applications the boat is everything. Well, maybe not everything, but a critical element to be sure. For example, out of Key West Captains Jose Wejebe and Ken Harris chase yellowfin and blackfin tuna, wahoo, dolphin, sailfish, tiger sharks, and other truly large pelagic fishes. They both use Conch 27

*The Conch 27 is the choice of several of several Keys guides for offshore work for tuna, dolphin, and billfish.*

custom fishing machines manufactured by Edy & Duff. These incredible boats are important elements in their success. Ken Harris

*Flats skiffs continue gaining popularity with good reason- they make excellent fishing platforms for a wide variety of applications.*

says, "It's the last boat I'll ever own."

Tarpon fishing in the Keys or along the West Coast also requires a boat up to the task. Seen on tarpon flats are the Silver King, the Hewes, the Dolphin, the Maverick and many more. All of these boats have a "poling tower" over the transom. The "guide" stands atop the tower with a pushpole, primarily used for steering while hunting fish. The poler's height gives him an excellent vantage point from which to spot the tarpon. Two or four stern mounted electric trolling motors provide propulsion along the flats. These motors are controlled by foot switches on the poling tower. Tarpon flats tend to be too deep for efficient poling, especially when windy (which is most of the time). The electrics allow an almost silent approach to the fish, giving the angler a decent chance at putting his

*Jonboats lack prestige, but have several advantages for backcountry and inshore work, including shallow draft and relative "indestructibility".*

fly in front of the tarpon.

For some reason jonboats get little respect. This is a shame since they really are useful in shallow inshore and backcountry areas. You can rig them for fly fishing very easily and they work extremely well for exploring hazardous areas, such as oyster clogged creeks or the rock-bottomed areas around Homosassa on the west coast. My 14 foot MonArk has been dubbed the "Bang-O-Craft" because of its countless scrapes with rocks and oysters. Its tough metal hide absorbs punishment without complaint. It just bounces off and keeps right on motoring along.

Car top boats are not seen as often along the coast as one might expect. Canoes in particular make excellent craft for getting back into areas that receive little if any fishing pressure. Two of the state's more well-known anglers, Chico Fernandez and Flip Pallot, use canoes for exactly this reason.

In addition to paddle propulsion, serious anglers fishing from canoes also carry a pushpole. The pole allows both anglers to stand up while searching for fish. The bow man carries the rod while the stern man pushes the boat. After the bow man connects, they trade gear, turn the canoe around, and switch roles. The canoe now goes backwards, the stern man handles the rod, and the bow man poles the boat. It may sound crazy but it works very well for skilled anglers. Give it a try!

Boaters need accessories, too. Use an anchor as our first example. It needs to hold the boat securely. More importantly, it sometimes needs to be abandoned quickly, especially when a big fish bites. When a big fish strips off backing FAST it needs to be chased right now, and pulling the anchor up wastes valuable seconds. Most Florida fishermen use a float on their anchor rope so they can chase fish like this in a hurry. The anchor can be unclipped and left where it is. At the end of the battle the boater returns to retrieve the anchor, or re-connects it to the bow of the boat.

Shallow water anglers need propulsion over the flats. Many anglers use a pushpole for this purpose. Relatively inexpensive and maintenance free, some anglers use nothing else.

Electric motors become more popular every year. You'll see both bow mounts and stern mounts in use. Bow mounts give better control of the boat and have the advantage that you only need one. They work in any depth water too, something that cannot be said of a pushpole. They and their operator always seem to get in the way of a fly fisher, though.

For effective use of stern mounts two (or even four) are

used. Most steering requires a pushpole. In other words, the stern mounted electrics help the poler, rather than replacing him the way the bow mount does. The angler gets the entire front deck to himself, with no one or nothing to get in the way. Some guides use a combination of bow and stern mounts.

Use whatever combination suits you best. When the time comes that you need the electrics, you'll know it.

## Guides

They should be your best friend, but might be your worst nightmare. Good ones are a bargain, bad ones a complete waste of money. Some anglers swear by them, others swear at them. The professional fishing guides of Florida are a diverse lot, and like any group of people anywhere hard to make generalizations about.

Anyone considering hiring a guide should ask him some questions before booking the day(s). "What do you charge?" is an obvious start. "What's included?" and "What type of fishing do you do?" are other easy questions. Most guides supply tackle, flies, and licence as part of the package. Ask before you go.

A question I'm often asked by potential clients is, "What type of boat do you have?" This question is important if three or four people would like to go out on one boat, but as mentioned earlier, fish are generally not impressed by the nameplate on the hull. Although it's true you don't want to fish from a garbage scow there are other, better things to ask about.

During your conversation with the guide, tell him what you want to do. If you will be in the area for several days and need help finding places to fish after your day together, tell him. If you have concerns about your casting and would like some instruction, tell him. Honesty now will save misunderstanding and ill will later.

If you can be flexible in your scheduling, ask what days are likely to be most productive. While the guide can't predict the weather or give guarantees, moon phase has a lot to do with fish behavior since it affects tides so much. The guide knows this and also has an experience base from past years on which he can speculate. Why book a date he knows may be unproductive?

If you don't know his reputation ask the guide for references. Often guides develop long term relationships with some of their anglers and fish them the same week every year. Guides with a lot of return business generally entertain and instruct in addition to finding fish. Others could find fish in a bathtub but get little if any repeat business because they're obnoxious. Although you may catch fish, you may still hate the entire experience!

Many guides now ask for a deposit to reserve dates, a reasonable request. If an angler changes his mind at the last minute, the guide loses out on a day's wages. Guides get none of the fringe benefits that most salaried workers take for granted. When they're sick or if the weather's bad, they don't get paid. They do not earn retirement pay. While it may look like peaches and cream to the angler, most guides work hard for their entire lives and seldom retire anywhere near what most folks would consider financial security. It's a tough way to earn a living, and guides guide because they love it. The financial rewards are few for all but the very best. So don't complain about the deposit, and don't forget to give a good guide a well-deserved tip.

## Hazards and Safety

Hazards? In Florida? Yes, accidents happen everywhere, and Florida isn't immune. Take a look at the hazards you may encounter on any trip in the Sunshine State.

Number one has to be insects, primarily mosquitoes, but biting flies and stinging insects can't be forgotten either. Insect repellant and protective clothing takes care of the biters. Controversy increases about the safety of DEET (the active ingredient in most insect repellants), but it definitely does repel insects. It also melts down fly lines, so be careful with it. Some folks like to use Avon's Skin So Soft or other non-DEET repellants. My own experience is that these do not work against anything but no-see-ums. I suspect the individual's attractiveness to and tolerance for bugs determines, in part at least, their effectiveness.

Nothing will repel a swarm of paper wasps should you be so unfortunate as to crash into their nest in the backcountry. Keep a careful eye out when travelling down overgrown creeks, and be prepared to clear out under power In a hurry should you hit one.

Next comes the sun. Sunburn is an ever present risk in Florida, and skin cancer rates continue rising everywhere. Protect yourself with sunscreen and protective clothing. Dr. William Barnard

*Waders need to watch for stingrays.*

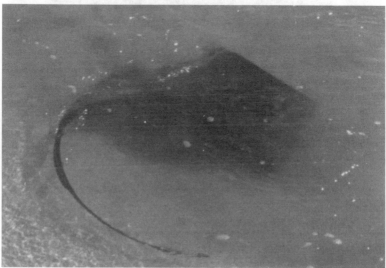

*When the thunderheads start heading your way, be smart and get off the water!*

tells me that he uses the highest SPF sunscreen available whenever he goes fishing regardless of the season, and recommended that I do the same. I pass on his advice to you.

Lightning strikes more people in the state of Florida every year than all other states combined. The majority of those hit are either golfers or anglers. A graphite fly rod could well be the finest lightning rod ever designed. Is any fish worth a million volt jolt? Find and get under shelter when those threatening thunderheads come rolling your way.

Waders need to concern themselves with three forms of aquatic wildlife. Stingrays are the most prevalent hazard waders face. Seldom aggressive, the rays cover themselves with sand or mud and thus are hard to see. Step on one and it will drive the stinger deep into your leg. The stinger then breaks off while the ray goes about its business, leaving you with an excruciatingly painful souvenir of your encounter.

Drag your feet while wading. Do the well-known "stingray shuffle." The ray will swim away if you touch the wing. This may startle you, but leaves no lasting mementos.

Alligators swim all through coastal Florida waters. Many folks assume, mistakenly, that gators live only in freshwater. Although gators are seldom aggressive, if you see a big one paying attention to you, get out of the water. Whatever you do, don't drag fish on a stringer while gators are around!

Gators often rest on the bottom in shallow water- be careful when you wade. I seldom see gators in central Florida coastal waters during the winter months. We never worry about them then. During the warmer months we watch much more closely and in waters where there are lots of them we are much more hesitant about getting out of the boat.

Sharks present almost no danger, unless you are dragging a stringer of fish. However, they certainly deserve respect, especially when the surf gets full of big ones. The mullet run will bring large sharks in close to shore. Consider fishing from the beach then!

Other boaters possibly present the greatest hazard of all. Florida has the highest boating fatality rate in the nation. Alcohol is often a contributing factor in boating accidents. Stay sober and consider wearing a life vest when travelling from spot to spot.

A well prepared angler knows the hazards and acts accordingly. In addition, common sense dictates always carrying a first aid kit. All anglers, all <u>adults</u> need to know know basic first aid techniques. Although you hope you never need them, you never know when you will. Take a standard first aid course at your first opportunity.

# Chapter 2 ANGLING TECHNIQUES

      Poling my canoe across the shallows on my first visit to Mud Lake the thought entered my mind, "There will never be fish in this shallow water." No sooner had the thought completed than a clearly visible fish appeared. A quick cast put the fly in front of it and the fish immediately charged and ate the fly. Five minutes later my hand grasped seven pounds of unhappy redfish, which was quickly unhooked and released. Several more redfish followed and Mud Lake fast became a favorite place to fish.

      This chapter examines in depth the various techniques used to catch Florida's saltwater gamefish. Many of the methods used here differ radically from those used elsewhere, necessitating more than just a little explanation.

      For starters, many of the fish often hunt for food in ridiculously shallow water. Redfish and bonefish in particular will look for crabs and minnows in water that does not even cover their back. It takes an enormous change in the mindset that "big fish only use deep water" to get the confidence to look in these shallow areas.

Much of Florida's saltwater fishing requires a substantial amount of hunting first, and the fly never enters the water until the fish are located. Let's take a look at how to find fish, then at sight-fishing, blind-casting, chumming, fighting and handling fish, and other important angling techniques.

## SEARCHING FOR AND FINDING FISH

The scenario- two anglers have a boat, and have begun fishing in a large bay in which neither have fished before. Do they have any chance of success?

It depends how hard they search. A situation like this often requires extensive hunting. Many tips follow which will hopefully make the hunt a more successful one.

Begin the search by moving fairly rapidly, looking for any signs of life, especially bait. An area showing obvious signs of life will much more likely hold fish than a location which otherwise looks good, but has no bait. Sharks and rays may also indicate fish.

It's also important to work different types of habitats until you find fish. Points with water movement (especially with fallen trees), creeks, creek mouths, the windy side of bays, the sheltered side of bays, deep bays, shallow bays, drop-offs, channels, and oyster bars, are all locations that could hold fish. Work them all in succession, using common sense to guide your search.

For example, don't try the south side of a bay with the wind from the north and the temperature in the fifties. A more likely location on a day like this would be a mud-bottomed, wind-sheltered shoreline with sunshine warming the shallows. The fish could maintain a comfortable body temperature here, and could be persuaded to eat a well-presented fly. The windy side of a bay might be good on a warm day. The wave action oxygenates the water, and blows baitfish against the windward shoreline.

As a general rule, work creek mouths when water flows out of, rather than into, them. The current carries bait and gamefish in general and snook in particular know that.

Try around oyster bars or mangrove shorelines on the rising tide. The fish like to hunt in areas not accessible to them when the tide was low. Both the oysters and the mangroves hold small baitfish as well as shrimp and crabs, all of which your saltwater gamefish hold in high esteem as edibles.

Search aggressively! If you don't find the fish holding on a particular habitat type, for example oysters, don't waste time fishing around other oyster bars unless you actually see fish working there. Cruise along the shoreline, trying to flush fish out. Don't be concerned about spooking a few fish like this if it helps you to figure out the type of habitat they're using. Please remember to be courteous to other anglers. Since outboard motors spook fish in shallow water, using this technique is the height of bad manners if there are other fishermen present.

Birds have long been used by savvy anglers to locate fish. Anytime terns start diving and screaming, it doesn't take much knowledge to figure out that fish are underneath piling into bait. Wading birds such as great blue herons or great egrets also feed on baitfish. Anytime several of these birds work together in one area, they indicate the presence of bait. Most of the time predatory fish like snook or redfish will be there too, and sometimes the birds and the fish play the bait off of each other. Congregations of wading birds can certainly mean more to the fly fisher than simple aesthetics.

One technique which almost always works, but which requires a bit of observation and patience, involves looking for guide boats. Often several guides will be drifting with the current, casting through a productive zone. Once they finish passing through it, they'll motor back upcurrent BEING CAREFUL NOT TO MOTOR NEAR THE FISHY AREA, and make another drift. If you watch what they are doing and closely emulate it without getting in their way or

*Feeding wading birds like these great egrets indicate bait, and possible gamefish.*

43

spooking the fish, they will usually not mind your joining them.

Guides get touchy about sports who ruin the fishing. Keep in mind that in shallow water an outboard spooks fish from a long way off. Treat others with respect and you will usually be welcomed.

## SIGHT-FISHING

Few angling experiences compare with actually seeing the fish in shallow water, casting to it, manipulating the fly, and watching the fish take. In order to succeed consistently you must have two items of equipment. The first is a billed or broad brimmed hat. The underside of the bill should be a dark color. The dark color reflects less light onto the face, reducing glare. You also need a pair of quality polarized sunglasses. The polarizing filters in the lenses cut reflection from the water surface, making it easier to see into the water. The right glasses are very important.

The right attitude is more important than the equipment. It takes a certain degree of mental toughness and perseverance to get up in a boat or wade all day and really concentrate, trying to read signs that indicate fish. Concentration definitely is the key here, for without it success is impossible.

When you concentrate you see more fish. Seeing more fish means more shots at fish. The odds dictate that with more opportunities, you have more hookups. So concentration is the key that unlocks the secrets of the flats. Now let's discuss what to look for.

Sometimes a fish betrays its presence in shallow water by causing disturbances on the water's surface. Fins, whether dorsal or caudal, are easy to spot, particularly when in motion. Sunlight sometimes reflects off of the caudal fins of tailing reds or bonefish, and you can see the flash from a surprising distance.

A fish cruising in shallow water pushes a wave up above it, a wave known as a wake. To visualize what this looks like, think of a submarine moving through the water only five feet below the surface. Would it make a disturbance on the surface? You bet it would! Obviously, fish are smaller than submarines, but the principle is identical. Wakes are easy seen when it's calm. They're harder to see if it's windy, but it can still be done. Although a choppy water surface has a chaotic pattern to it, moving waves have a pattern. They all move in the same direction. The heights are all in a certain range. ANYTHING that breaks this pattern, that looks even slightly different, could be a fish and should be investigated, either visually or by casting up ahead of it.

*Don't expect to see the whole fish while sightfishing!*

The importance of looking into the water was stated earlier. Most fish on the flats do not put up flags telling their enemies of their whereabouts. Fish enter shallow water looking for a meal, but they still try to hide as best as they can. If you want to see them, you must train yourself to look and to see.

Again, look INTO the water. This is most easily done with little or no wind, the sun high in the sky and at your back, no clouds, and a light colored bottom. That you need water almost goes without saying. Tilt your head both ways to find the maximum effectiveness of your sunglasses.

Avoid staring at one spot! Keep your eyes scanning the bottom, looking for breaks in the patterns you see there. Scan in a pattern, back and forth, from close in to the limit of visibility, then back in close again. Develop your peripheral vision as well. Use good sighting conditions to train yourself. Believe me, your skill and your ability improve as you practice.

What do you look for? Anything that might be a fish. There are different kinds of clues. Muds are easily seen and are almost always caused by fish. Although sometimes the fish making them will only be mullet or stingrays, gamefish often follow both. Always investigate with a cast or two.

Look for any movement that breaks the patterns. The ubiquitous waves cast moving shadows on the bottom. Wave patterns have already been mentioned. Keep scanning with your eyes, looking for any movement contrary to the patterns produced by the waves. Sometimes you see movement of the fish itself, sometimes you pick up the shadow cast by the fish onto the bottom. Either way, you know it's there. Large tarpon over light sand bottoms are about the easiest of all fish to see this way. They look like big logs cruising through the water. Seeing bonefish and seatrout is most difficult.

Look for flashes. When fish turn or roll on their sides, particularly while they're feeding, their sides catch and reflect light. This lasts for only a brief moment, but is easy to see and is a dead giveaway to the presence of fish.

Look for differences in color. The light copper color of their pectoral fins are often the only visible clue to the presence of redfish when they cruise over a dark grass bottom. Bonefish have a peculiar emerald color, unique and sometimes hard to see. Tough to spot, permit have silvery sides that reflect the bottom with incredible effectiveness. They do, however, have a dark outline which can be discerned by careful observation. Check out everything which might be a fish!

*In addition to their wariness, seatrout are one of the most difficult fish to see while on the flats.*

Watch underneath birds like pelicans or great blue herons when they fly close to the water surface. As they pass over fish, the fish spook and jump, as if someone yelled "BOO!" at them without warning. I've taken some fine fish after a wading bird in flight tipped me off to their presence.

Sometimes your ears can direct you to your quarry. On a cold, windy day one winter I had an angler from Buffalo, N.Y. out on what I thought would be a futile search for fish. I heard a splash and went to investigate, expecting to find mullet. We were happily surprised to see a big redfish tail waving at us in the chilly breeze. Tailing fish splash and quiet anglers can hear this.

Another thing to look for are fishy-looking shapes. Sometimes the fish lay up. They're not cruising. They're not moving. They may be in an ambush mode, or sleeping, or just sunning themselves, but they certainly are motionless. Needless to say, they're hard to see when they do this.

If you see something that looks like it might be a fish, cast to it! Many times I let my curiosity get the best of me and approach too closely. The fish lets me know that it actually is a fish and not a piece of wood by streaking off towards deeper water, leaving me feeling pretty foolish.

You can't always see the entire fish. Seatrout are one of the hardest of all fish to spot. Their dark backs blend in perfectly with grass. They often lie motionless over grassy bottoms, particularly around the edges of sandy areas. While they do this they are almost impossible to see. Often the only clue you have to a trout's presence is its tail, a little lighter in color than the background, with a darker band along the back edge. Check it out with a cast!

Seatrout, especially the larger specimens, are one of the spookiest of all fish. They seldom let you get very close, and rarely eat after they flush. A good cast is the best form of investigation, unless you'd rather see fish than catch them. Most of us prefer catching them.

One time I spotted what I thought was the motionless tail of a redfish in Mud Lake, a shallow, brackish Everglades pond. I cast beyond where the head should be, and was rewarded with a strike. It turned out to be one of my most unusual catches ever, a sawfish of about twenty-five pounds. Never ignore anything. Remember, you're a hunter and have to behave like one.

Try these techniques and practice. Practice a lot! As your seeing skills develop, you derive a lot of pleasure and pride in being able to see things that others can't. Not only will you catch more fish, you get more enjoyment from your fishing. You'll be amazed at all the sights you were missing!

*Charlie Chapman releases a redfish he saw cruising over a grass bed.*

## Blind-casting

Imagine for a moment in your mind's eye the perfect bonefishing scene. You stand on the bow of a guided skiff. A gentle, cooling breeze ripples the surface of the shallow, crystal clear water. Bright sunshine illuminates the white sand bottom, clearly displaying the school of hundreds of bonefish greedily tailing for crabs and other crustaceans. The biggest bone of all time devours your perfectly presented fly, and you're off to the races.

Now let's talk reality. The highest tide in ten years picks the same weekend as your bonefishing trip, covering the flat with three feet of water. There's heavy overcast with intermittent rain squalls. A hard wind is blows at 20 miles an hour with gusts. What can you do? Can bonefish still be caught?

All of the above situations have happened to me, from heavenly to hellish. And with perseverance and some luck, bonefish can be caught in all of them.

Let's face it, most of us would rather sightfish. It's more interesting, and more exciting. But Mother Nature doesn't always cooperate. Wind, clouds, and high water can conspire to make sighting conditions less than ideal. If you want to hear the magic song of a reel in stress, you fish anyway. Simply deal with lousy conditions by blindcasting.

Let's discuss a few general rules for blindcasting. It really involves more than just mindlessly casting a fly out into the water. First, if fishing a flat, pick a flat where fish you know fish feed. Obviously you won't catch any fish where there are none. All other things being equal, the fish feed on their favorite flats when weather conditions allow. If you're there too you just might get a couple.

Next, use the tips described in the sightfishing section to search the water you can see into for fish. If you see any, cast to them! There's no sense in turning down any good opportunities.

Keep casting your fly into the water where you cannot see. Although it depends on your direction of movement relative to the position of the sun, this will usually be the deeper water. Fish are in there, so just keep casting.

Make long casts. You cover more water this way, giving more fish the chance to see your offering. You may periodically line fish, and you'll see the boils they make as they flee. You may look at it as a fish you won't catch, but instead look at it as proof that you are working the right area. Spooked fish mean the fish are there! If you just keep casting you'll get some.

In many locations in the state you may not be fishing flats. Bass fishermen in freshwater tune in to the concept of structure. Many saltwater fish relate to structure, too. Stumps, docks, oyster bars, rocks, wrecks, points, fallen timber, drop-offs, creek mouths, seawalls, edges of grass beds and sandy bottoms, all of these types of irregularities and more attract and hold many species of fish. In snook country, points of land extending out into a current often hold fish, and if a fallen tree lies there so much the better. Experienced anglers recognize fishy looking areas. Use your judgement and trust your instincts.

**Teasers**

Most anglers associate teasers with offshore fishing, and certainly the concept has reached its most rapid evolution in the arena of fly fishing for billfish. Billfish teasers often resemble a large popping plug without hooks, but it could be a freshly dead or frozen baitfish such as a ballyhoo rigged without a hook.

The teaser is trolled about 100 feet behind the boat until a fish rises to it. The teaser is then manipulated to excite the fish and lure it to within fly casting range, usually only about 30 to 40 feet behind the boat. At this point one of two things happens, depending on whether the teaser is a real fish or an artificial.

When teasing with an artificial, the reeler gives it a mighty jerk, pulling it into the boat. The fly fisher yells, "Neutral!" and the captain takes the boat out of gear. In the meantime the excited fish frantically wonders where the teaser went. The fly fisher delivers the fly, and hopefully the fish eats the fly and a hookup ensues.

When teasing with a baitfish, a similar thing happens except that the reeler allows the fish to mouth the bait before pulling it away. After the fish gets the flavor of the bait in its mouth and loses it, delivering a fly anywhere near the head of the fish usually results in an immediate and vicious strike. The vast majority of fly-caught billfish succumb to this technique.

Teasing can be used inshore too. Large jack crevalle are tremendous fly rod targets, but usually flies are simply too small and move too slowly to interest them. A pair of anglers can team up to catch these fish.

Get a large popping plug and remove the hooks. Tie this modified plug on the line of a spinning rod (if you don't own one of these you can usually borrow one from one of the neighborhood kids). The "teaser" casts the plug out where the jacks are and reels it in as fast and as noisily as possible.

In the meantime the fly fisher has his line in the air, with a

*With a large hookless popping plug and a large hooked fly, various species of fish can be teased up and taken with fly tackle.*

large popping bug or streamer on the business end. When the jacks start chasing the plug, the fly fisher drops his bait on the plug while the teaser simultaneously pulls it from the water.

Smart snook anglers in the Palm Beach/greater Miami area tease, too. Many bridges over canals and rivers in that part of the state shelter some enormous snook. These fish feed mostly at night, and prefer large mouthfuls. Fly fishers using standard techniques have little chance of success. But two fishermen working together can sometimes hook up with these monsters, although landing them around these bridges when the fish have those pilings to work with is another thing altogether.

Equipment needs for bridge teasers are basic. All you need are a few live mullet in the six to eight inch size range, a large rigging needle, and a stout cane pole to which is tied a section of 50 pound (more or less) monofilament. At daybreak (this is an early morning operation) use the rigging needle to tie the mullet to the line on the cane pole. The teaser then works the mullet around the bridge pilings, tempting the snook to come up and blast it. If the snook cooperates, the teaser pulls the mullet away, then puts it right back down again. When the snook comes back, the teaser might let the snook mouth the bait, but then pulls it away again. The idea is to get the fish so angry that when the fly fisher finally tosses the feather duster over, the snook is ready to smash anything. It works.

## WADING

Tails, fish tails, reddish bronze tipped with a bluish tinge, protruded from the water's surface all around us. Although the fish were obviously feeding, while in such in shallow water they were very spooky. Every time we maneuvered the boat close enough for a cast the tails would vanish, while further away beyond casting range tails continued to wave. Frustrating!

Fortunately, both Joe Mulson and I had with us the needed piece of equipment that would allow us to get close to our wary prey. No, it wasn't a spinning rod with a long cast spool. Joe and I were wearing chest high waders. We simply abandoned the boat and went after the reds on foot.

One of the most effective ways to approach game fish, as well as one of the most enjoyable of all the ways to fish involves getting into the fish's element and wading. The angler has a low profile and keeps the disturbance of the water to a minimum, allowing him to sneak up on feeding fish without spooking them. It's

John O. Thompson waded his way to this big black drum.

often possible to hook shallow water reds with literally just the leader out of the fly rod's tiptop. The fish come so close, all one need do is to dangle the fly in their faces. Exciting fishing!

For many species of fish which swim in our salty inshore areas, wading in many situations will actually be more effective than fishing from a boat. For example, in areas where redfish are heavily pursued by anglers in boats, they soon learn that boats are trouble. Getting into casting range from a boat can be tough. A wading angler who tries to be quiet can literally wade right up to the fish.

On many days in the winter and spring, strong winds make even the most skilled boat handler want to scream in frustration. Fly fishing is difficult when the boat is moving too fast because of strong winds. It's tough to strip the line fast enough to keep contact with the fly. A wading angler can fish in almost any kind of breeze.

In Florida during the summer months, shorts and some

*Two brands of neoprene wading booties.*

type of protective footwear are all that you need for comfortable wading. I stepped on a flounder one time while wading barefoot, and although nothing happened as far as injury goes, the incident convinced me that some sort of shoe was really a good idea. Crabs, sea urchins, shells, broken bottles, and other hazards to the feet make barefoot wading a stupid thing to do.

The best footwear for wading are neoprene wading boots. These are similar to dive boots, but have a stiff plastic sole which give support and protection to the foot. Orvis makes a great one. Since they're ankle high, they also keep sand and shells out, and resist the suction effect that soft bottomed areas sometimes dish out. Take it from me- losing your shoe in bottom ooze in thigh deep water is not fun.

In central and north Florida, waders make winter wading possible. Those who wade only occasionally only need the boot foot type of nylon wader. Red Ball waders give several years of service. For those for whom wading is a way of life, stocking foot neoprenes are the only way to go.

Stocking foot waders need wading boots. The area fished dictates the type of boot worn, and some anglers may need more than one type. Freshwater trout fishermen are familiar with felt-soled wading boots. These work best where slick, algae coated rocks cover the bottom. Some anglers wear chains or crampons when working around treacherous rocky areas. On soft muddy bottoms chains aren't needed and muck sticks to the sole of the felt boots and makes wading tough. In this type of area, the hard soled neoprene wading booties like those mentioned above work much better. You may need to purchase a second pair for use with the neoprene waders, a size or two larger than your shoe size.

Waders also need to carry all their paraphernalia. In the winter wading vests provide a terrific way to carry tackle and accessories. Many fine vests are on the market. Make sure the one you buy has enough storage space for everything that you need.

Often in the summer vests are too hot to be comfortable. The only thing to do is carry less stuff. Some fishermen carry extra flies on their hat, others carry accessories in an over the shoulder type of bag. Nu-Mark Manufacturing, a tackle manufacturer in Houston, specializes in accessories for the wading angler. Look for their products at your favorite tackle store.

What accessories will you need? This depends on the type of fishing done. Anglers need extra flies, fly boxes, floatant for hair bugs, pliers, and a glove for handling fish as an absolute minimum. Material for making shock leaders, water, food, smoking materials (for those who indulge), and more get added to the essentials. You end up carrying a lot of stuff. It adds up fast if care is not used.

What techniques can waders use to find fish?

Oftentimes waders use a boat to find fish, then anchor up, slip out, and start wading. Two (or more) wading anglers work a long stretch of shoreline by "leapfrogging", that is, one angler hops out of the boat and starts wading. The other takes the boat downwind (or sun or tide) several hundred yards, then anchors it. He starts wading. When the first angler reaches the boat, he takes it a few hundred yards down the shoreline and they repeat the process. If four anglers do this, they can work new water all day long and never have to fish alone. If one is right-handed and the other's a lefty, it works even better.

If while wading down a flat the fish seem scarce, do what guides do and zigzag. Go in close to shore and then work farther out. The fish may be on the flat in slightly deeper or shallower water. By looking in different depths on the flat your chances of finding fish improve greatly.

Of necessity much of the angling time spent wading consists of casting blindly. In general, flies that make noise, especially surface baits like poppers, often work the best for two reasons. First of all, watching and working a popper that you can see is more interesting than retrieving a subsurface lure or streamer that cannot be seen. Secondly, the noise a popper makes attracts fish that might never see an underwater bait. They hear the popper and come to investigate. And although this is somewhat of an intangible, surface strikes are so much more exciting than underwater ones. Keep in mind that poppers won't work for some species.

Cast to any areas that you think might hold fish. Cast along oyster beds, rocks, stumps, pilings, drop-offs, the edges of grassy and sandy areas, or any other area or structure that might hide a fish. In addition to increasing the odds for a strike, your targeting specific locations before every cast improves your casting skills and this pays big dividends on future trips.

*Wading is an excellent way to work shallow areas with spooky fish.*

Always look for signs of fish while wading. If fish are seen, try to get into the best possible position from which to cast. Sometimes you have to take any shot that's offered, but other times the fish move slowly and you can get a head on presentation, the kind most likely to produce a strike. Remember that the first cast is usually your best opportunity. Try to make it count.

Lastly, use care and common sense when wading, especially in new areas. Make sure the bottom is firm enough to hold you before hopping out of a boat. On the Gulf side of the Keys, and in most places in Everglades National Park, the bottom is very soft and the muck is very deep. If you just jump out you may find yourself up to your waist in marl with no easy way to get out. Also, if you step off a drop while wearing waders you will discover to your dismay that waders were not designed with swimming in mind.

In our southern waters, stingrays are a cause for caution. Do the "stingray shuffle", never lifting your feet from the bottom. Kicking the ray's wing will cause it to swim away. Pinning it to the bottom will lead to a pierced leg.

In waters with sharks or alligators (and where aren't they?), dragging a stringer with fish invites huge trouble. Most fly fishers don't kill many fish anyway, and these predators provide another good reason not to. And finally, although wading can be done as a solo act, safety considerations dictate that you fish with a buddy. So find another fishing maniac and go chase those fish together!

## CHUMMING

When all else fails, attract the fish to you. Use chum. Depending on the fish you want there are several different approaches to this technique. The best way to do this for bonefish is to use live shrimp and a chumming tube. Allow me to explain.

The least troublesome way to chum for bonefish, redfish, or other flats fish involves breaking live shrimp into pieces and just throwing the pieces out where you want the fish to show up. The trouble with this is that every fish in the area that eats shrimp gets a free meal. Most of these fish are little guys like pinfish. You won't want to catch most of these fish, and your chum won't last very long.

A chumming tube is a piece of PVC pipe. A one and a half inch diameter piece about twenty inches long is plenty, but any PVC scraps you happen to have will do. Cap one end permanently by using PVC cement. Use a drill to fill the pipe full of approximately quarter inch holes. Hole size isn't critical. Put another cap on the other end, but don't cement it on. Drill holes through the pipe and cap so that a nylon cord can be tied through the holes to tether the tube to the boat and hold the cap in place.

Next, find a known bonefish flat. Anchor the boat about 30 feet upcurrent of a white sand patch. Take 25 or so live shrimp, break them up into pieces, and put them into the chum tube. Add six or eight whole live ones, too. Put the cap on, tie the tube to the tether line, and heave it out onto the near side of the sand patch. The chum now does its work. Bones can smell the shrimp from a long way off and will follow the odor to its source. At this point the fly fisher waits and watches for fish to come into the chum line. When he sees them, a fly imitating a shrimp is delivered. Many, many fly fishers caught their first bonefish this way.

Anglers fishing for bluefish use a similar technique, using ground up fish (usually menhaden) instead of shrimp. The chum "soup" is ladled sparingly over the side of the boat in an area where bluefish are known to be. The blues come into the chum line, and the angler works the fly into it. The fly for this is the bloody chum fly, a hunk of brown marabou tied to the hook. Dead drift the fly with the chum. Any motion imparted to it only puts the fish off.

On Florida's west coast guides often chum fish into feeding frenzies by using "whitebait", or pilchards, which they catch in

*A chum tube and some of the shrimp that go into it.*

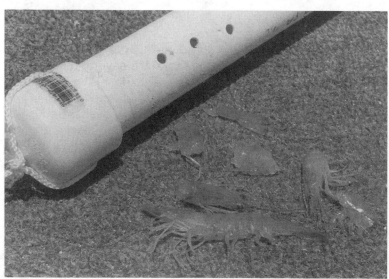

cast nets. They anchor the boat up current of a location where redfish, snook, and sometimes seatrout are known to be. They then throw handfuls of the live baitfish hard onto the water's surface, stunning them. As these injured and struggling minnows drift down current, predators who recognize an easy meal when they see one start feeding on them. Ten minutes or so of this, and the fish will hit almost anything thrown their way.

Down Key West way, offshore guides Jose Wejebe and Ken Harris use pilchards to lure yellowfin and blackfin tuna, large sharks, wahoo, dolphin, billfish, and other pelagic species within casting range of fly rodders. Wejebe's boat has a live well of over 100 gallons, into which he will put the 1000 to 2000 baitfish needed for a single day's chumming.

Many anglers will fish around shrimp boats as they shovel by-catch overboard, or will purchase by-catch (cold beer is the medium of exchange!) from shrimpers to use as chum. Again, many pelagic species (especially bonito and blackfin tuna) follow these boats, waiting for the smorgasbord of small dead fish that shrimpers throw away after every time they pull their nets.

Captain Jake Jordan does his fishing out of the World Class Angler on Marathon Key. Although Jake fishes for permit, bonefish, and tarpon in shallow water, he's best known for pioneering deep-water fly fishing techniques for permit over spring holes in the open Gulf. These fish school up on the surface over the spring holes he fishes. The water there will be from sixty to over one hundred feet deep, so dropping your crab fly to the bottom isn't too practical, and is unneccesary anyway.

When Jake locates a school of permit, he dips a live, silver dollar sized blue crab out of his bait well, and tosses it into the middle of the milling permit. He says the crab instinctively heads for the bottom, and will make it down ten feet or so before a fish gobbles it. He gets another crab and tosses it out. This one will only make it down about seven feet. The next one only makes it a few feet down, and pretty soon the fish are racing each other to hit the crabs before they hit the water.

The angler, meantime, picks the fish to which he wants to cast, and when the school is sufficiently worked up, he delivers his fly. Jake's clients have taken several permit of over thirty pounds by using this technique, so it's obviously effective. Jake claims that the pattern out here is relatively unimportant, too. The fish are so worked up from the free handouts that they forget to be fussy. If the fly looks remotely like a crab, they jump on it.

In all the discussions above, regardless of the fish being sought or the technique used to chum them, the common denominator is simple- in order for chum to work there must be fish present. Chum will not pull fish into an area they are not using. If the fish are there but being uncooperative, chumming can turn a mediocre day into a great one.

## HOW TO FIGHT FISH

"There's a fish at three o'clock!" Captain Tommy Locke directed my casting from his position on the poling tower. I couldn't see the fish in the glare of the early morning sun, but I cast where he told me to. The fish inhaled the fly and in a heartbeat I was hooked up to the biggest fish of my life.

Forty minutes later this magnificent fish was alongside the boat, where Captain Jim Weber lip gaffed and released it. Jim and Tommy both estimated its weight at 130 pounds. After some resuscitation the fish swam away strongly. I felt like I needed an oxygen tent, but I had whipped this fish in a relatively short period of time. We were all very pleased with the vigor the fish had shown as it disappeared into the emerald waters.

Regardless of their size, fish to be released benefit greatly from a short, hard fight. Most of us can recall (even if it was way back there when we had physical education classes in school) overexercising. The next day our muscles were sore and stiff, making it difficult and painful to move. For most of us this was not a life threatening situation. But a fish played too long develops the same lactic acid compounds in its muscle tissue that we do when we overexercise, and a fish that can't move well often falls prey to one of its many enemies.

Oxygen dissolves better in cold water than warm. While here in Florida we never find truly cold water, the cooler temperatures of winter often put more fight into the fish we catch, particularly redfish. Fish caught at this time of year suffer less stress because of the relatively plentiful oxygen supply in the water. Without having done any research on the subject, common sense leads me to believe that post-release mortality is lower during the winter months.

In summer, fighting fish hard is more important simply because the water hass less oxygen. The fish is in a situation somewhat analogous to the marathon runner who trains at sea level and then has to run a race at 10,000 feet- there is simply not enough oxygen. Concerned anglers will put it to the fish during summer in

*This vertical rod position puts very little pressure on the fish. All it needs to do to resist effectively is spread its pectoral fins.*

consideration for their quarry, and bring the fight to a conclusion as quickly as possible.

Why else should anglers try to fight the fish hard and fast? The least altruistic reason is that the longer you fight it, the more likely it is to get away. The hook wears a larger and larger hole in the tissue and a brief moment of slack allows it to fall out. Abrasion on the leader leads to breakage. The angler tires and makes a mistake which lets the fish break off. It makes more sense for everyone, or everything, involved to beat the fish quickly.

So let's take a look at six general rules for fighting fish which hold for any type of tackle, and which lead to a higher success rate for any angler lucky enough, or skillful enough, to hang a big fish every now and then.

-Rule 1) Use the heaviest line that's practical. Why use six pound tippet if ten pound will work just as well? I take exception with anglers who tell me ultralight tackle is more "sporting". They may have more fun with it but it really beats up on the fish. I was speaking with a guide recently who told me that his client fought a 30 pound plus redfish for an hour and a half on fly tackle before the hook pulled out. My response was the guy should learn how to fight fish. The guide said he did a good job but was using six pound tippet. WHY? Why would anyone chasing 30 pound reds use six pound tippet unless he was specifically trying for a world record? In my own saltwater fly fishing I never use less than twelve pound tippet with the exception of bonefishing.

-Rule 2) Set the drag correctly. When using fly tackle set the drag at 25% of the breaking strength of the tippet. To determine the drag setting get a good scale and tie the leader to it. Then tie the other end of the scale to a tree or some other immovable object. Point the rod directly at the scale and pull until the drag starts to release. The reading on the scale is the actual, measured drag setting on the reel.

-Rule 3) Learn to put maximum pressure on the fish. While we're still tied to the tree, start putting some bend in the rod while holding the reel to prevent drag slip. How much pressure can you put on the line before it breaks? Try this two different ways.

First, use the method already described, and second, try lifting a ten pound mushroom anchor off the floor while standing on a table. Use twelve-weight fly tackle with 16 pound class tippet. Using the scale, with all their strength, the maximum pressure most anglers will put on that 16 pound tippet will be only twelve pounds or so. During the demonstration with the anchor described earlier, most of us just barely moved the anchor. The obvious conclusion is that with 16 pound tippet the average fisherman will never break the line no matter how hard he pulls on it, and with twelve pound tippet

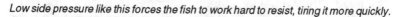

*Low side pressure like this forces the fish to work hard to resist, tiring it more quickly.*

we can use 90% of our pulling strength and still be safe.

While your neighbors might call for the men in the white coats if they see you fighting trees with your fishing tackle, if you want to learn to put maximum pressure on the fish you catch there are few things that are more valuable.

-Rule 4) When the fish swims away, don't try to stop it. While you probably can't pull hard enough to break a 16 pound class tippet, plenty of fish can. If the fish surges or makes a run and you try to stop it, something will break. While the fish runs it uses up its energy reserves. Let it go.

Snook fishing around mangroves or other structure provides one exception to this rule. If a fish runs toward the roots, you have a decision to make. If he gets in there, he's gone. Should you try to stop him?

I vividly remember trying to stop a fish in the Everglades that I had hooked on a surface plug. I locked up the reel, trying to keep that fish from the trees. The eight pound test line went slack and the plug floated to the surface. I reeled it in and checked it- the hooks had straightened before the eight pound line broke.

-Rule 5) Either you or the fish should be gaining line. When the fish stops its run, you should immediately attack it and start gaining line. Never let up or let the fish rest. While neither of you takes line, he is resting. He recovers faster that you, so a standoff only prolongs the fight. Show the fish you want to win. Like Billy Pate says, "You have to want the fish more than he wants to get away, and the fish thinks he's going to die."

-Rule 6) Learn to use side pressure. In shallow water, or if the fish is at the surface in deep water, pulling up on its head does little or nothing to tire it or break its spirit. The fish spreads its pectoral fins and resists with almost no effort. If you pull to the side, or better yet pull down (the famous "down-and-dirty" move) the fish has no defense and has to use muscle power to overcome the pull. Furthermore, once it has been rolled over once or twice, the fish will give up more quickly. Always pull opposite to the direction the fish is moving. In other words, if the fish is moving to the left, pull to the right and vice versa.

Learn these six techniques for fighting fish. Fish you release will have a better survival rate, and those around you will know that they are in the presence of a world class fisherman.

## HANDLING FISH

Before you beat the fish, you decide whether to kill or release it. The only good reason to kill a fish involves eating it. I think killing a trophy fish to eat it is a tremendous waste. Eat the smaller fish and release the trophies so they can pass on those genes! At the very least put table-bound fish on ice immediately for maximum quality. Most fish headed for the table benefit from being bled and gutted before being iced down. Some, like bluefish and mackerel, become almost inedible without this treatment.

Handle fish you intend to release as little as possible. Many times just letting small fish shake in the water at boatside or at your feet will free them with no handling whatsoever. You can safely handle most small fish that won't unhook themselves with a bare, wet hand. Roll the fish on its back and remove the barbless hook. Most times it comes out easily, unless taken deeply.

Larger fish require a different approach. I use a cloth glove covered with squiggly lines of rubber to handle most of the fish I catch. With this glove to protect your hand you can "lip" many species of fish just like you would a largemouth bass. Redfish, seatrout, snook, and smaller tarpon and cobia can all be handled this way. The glove protects your hand while you "tail" some of the other species, like larger jack crevalle, permit, dolphin, kingfish, and smaller tuna.

Really big fish usually require the use of a gaff. A lip gaff is recommended for tarpon too big to handle any other way, large barracuda, large kingfish, and large tuna headed for release. After piercing the thin membrane behind the lower jaw, pin the gaff against the underside of the boat gunwale, preventing the fish from jumping off the hook. If you intend to kill the fish use a body gaff.

I try never to use a net unless I'm going to kill the fish. Nets remove the slime layer and often damage the eyes as well. Their use is not recommended for catch and release anglers.

If you want to photograph a catch, please keep in mind that fish suffocate when kept in the air. Have the camera equipment ready before the fish comes along side. Once you remove the fish from the water, work quickly! If you hold your breath while you work you have a better idea of when the fish needs to breathe again, too.

If you want a mount, get a few photos so you can get accurate color rendition and tape the fish to get its length and girth. Almost all taxidermists use fiberglass mounts these days. Glass mounts look better and last longer, and allow you to release your trophy unharmed. Let another angler experience the same thrill!

# Chapter 3- THE FISHES

Anglers visiting Florida's saltwater for the first time could easily compare their experience to that of finding a treasure chest. Most everyone has heard about the "Big Three"- tarpon, bonefish, and permit- but so many other fish here take flies and are either fun, interesting, challenging, or all three combined to catch, that to just discuss the most popular species would be a disservice to the reader. Instead, this chapter takes a look at most of the common fly caught species with information about specialized tackle, techniques, times of year, and various other interesting tidbits. I intend to try to paint as complete a picture as possible in the short space allowed in this book.

## BARRACUDA *Sphryaena barracuda*

*Capt. Nat Ragland with a smallish sized cuda. Photo courtesy of Bill Elliott.*

    The barracuda, or cuda for short, is one of fly fishing's most underrated gamefish. Lightning fast and possessing keen eyesight, big cudas (anything over about 15 pounds) don't get fooled easily. Although they lack stamina, the speed of their runs and spectacular leaps make barracuda very exciting fish to catch.
    Cuda can be sightfished on flats in a manner similar to tarpon or bonefish. The best time for this is during the winter, when the big cuda come into the shallows to sun themselves.
    Cuda require a somewhat different approach than other flats dwellers. The fly should never land near (within about five feet)

the fish, but rather is cast beyond the cuda 10 feet or so and then stripped as fast as possible in hope of enticing a strike. If the fish follows without striking, the fly is moving too slowly. Sometimes pulling the fly from the water and casting it back out so that the fish intercepts it as it returns to its resting place works well. Sometimes the rod needs to be tucked under the arm and a two-handed retrieve used in order to give the fly sufficient velocity.

Another way to entice a flats cuda to strike is to cast the fly, then immediately backcast and pull the fly from the water. Repeat this from four to six times. Then, let the fly fall and retrieve it quickly. The cuda gets so excited by seeing all these flies blast by that he just crushes it on that last cast when you retrieve normally. Remember, though, if the cuda sees you, and they see quite well, the chance for a strike greatly diminishes.

Cuda can be caught by blind casting on the flats. They tend to use sandy holes in grass flats as ambush points. If weather or sky conditions don't allow sight fishing, long casts past sandy areas and rapid retrieves will often raise a few fish. Expect to work hard!

You can fish cuda over wrecks or around channel markers, channel edges, or other structure, using the same techniques already described. In these offshore situations, chumming with live baitfish like pilchards or sardines will usually get them in the mood.

Cuda flies tend toward the long and thin, usually made from synthetic materials. A fly from six to eight inches long tied on a 1/0 hook is a good choice. The bulk of the fly seems to be relatively unimportant, so the fly should be no thicker than a pencil. Bright colors work best most of the time. Remember to use three to four inches of single strand wire or most fish you hook will be off with your fly before you ever knew they were there.

Cuda will also take poppers. The same rules apply. Long and thin, fast movement, long casts, and bright colors will bring the most action. Don't use poppers you value- they won't last long.

The all around rod described in Chapter 1 makes an excellent cuda stick. The fish gives the best account of itself on the lightest tackle practical. Seven weight outfits toss the cuda flies an adequate distance if the wind isn't too strong.

The best locations for sight fishing cuda on the flats include all of the Keys waters and Biscayne Bay. On the east coast they will sometimes be found inshore, but this fishery lacks consistency. Rare in the Everglades and inshore on the west coast, cudas can be found in most offshore waters from about Cape Canaveral/ Tampa Bay south, especially during the summer months.

Although barracuda flesh has excellent taste and texture, the fish often carry ciguatoxin, a nerve poison that can be fatal. Handle all your barracuda carefully (those teeth are every bit as dangerous as they look) but gently, and after getting a photo or two release them to fight again another day.

## BLACK DRUM *Pogonias cromus*

Black drum are not usually thought of as a fly rod fish, and sometimes (well, maybe most of the time) they completely ignore flies. But in the Banana River Manatee Refuge, during the winter months, big black drum tail on the flats and will eat certain flies with a surprising degree of consistency. These fish start at 20 pounds and go up from there! I don't know just how big they get, since the

*Barry Kent holds a big black drum he took with a Clouser minnow.*

biggest ones always seem to break off.

Should you visit this area, throw Clouser minnows in brown or black, or crab imitations in brown. Drop the fly close to the fish and allow it to sink to the bottom, then move it very slowly. Keep working on the fish until it eats or moves off. Sometimes, if it's tailing, you can chase an individual fish for as long as ten or fifteen minutes before it finally sees your offering and decides to take!

Once hooked most of these fish fight like bulldozers. Unless you want to be messing with one fish for a long time use a heavy tippet (15 pound) and put it to him immediately. I try to keep them from running at all, but on the other hand I break off quite a few fish and sometimes end up with bloody knuckles. Even with this approach, expect a hard fought 10 to 20 minute battle.

These big fish aren't edible unless you enjoy eating coarse flesh with parasites. Revive your catch, which won't take long (these fish are RUGGED) and release it so it can make more baby drum.

## BLUEFISH *Pomatomus saltatrix*

Unfortunately, most of the time Florida bluefish just don't create the same type of excitement that they do up north. Since the average Florida bluefish only weighs between one and two pounds, that isn't really surprising. Every spring though, a horde of big, hungry choppers migrates north along the east coast following baitfish schools. If easterly, especially southeasterly, winds push the bait near shore the blues will be right along the beaches, terrorizing mullet, bathers, and anything else in the water.

Inlets seem to attract these fish as much as anything else. Coming up the coast, St. Lucie, Ft. Pierce, Sebastian, Ponce, and Matanzas Inlets, Port Canaveral, the St. Johns river mouth and Nassau Sound are all possible sites for the blues to come ashore. Some years they never do come in, and are north of the Florida state line and probably up to Hatteras before ever making landfall.

The smaller blues hang around inlets and river mouths along the east coast all winter. They move into river systems and we've caught them in the Indian River system as far from the ocean as the power plants in Titusville, at least 30 miles from Ponce Inlet. Like their bigger relatives they strike pretty much anything when they feed. Heavy mono leaders and durable, flashy flies imitating minnows are suggested. Poppers sometimes bring some very exciting fishing.

Bluefish also run along the west coast. These again tend to

*An angler displays a typical Florida bluefish. Photo courtesy of Capt. Mike Holliday.*

be smaller fish. Up in the Panhandle bluefish are caught all summer, but along the rest of the west coast it is a winter and spring fishery, concentrated around cuts and passes.

## BONEFISH *Albula vulpes*

Somewhat surprisingly, bonefish can be very easy to catch with flies. As could be expected, they can be practically impossible, too. Among the biggest found anywhere, Florida bonefish average about six pounds.

Bones can consistently be found from Biscayne Bay south into the Keys to about Big Pine. South of there the population seems to thin somewhat. They feed on small fish, various crustaceans, marine worms, and other invertebrates, and classic angling for them takes place on shallow flats where they feed, locations where

*Bill Elliott with a nice bonefish. Photo courtesy of Bill Elliott.*

anglers typically watch all of the action.

Fortunately for the boatless, lots of good wade fishing can be found in the Keys and even around Miami. Ocean side flats tend to be firm and support the weight of even husky fly fishers. Waders, as always, have the advantage of stealth on their side, a big help in heavily fished Keys waters.

Good bonefishing can be found all year long, weather conditions permitting. During the winter periods bones tend to feed between fronts, especially after the afternoon sun has warmed up the water a bit. Spring is good and fall is probably the best time to fish for bones. You'll find the best summer fishing in the morning, as intense heat and sunlight during the day make the flats uncomfortable for fish and angler alike. Evening fishing during the summer months also produces.

During the spring and fall the fish feed on the flats any time of day. It gets windy this time of year and if the water gets muddy the game ends. Good weather often brings tremendous fishing. Relatively few people fish the Keys during the autumn. You may have the entire flat to yourself.

During the winter, water temperature again becomes critical. During cool weather, fish during the afternoon hours. The water will be warmest then.

Given the choice fish an incoming tide (winter excepted).

Also, whether fishing in a boat or wading, try to move with the current, since the fish always move into it. So by "going with the flow", casts to fish will generally be head-on shots, too- the best kind.

Expert bonefisherman Chico Fernandez describes bonefish feeding behavior this way: "When the tide is low and the fish first move onto the flats, they are hungry. After they've been feeding for a few hours they become much more selective." It makes sense. Bones are usually easier early in the tide.

This having been said, sometimes time of day becomes more critical than tide phase. Again, normally this occurs during summer, when morning fishing is best, and during winter, when evening fishing is best.

If you must fish during the day in the summer, fish an incoming tide. Cooler ocean water coming onto the flat allows the fish a degree of comfort they would not have otherwise. The situation reverses during the winter. The sun warms up water that's been on the flat a while enough to allow the fish to use it. This happens during the later stages of the incoming tide and the early stages of the outgoing.

Slowly wade or pole with the current looking for anything which might be a bonefish. If there are no fish tailing or pushing wakes look for muds. Muds are made by feeding fish. Make your casts fall short a few feet, letting the fly sink to the bottom if necessary. The fly will be between you and the fish, but they're moving toward you. As soon as you think they can see it, move it slowly. Make sure that you keep watching the fish!

If they see it there will be no doubts about it. They do one of three things- flee in abject terror, come check it out and refuse it, or come check it out and eat it.

If they flee, the fly was fouled with grass, or moved at them, or was too close to them before it moved. If they refuse it, check the fly. If it is not fouled with grass or algae, change to a different size or color. If they eat it, set the hook GENTLY. When the fish takes off, it takes care of hook setting, believe me.

If you see fish pushing up a wake, cast several feet ahead of it and move the fly SLOWLY. Sometimes when the fish are pushing a wake, they swim fast, with an obvious agenda, and aren't interested in eating. If they don't strike don't let this bother you- they probably wouldn't have taken a live shrimp!

Tailing fish are eating, though. A small crab fly made from wool, or my Fuzzy Crab pattern, are good choices for this situation. These flies hit the water with a soft, seductive "splat", sink rapidly

*A sampling of simple, effective bonefish flies.*

into the feeding zone, and perfectly imitate a favorite bonefish food. Crab flies don't even need to be moved. If the fish sees it and wasn't spooked by the presentation they usually eat it immediately.

If this is your first bonefish, at this point your life may change forever! First, clear the line. If it fouls on anything the leader instantly breaks, you have a super adrenaline rush, and you own one less fly. Once the fish is on the reel extend the rod high into the air. The fish run right along the bottom. You want to hold the line up to prevent the leader from fraying on coral, rocks, or sea fans.

Let the fish go. If you try to stop it he'll break off. Make sure the drag is set only tightly enough to prevent a backlash.

Once that first incredible run ends he will take a couple shorter ones. Once you've beaten him, handle the fish gently. Leave him in the water if possible. If not, hold the fish parallel to the water's surface and belly up. They have no teeth or spines and are quite safe to handle. Remove the fly (barbless hooks are recommended), revive him until he can swim away, and release him to grow and thrill another fisherman. And congratulations to you!

All of the above supposes that you have good visibility. But if you fish early or late in the day, or if it is overcast, or if you are not used to looking for fish, seeing bonefish in the water can be very difficult. They can still be caught. Try blindcasting for bones.

*Bill Cleveland demonstrates the classic bonefish fighting technique. The rod is held high in the air to keep the leader from fraying on obstructions on the bottom.*

All other things being equal, the fish feed on their favorite flats when weather conditions allow. If you're there too you might just get a couple.

When you use this blind casting technique for bonefish, fly choice is important. You want a fly with which you can cover a lot of water reasonably quickly. The Clouser minnow works well for this. Search the water you can see into for fish. If you see any, cast to them! There's no sense in turning down any good opportunities.

Keep your fly in the water into which you cannot see. Generally this will be the deeper water, but fish feed there as well as in the skinny stuff. Keep casting! Fish every cast as if you expect to hook a fish. Sooner or later you will.

Make long casts. You cover more water this way, giving more fish a chance to see your offering. Also, oftentimes the fish follows your fly for quite a distance before finally making up its mind. Long retrieves give them the opportunity to do this.

Once you hook up, play the fish as explained above.

## BONITO *Sarda sarda*

Fly fishers take bonito all along the east coast during the summer months. Many are taken inadvertently while fishing for other species, and in this situation they are often considered a nuisance catch. Some anglers target bonito though, using pilchards or other baitfish to chum them up.

Once the bonito are chummed up they are not fussy about the fly pattern, and any white fly imitating a minnow works. Their strike is spectacular. They may see and charge the fly from 30-40 feet away and have a good head of steam up when they hit it, often

*A bonito like this one will work your buns off. Photo courtesy of Bob Huttemeyer.*

coming clear of the water.

The first run is something to experience. They sound and then go out from the boat. Like all members of the tuna family they are fast, strong swimmers. This run will test, and sometimes break, your tackle. The fight tends to be long and tough.

Using live pilchards as chum you can keep the bonito around your boat all day. However, at the end of such a day you'll probably need an application of muscle cream!

## COBIA *Rachycentron canadum*

Cobia rank as one of Florida's most exciting inshore game-fish. Found along both coasts in water as shallow as three feet out into depths of over 100 feet they often eat flies with little hesitation, although on some days they completely ignore feathered offerings.

Cobia love structure and often cruise around channel markers, buoys, floating debris, ocean going ships at anchor, and other inanimate objects. They also swim with other "denizens of the deep". Along the Atlantic coast they often swim with manta rays off the beaches. They sometimes associate with sea turtles. I've seen big cobia swimming with manatees in Charlotte Harbor, and in the Homosassa area they follow stingrays in shallow water in the early spring, making for a great sight fishery before tarpon season starts.

These fish, like many other fish found off the beaches, can be chummed up with live baitfish. The baitfish get them feeding and then they're much more likely to hit a fly.

Cobia make seasonal runs up and down both Florida coasts, heading north in the spring and to a lesser degree south again in the fall. During these migrations angler excitement rises to a fever pitch. The St. Andrews Fly Fishers up in Panama City time their annual fly fishing show to coincide with the cobia run. There's no sense in having a fishing show without good fishing available! Personally, I think it shows darned good planning.

At least a nine-weight outfit is usually used to chase these fish. Cobia get big, over 100 pounds, and they're strong. Plenty of backing is needed. Their mouth is rough. Use a 40-50 pound shock tippet.

Cobia eat a wide variety of marine organisms. They hold small fish, shrimp, crabs, and squid in high regard. Consequently, flies imitating any of these foods (or even nothing in particular) all work well. For example in Homosassa dark colored flies, especially rabbit strip patterns, are popular. Up in the Panhandle they like big

*Jim Weber with a nice cobia taken from the shallow waters off Homosassa.*

white ties, sometimes with some pink thrown in. These flies supposedly imitate squid, another favorite cobia food.

Unfortunately, there's not much of a catch and release fishery for cobia. Excellent on the table, they seldom get released once they grow larger than the minimum size limit of 33 inches.

## DOLPHIN *Coryphaena hippurus*

The dolphin rates high as an offshore fly rod target. They strike explosively and their fight is spectacular with frequent acrobatic leaps. In addition, their stunning coloration and high quality on the table make them extremely popular.

They are usually found by trolling, but any type of offshore flotsam often holds dolphin, especially in the summer months. A minnow imitation or popping bug thrown near the floating material

*A typical Florida dolphin. Photo courtesy of Capt. Mike Holliday.*

will usually garner a savage strike. Once a fish is hooked, other fish in the school often follow it, making multiple hookups possible and prolonged action a distinct possibility.

Nine-weight tackle is considered light for dolphin. The average east coast fish ranges from 5-15 pounds, but they get much larger, up to 50 or even 60 pounds. Plenty of backing is needed on the reel, as they make long, fast runs when hooked.

Like many other fish, dolphin respond well to chumming, using small baitfish like pilchards. Once they are in a frenzy behind the stern, the fly fisher has an easy time getting them to strike.

Dolphin grow fast and are short-lived. They mature sexually at the age of nine months and rarely live longer than four years.

## JACK CREVALLE *Caranx hippos*

Crevalle of over six pounds or so are one of my favorite fish. Big, fast, tough, and aggressive, they like to eat flies, and they are common enough that catching one doesn't require an exodus to some far-off location.

The late A.J. McClane had this to say about the crevalle: "One of the several things in the crevalle's favor is the fact that it's a first-class light-tackle fish which can be caught on fly gear. Small crevalle of 6-7 pounds are gregarious and travel in schools. As they become older, big jacks occur in pods, or sometimes you'll see a single or a pair 'running' at top speed.

The individual crevalle takes its feeding seriously. Here and there one mullet will rise above the surface, doing front and back flips, then leaping madly in all directions with a telltale swirl countering each shift. If the hapless baitfish is lucky, it may elude the jack for two or three jumps, but sooner or later the mullet will land in the crevalle's jaws. You can actually drift through acres of frantic mullet and observe this single-minded pursuit."

McClane added this about the jack's fighting ability: "In common with the permit, large jacks always seem to have an extra ounce of energy in reserve. Their tactics are dogged and unrelenting. It's not uncommon to play a 20 pounder for an hour or more on light tackle."

*Walt Jennings with a nice jack crevalle.*

You can find jacks throughout the state, both in inshore and offshore waters. They like patrolling around structures like seawalls and jetties, and are attracted to inlets and river mouths. When they corner or surround a school of baitfish little doubt remains about what's going on- the bait leaps frantically into the air as the crevalle churn the surface to a froth. This makes for heart-attack action as long as the fish stay on top!

Large colorful streamer flies work well for jacks but for the maximum excitement from these fish use popping bugs. The strike from a good sized jack is tremendous and is half the fun of catching them. The bug has to move fast though- they usually don't show much interest in a slow-moving bait.

When fishing off the beaches chumming with live baitfish is an excellent way to catch large jacks. Fifteen and twenty pounders will stay right under the boat as long as the handouts continue. They will definitely work you and your fishing buddies to exhaustion.

## LADYFISH *Elops saurus*

A lot of fly fishers have said if ladyfish grew to 25 pounds they would fish for nothing else. Small ladyfish can be a nuisance, but when this animal hits three pounds it fights far out of proportion to its size. After hookup it takes off on a lightning run, which usually ends with a spectacular leap. They're fast, they jump, they're tough, and they take flies eagerly. Too bad they only grow to about five pounds!

These bigger ladyfish school in certain areas and seldom use others. Two hotspots during the winter are both of the electric generating station outflows, south of Titusville on U.S.1. It is not unusual here to hook and lose two or three of these beasts on a single cast. The current all-tackle world record ladyfish, a five pounder, was caught here on fly tackle by Captain Ron Rebeck. The St. Lucie River holds some good concentrations of big ladies, as does the Loxahatchee.

Ladies have very abrasive mouths and are rough on flies. Fortunately, they hit almost anything. When I fish at the Titusville power plants during the winter I clean my fly box of all the uglies, the failed experiments, the flies that are just too beat up to use for anything else. That having been said, Clouser minnows in chartreuse and white are always a good choice. Coating the fly's head with epoxy will extend its life significantly. In many areas they also hit surface bugs, always an exciting way to fish.

*Matt Van Pelt holds a ladyfish he caught at the Titusville power plant outflow.*

Light tackle maximizes the sport with ladyfish. A six-weight does a good job. Be sure to use a good long length of 30 pound mono as a shock tippet. The mouths of the ladies wear the shock out quickly and you have to cut off and re-tie your fly frequently.

Ladyfish are rumored to be edible. However, I don't know anyone who knows anyone who eats them! So handle your ladies gently and release them as quickly as you can. And be sure to bring a towel- the ladyfish is a slimy creature, and you need the towel for cleaning that slime from your hands.

**THE MACKERELS** *Scombridae* family

Florida waters hold three different species of mackerel- Spanish, cero, and king. You find Spanish and kings along both coasts the length of the state; ceros are found mostly from Miami south into the Keys. Ceros and Spanish are quite similar- schooling fish that average three to six pounds, are found in ocean waters from right off the beaches to several miles offshore, and feed primarily on glass minnows, pilchards, sardines, anchovies and other small baitfish. From here on when I mention Spanish I'm talking about both fishes.

King mackerel (or kingfish) range in size from "snakes" in single digit weights, to "smokers" of 50 or 60 pounds. They are usually found farther offshore in water more or less 100 feet deep, around wrecks, buoys, or other structure, offshore from inlets, or other areas where their primary food (menhaden and other large baitfish) is abundant.

Spanish make excellent fly rod targets when they work on bait schools. Terns are especially helpful in pinpointing schools of Spanish. Small flies imitating glass minnows or other small bait work well, flies like the Glass Minnow pattern, small Clouser minnows, or the Surf Candy pattern. Although Spanish (and all the other mackerels) have sharp teeth, if you use a wire trace you'll get many fewer strikes. Thirty pound mono gives a reasonable compromise between strikes and cutoffs. Bring a lot of extra flies!

For anglers without boats, Spanish can often be caught from the beach, especially around sunrise and sunset. Rod Smith, Gary Berkson, and I were casting for snook off Satellite Beach one summer morning. The snook were uncooperative and we could see the Spanish going nuts on glass minnows just out of casting range. We took the canoe off my car and launched it through the surf and caught several nice mackerel on Clouser minnows.

Spanish are good eating, especially so if they are bled and put on ice immediately. They don't really freeze very well, so don't fill the boat up with the idea of saving them for a rainy day.

Kingfish are another animal entirely. For one thing, few kings are caught from shore- a boat is pretty much a necessity. Secondly, you are not likely to find kings at the surface feeding ravenously the way Spanish do. Without a special approach, fly fishing for them successfully is difficult to accomplish at best, and could probably be considered impossible.

What the serious kingfish angler needs in order to catch them on flies (and this should come as no surprise) is a livewell filled with pilchards or other small baitfish. The successful fly fishing king mackerel angler chums the kings within casting range of the boat. Once they're there actively feeding, catching them follows naturally.

*Joe Mulson pulls in a Spanish mackerel caught off Cape Canaveral.*

Captain Tommy Locke specializes in catching kings on flies. Based in the Boca Grand area, Tommy fishes along the buoy line leading out into the Gulf from Boca Grand Pass when the kings are running. The buoys serve as fish attractors.

Tommy tosses pilchards over a few at a time until he gets the kings' attention. They literally boil on the pilchards right behind the boat. While in this frenzy the kings take a white fly resembling a pilchard without hesitation. You'd better have a wire trace between the fly and the leader. Kings have sharp teeth.

You'd also better have a lot of backing on the reel, and prepare to reel a lot of line. Kings swim long and fast once hooked up, and the bigger they are the longer they go. They don't call them smokers for nothing! Tommy's anglers have taken kings over 40

*Captain Tommy Busciglio with a nice fly-caught permit. Photo courtesy of Bill Elliott.*

pounds while doing this.

Tackle for these big kings starts with nine-weight rods, which are definitely on the light side. Ten- and eleven-weight tackle gives the angler better lifting power when the fish sound.

While Capt. Locke uses this technique in the Boca Grande area, other charter captains use the same technique elsewhere along the coast. In order to work effectively, there must be some thing present to concentrate the fish- a reef, a wreck, a buoy line, a spring hole, or some other type of structure.

King mackerel make excellent table fare.


## PERMIT *Trachinotus falcatus*

Permit are one of the great trophies of the Florida Keys. A Keys Grand Slam consists of catching of a bonefish, a tarpon, and a permit on flies all in the same day. Most anglers who try and fail to achieve this distinction stumble over the permit more often than the other two.

Up until about ten years ago permit were an extraordinarily rare fly rod catch. Due to the efforts of guides like Nat Ragland and anglers like George Anderson and Del Brown, catching permit on flies, while still not easy, happens reasonably often.

These "permit pioneers" recognized that permit love eating crabs and also recognized that sink rate was an important factor in fly construction. They then designed crab imitations that permit actually ate. Ragland developed the Puff, Anderson developed the McCrab, and Brown developed the Merkin. These flies revolutionized fly fishing for permit.

Anglers who want to catch a permit on a fly are strongly advised to hire a guide. I typically prefer the do it yourself approach and the desire to help others who feel the same way was one of the driving forces behind my writing this book. However, I tried on my own unsuccessfully for years to take a permit on a fly. I hardly ever saw them, much less got them to eat my fly.

Having said all that, you may want to try anyway. Like kingfish tackle, a nine-weight is considered light for permit. Unlike kings, no wire is needed, and a shock tippet is actually a handicap. A 14 or 16 pound test tippet supplies all the protection you need.

Look for permit near the edges of flats, or near rock piles. Sometimes the fish "fin out", lying just beneath the surface with the tips of their dorsal and caudal fins in the air. They often tail, rooting in the bottom for crabs just like bonefish do. You'll see them cruising along the flat in water three or four feet deep.

Guides differ in their recommendations on how far to lead the permit, but all of them agree on the following point- once the fish sees the fly (a crab imitation, of course) that fly should be allowed to drop to the bottom and should not move again until the fish has either taken it, or refused it and started swimming off. If the former occurs, strip strike with the line hand to make sure the fish actually has the fly. Once you determine that the fish is actually on, use the rod to strike several more times. The mouth of a permit has about the same consistency as the tires on your car. You really need to stick them.

If the fish refuses your fly, all is not lost. When it starts to swim off, move the fly just a little and see if it comes back. If it does, do not move the fly until it takes or refuses. You might have to play this game a few times. If the fish really does move off, try to get the fly airborne and deliver it out front again. Don't give up until the fish is out of sight!

If you are lucky enough to hook up, prepare for a long tough fight. A good sized permit can easily be over thirty pounds. Like other members of the jack family, permit are incredibly strong. They run like a bonefish when hooked, but swim much farther than bonefish do. If hooked near the edge of a flat the permit usually heads toward deeper water.

In one way, they are kind of like snook or largemouth bass. If they can tangle your line up on a snag, they will. They will find plenty of snags between the flat and deep water, things like sea fans, coral heads, crab trap lines, and others. They also rub their snout in the bottom, trying to dislodge the hook. They successfully use their broad sides to resist to the utmost. If you are lucky enough to boat the fish, it may be miles from where you hooked up.

Permit are reputed to be delicious on the table, but most serious fly fishers would rather lose their casting arm than kill such a magnificent fish.

### REDFISH *Sciaenops ocellatus*

Redfish keep more guides working than any other fish in Florida. Hard to find only a few years back, redfish populations made an incredible recovery after being protected from commercial gillnet fishing. Schools of hundreds of redfish averaging ten, twenty, or even twenty five pounds are common sights on flats all over the state. Singles, doubles, and small pods of fish are often found too.

You may see them laid up on the bottom, pushing up wakes, tailing, or "backing", that is, feeding in water so shallow that they are not even covered and their backs are out of the water. Best of all, redfish eagerly (well, most of the time) gobble flies of all kinds, including all the various minnow imitations, poppers and sliders, and flies imitating crabs, a favorite redfish food.

Reds are made to order for the do it yourself angler. Various techniques work well for reds, and they're found in most parts of the state. You can catch them from the beach, by wading on shallow flats, or of course by casting from a boat. Typically fished for with flies in water from six inches to three feet deep, they make a superb fly rod target.

Tackle for reds typically includes rods in the seven- to nine-weight range. Line choice depends on where you fish, but for flats floating weight forward lines work best. A leader about the length of the rod, a section of 20 pound shock, and the fly of your choice complete the rig.

Popular flies for reds include bendbacks, deceivers, seaducers, popper/slider types, divers, Clouser minnows, and crab patterns. As mentioned earlier, reds usually aren't too fussy. If you have a fish refuse, change to a smaller and/or darker colored fly.

*The author with a beautiful redfish. This fish was tailing when it took a Fuzzy Crab.*

Effective fly sizes range from #4 at the small end to 2/0 at the big end. Larger flies are better when it's warm. Choose smaller darker flies in the winter.

Florida currently protects red drum with a slot size limit and a closed season. Fish smaller than 18 inches or larger than 27 inches must be released. Legal-sized fish make for excellent eating.

## SEATROUT *Cynoscion nebulosus*

At one time seatrout were the most popular sportfish in Florida. Years of too liberal bag limits and heavy commercial fishing pressure has taken its toll, and finding large seatrout is fairly rare. Finding a concentration of large seatrout is VERY rare. Hopefully, now that the net ban has passed the trout will recover as spectacularly as the redfish did, and in a few years the Indian River Lagoon in the vicinity of Cocoa will once again be known as the "Seatrout Capital of the World".

Seatrout feed primarily on other fish and shrimp. Therefore, the fly fisher should try to imitate these foods. All of the popular minnow imitations will work well, and trout have a weakness for brightly colored flies. Hair bugs or other types of poppers also produce. And of course seatrout are suckers for flies that mimic shrimp. The fly fisher can successfully use a wide variety of flies.

Seatrout are unspectacular at the end of the line. A Pfleuger Medalist 1498 is all the reel needed. In other words, state of the art tackle is unnecessary. Really nice trout will make runs, but they won't be very long. The only reason you would need more than fifty yards or so of backing is if some other type of fish ate your fly instead

*Susan Kumiski with a nice trout caught in the Mosquito Lagoon.*

of a trout. This is a very real possibility, so don't get complacent!

Rod size is determined by wind and fly size more than anything else. A seven weight will usually be ample, and nine-weights overpower most trout hooked nowadays.

Waders (and everyone else who looks) find trout on grass flats all over the state. Trout like areas of mixed sand and grass bottom, and use the edges between the two as ambush points. Sand holes in grass flats make good targets for your fly when fish can't be seen.

Blind casting over healthy grass flats with any type of surface fly can be extremely effective, especially early or late in the day. On the flats big trout will often be found cruising under schools of finger mullet, waiting for one to make an error. Cast around and into these schools. When mullet make muds, seatrout will definitely be in the vicinity, looking for an easy meal.

When iced down after capture, seatrout will make an excellent meal. In deference to the restoration of this particular fishery, if you are so lucky as to catch any trout more than about twenty inches long, please release them so they can spawn and boost their population for the future.

## SHARKS Phylum *Chondreicthyes*

*SHARK!* To the average person, the word is synonymous with fear bordering on terror. To the angler though, sharks supply a source of wonder. We marvel at the grace they show as they move through the water, even as we try to keep our distance. We are no strangers to fear either, we fishermen. It makes no sense to look for trouble.

Many different species of sharks swim in Florida waters. Several make exciting fly rod sport. Some, like the nurse shark, are relatively dull, sluggish creatures. Others, like the hammerhead, often grow to lengths which make them longer than the boats from which the anglers are fishing. Tangling with a fish like this from a small boat could prove exceedingly dangerous!

Several species of sharks patrol shallow flats and can be stalked and cast to like others flats fish. Blacktips, lemon sharks, and bull sharks all like to hunt in the shallows and use water so skinny their backs are exposed to the air. They are extremely spooky in these shallows and you need to use the greatest skill in stalking and care in presentation in order to elicit a strike.

They take brightly colored streamer flies, if you place the

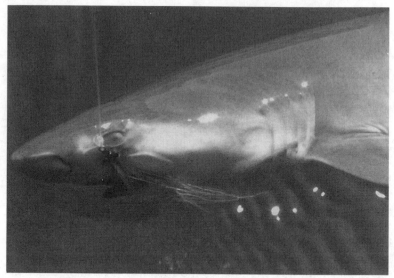

*Although it's not the greatest shark fly, this blacktip took a Clouser minnow.*

fly off to the side of their head where they can see it and turn on it. Joe Mulson and I had shot after shot at some blacktip sharks one time while in Everglades National Park. We watched in frustration as the shark would come up behind the fly ready to eat and would lose sight of the fly after getting it under its snout. The poor shark kept trying to eat this morsel and opened up and missed time after time! I still don't who was more frustrated, the shark or us.

You can also sightfish sharks with poppers on slightly deeper flats. In very shallow water the popping of the fly spooks the shark, but with a foot or more of water under them they become much more aggressive. You'll find watching a shark tracking and then attacking your popper tremendously exciting!

Finally, whether on the flats or offshore, sharks respond very well to chum. Get a small barracuda or a blue runner and partially fillet both sides. Hang it in the water. The current will spread the scent and sharks will follow it to your boat.

Tackle for shallow water sharking depends on the anticipated size of the shark. For smaller sharks to fifty pounds or so seven- to nine-weight outfits work well. Blacktips, bulls, and lemons all reach triple figures in the poundage department, though. Going after these brutes without sufficient firepower is sheer folly. When one of these sharks realizes it's in trouble in the shallows it streaks off for deeper water as powerfully as any other fish is capable of doing. Under the best of circumstances you'll be in for a long, hard fight. Go undergunned and you've probably lost before you start.

Bigger sharks can be had offshore. They are usually chummed in by using live baitfish or a combination of live bait and ground menhaden, balao, or other oily fish. This can be very serious business, with sharks the size of the boat entering the chumline a distinct possibility.

The legendary hammerhead called Old Hitler may be encountered. Old Hitler has been seen in various locations in Florida, usually during the tarpon run. These locations include Boca Grande Pass and some of the Keys bridges. This monster's length is estimated at between 17 and 21 feet. Hooking a shark like this on a mega fifteen weight would still be folly- he might never realize he was hooked!

Captain Tommy Busciglio told me one the best true shark stories I've ever heard. Tommy was fishing with clients in the Marquesas Islands off of Key West when they came upon a large school of hundred pound plus tarpon. These huge "baitfish" had been packed into a tight ball on a deep flat by three hammerheads between 12 and 15 feet long. While two sharks kept the tarpon corralled, the third would charge into the pack and eat. The tarpon were showering like gigantic terrified mullet as these sharks took turns feeding. Tommy said it was the single most awesome thing he's ever seen in a lifetime of fishing.

Hooking a shark like that from a small skiff in shallow water would be indescribably exciting. But imitating a six foot long tarpon with a fly (and casting it if you could) would be difficult at best!

Needless to say, regardless of the type of shark you chase or where you choose to chase them, you need some wire on the business end of the leader. Some anglers prefer single strand, but for big sharks it can easily kink and break during the battle. About twelve inches of plastic coated Sevenstrand works better for the big boys. A small swivel between the wire and the class tippet will help prevent line twist while fighting the shark. Blacktips especially like to spin during their often spectacular leaps!

When tying flies for sharking, use bronze hooks. The fly isn't worth your fingers. Cut the wire leader and the bronze hook will quickly rust out, leaving no permanent damage to the fish.

## SNAPPER *Lutjanidae* Family

Snapper aren't usually thought of as fly rod targets, but in Florida both the mutton snapper and the mangrove snapper sometimes fall to fly rodders. Muttons in particular like to follow stingrays along Keys flats, and when they do this they are at their most "catchable" by fly fishers. Ordinarily it's difficult to fool a mutton with a fly, but when following a ray that's kicking up some groceries it's much easier to convince them to take. Flies similar to those used for bonefish or permit do the trick.

Small mangrove snapper are commonly caught while fishing for other species, especially in the Everglades and Keys. Bigger ones (more than a couple of pounds) are suspicious of everything. They respond well to frozen chum blocks though, and can be taken with flies dead drifted behind the boat with the chum.

Both mutton and mangrove snappers are delicious.

## SNOOK *Centropomus undecimalis*

If snook ranged all over the United States the way black bass do, they would undeniably be the most popular fish in North America. They certainly hold a special place in the hearts of Florida fishermen. They make a superb fly rod target. They take flies readily

*These anglers show off a nice mutton snapper. Photo courtesy of Bill Elliott.*

(when they're in the mood), they're strong, they're tough, they jump, they use structure to break you off, and they get fairly large (over 30 pounds). Quite simply, they are one of Florida's most popular and challenging game fish.

Snook inhabit shallow coastal waters, estuaries, and brackish lagoons. They may range into fresh water, especially during the winter months. They can be caught by both sight-fishing and blind-casting along beaches, off beaches by chumming with live bait, in passes, along mangrove shorelines, blind-casting, sight-fishing, or chumming on flats, in creeks, around oyster bars, etc. They have many of the same habits as the aforementioned black bass, take many of the same flies, and can be caught with the same tackle.

Like bass, snook seldom make long runs. They lunge with incredible power for bridge abutments, pilings, roots, or whatever

*Capt. Gregg Gentile with a fine St. Lucie River snook.*

else is available to them. If they reach the cover the game usually ends. Once in a while a stupid snook gets hooked and heads out to open water, but such dumb specimens usually don't live long, since they make a fine table fish.

Snook are found roughly from Tampa Bay on the west side and Port Canaveral on the east side south. Snook are caught north of this line on both coasts, but it becomes a very specialized fishery requiring local knowledge. Although you just might get one, you certainly don't fish in Mosquito Lagoon expecting to catch snook!

Tackle needs as usual are dictated by the size of the fish targeted and the type of terrain to be fished. Fishing for big fish around mangroves requires a rod and leader system with guts. Nine weight rods do nicely. If you hook a big fish near mangroves he'll likely try to run in there. You've got to try and stop him. A wimpy leader will just give. A strong one of sixteen pound test will give you some hand-sizzling action, and although those line burns smart, this leader is much more likely to hold the fish.

Snook possess raspy, abrasive lips and a slick leader (and hand) cutting device on their gill plates. You must use a shock leader. Different opinions exist on what the optimum thickness is for this shock, but 30 pound mono is probably the most popular choice.

Even if the fish run large a skilled angler snook fishing on grass flats could easily get by with a seven-weight. With nothing to tangle the line on, the fish will make short runs and jump until she tires. Then she's yours! That's all there is to it!

Snook are protected by rather strict laws on bag limits, minimum and maximum sizes, and closed seasons. Laws change all the time. Check at a nearby tackle shop about these laws if you want to keep a fish. Catch and release angling is allowed anytime.

## TARPON *Megalops atlanticus*

In my humble opinion tarpon of any size are the supreme shallow water fish. First of all, although smaller tarpon are as game as any fish, tarpon get to be as large or larger than the average angler. Second of all, tarpon are often sightfished in water so shallow and clear that the angler can watch the entire drama of the fish tracking and eating the fly which as another point they take quite willingly (on occasion). Thirdly, tarpon after being hooked make these incredible, indescribable leaps, tailwalks, and other out of water displays, sometimes so violently that they severely injure themselves. Their response to being hooked is so extreme that they

*The author with a "baby" tarpon from the Sebastian River.*

sometimes leap into the angler's boat, trashing gear, injuring occupants, and occasionally causing smaller craft to capsize!

Tackle needs depend on the size of the tarpon being targeted. As one might expect, fishing for tarpon in the 80 pound and up category requires specialized tackle like eleven- and twelve-weight rods, matching high quality reels, and specialized lines and leader systems. Very skilled anglers could take on and beat tarpon in the 50 to 70 pound range on nine- or ten-weight rods, but most anglers shouldn't go after these fish undergunned. It puts too much stress on the fish to fight for a long time, making them susceptible to attack by their mortal enemy- big sharks. Stu Apte routinely whips even very big tarpon on twelve pound tippets in 20 minutes or less. Doing this is in the best interests of the fish.

Tarpon eat almost any type of fly designed for use in saltwater. Specialized flies tied for tarpon are based on the Keys style tarpon sreamer, developed by Stu Apte and others in the Florida Keys. Typically, they're tied on hooks from size 3/0 to 5/0 for big fish of over 100 pounds. This style is far from the only kind of fly that the silver kings will eat. The popularity of this style stems from their tendency not to foul. Smaller flies are becoming more popular. Flies for big tarpon are usually pre-rigged to the leaders and stored in a "tarpon box" to keep them from tangling.

Leader systems for the bigger fish are quite specialized too. Most anglers prefer the "big game" style of leader with a (usually) 100 pound mono shock tippet, a section of class tippet of 12, 16, or 20 pounds, and a long (five to eight feet, or sometimes even more) butt section connected to the end of the fly line.

Although the Keys and Homosassa have justly deserved reputations as tarpon fishing meccas, tarpon can be found anywhere in the state during the summer, sometimes in surprising places. The big fish are attracting a directed fishery all along the west coast during the traditional "tarpon season" during May and June. Smaller fish can literally be found almost anywhere, sometimes all year long. In the fall tarpon of all sizes follow the mullet run down along the east coast beaches. Hanging a hundred pound tarpon from the beach would make for an exciting but short fight!

Many anglers fish for years for big tarpon without success.

*Keys style tarpon streamers pre-tied to leaders and stored in a tarpon box.*

To catch big fish consistently, you really need to hire a good guide. Even then, bad weather can ruin the fishing in a flash. Many, many anglers have spent a week fishing for tarpon with the best guides in the business and never hooked a single fish. I spent seven years trying myself before I got that first 100 pound fish. So when things look bad and the fish won't bite and you're tempted to blame the guide, the weather, the moon phase, or (heaven forbid!) even yourself, DON'T. Just remember that the answer to the anguished question "WHY???" is, "Because they are tarpon".

Many tarpon kill tournaments used to be held in Florida. Almost all of these have been replaced by release tournaments, in which all fish are measured and released. Anyone wanting to kill a tarpon must first purchase a tarpon tag, similar to a hunter's deer tag. This tag costs 50 dollars. All taxidermists now make fiberglass mounts, so there is absolutely no reason to kill them for mounting. Besides, in the U.S. tarpon are not used as a food fish.

Tarpon are very delicate fish, surprisingly so for one which reacts so violently to the sting of the hook. If you are lucky enough to catch a silver king, try not to remove it from the water. Take as much time as necessary to revive it. And the thrill you get as you watch that warrior swim away will be as intense as the thrill you got when he rocketed out of the water on that first breathtaking leap.

*Captain Jim Weber up to his armpits in his work, reviving a big tarpon.*

97

*An angler strains to lift a big tripletail caught along the buoy line at Port Canaveral.*

## TRIPLETAIL *Lobotes surinamensis*

Most fly fishers have never heard of the tripletail, never mind catching one. This really is a shame. A common if unusual looking fish, tripletail readily take a well presented fly.

Tripletail are found along both Florida coasts, usually off the beaches but within sight of land. They like to hang out around any floating objects in the water, such as buoys, boards, mats of seaweed, or other objects. I've even seen them under dead jack crevalle which had been discarded by mackerel netters. They often lie on their sides directly underneath the object in question, looking like anything but a desirable gamefish.

During the stone crab season in southwest Florida, tripletail specialists make it a point of running the line of crab trap buoys first thing in the morning. They check each buoy with several casts to see if there are any tripletail present. This is really exciting fishing, for when a big tripletail gets hooked he tries to foul the leader in the buoy line. Stopping them is difficult, and lots of big 'tails break off.

What is big for a tripletail? They routinely reach double digit weights, but any fish over 20 pounds is a nice one. The all tackle world record exceeds 45 pounds. These fish are very strong and will sometimes even jump.

Tripletail seem to eat most types of flies with equal vigor. Seaducers, Clouser minnows, shrimp patterns, even popping bugs, all work at times. The standard eight- or nine-weight outfit performs well. Tripletail have firm white flesh and make fine eating.

## TUNA  *Thunnus* species

Tuna! What exciting fly rod fish! Here in Florida three species of tuna are of interest to fly fishers- the blackfin (*Thunnus atlanticus*), the yellowfin (*Thunnus albacares*), and the little tunny, or false bonito (*Euthynnus alletteratus*). While the little tunny can be caught quite close to shore, the blackfin and the yellowfin are usually taken well offshore, either by following the bycatch trail of shrimpers or by chumming the fish into range with pilchards or other small species of baitfish.

Anyone chasing tuna of any type had better have top quality tackle, especially a quality reel. These fish swim as fast as almost anything else in the sea, and go for quite a distance. Additionally, yellowfins, due to the size they attain, can easily and rapidly strip any fly reel currently in production. The largest tippet class fly rod world record for the yellowfin is around 60 pounds, but the all tackle world record is close to four hundred. You can see there might be a problem if you hook a fish like this on fly! You'll have about eight seconds of reel-smoking ecstasy. Of course you'll have to replace leader, line, and all the backing, but it sure was fun!

Anyone wanting to catch little tunny could find some near shore during the summer months, especially with the help of live baitfish chum. While experienced offshore fly fishers could probably track down some blackfins or yellowfins and have the proper gear for them, anglers not experienced in this type of fishing who want to try it should hire a guide who specializes in offshore fly fishing. Although tuna are caught all along the east coast, most of this activity centers in the Keys, especially Key West. In the next section of this book details will be given about who fishes tuna and when

*Tuna like this are a superb fly rod fish. Photo courtesy of Walt Jennings.*

the best times are.

Many people find the little tunny's dark flesh unpalatable. However, yellowfin and blackfin tuna make excellent eating.

## MISCELLANEOUS FISHES

Other fish swim in Florida's salt, fish not often taken by fly fishers and so ignored in this work until now. While chumming offshore, especially over wrecks, some surprises should be expected to show up in the chum line. Fish like wahoo, amberjack, African pompano, even sailfish are all distinct possibilities.

Bob Huttemeyer told me about a morning he was fishing for bonito and hooked one of about 15 pounds (on conventional tackle). Suddenly a magnificent blue marlin appeared, then attacked and ate his fish. Now he was hooked up to a several hundred pound marlin, fishing from a small boat, using fifteen pound test line. This "Old Man and the Sea" drama lasted well into the afternoon, when the marlin finally got serious and broke the wimpy line. Especially when fishing offshore, always expect the unexpected!

A few surprises may await inshore too. Unfortunately these are usually much less spectacular than blue marlin! You may take flounder while fishing for reds or seatrout, always a pleasant surprise. Other species may take your fly. Fishing with a hairbug for baby tarpon in Sebastian River one time, I had a strike. The fish was hooked and it was immediately obvious that it was not a tarpon. Much to my dismay, a minute later a hardhead catfish came alongside the boat, my hairbug stuck in its jaw. Sailcats and lizardfish are other types of unexpected (undesired?) inshore fish known to take flies.

## THE QUICK REFERENCE GUIDE

On the next two pages you'll find a quick reference guide which tells you in a flash which tackle and flies to use for the most popular species of fish. Allow a few words of explanation, please-
-Rod weights- the most commonly used rods to take the species in question. Experienced anglers can use lower weights. Less accomplished anglers can use them with perfect weather conditions.
-Line type- the most commonly used line. Due to space limitations a simple code is used. F= floating, FS= sinktip, and S= sinking, from intermediate to Wet Cel #4. Understand all lines are weight forward types.
-Leader- again a code was needed. T= tapered, using the standard leader formula described in chapter 1. Use the strength class tippet you prefer. This usually ranges between 12 and 16 pound test.
-Fly type and size- self explanatory.
-Water temperature- the first number tells the lower avoidance temperature, the second tells the upper avoidance temperature. Fish will be hard to find and usually won't eat near these extremes. The best temperature tells that temperature at which the fish stay most active.

When the water temperature is below the optimum range but warming fish will often feed. When the water temperature is above the optimum temperature but cooling fish will often eat. When the temperature changes toward either the high or low extremes, fish will be hard to find and even harder to fool with a feathered fake.

| SPECIES | ROD WEIGHT | LINE TYPE | LEADER | FLY TYPE AND SIZE | WATER TEMP. |
|---|---|---|---|---|---|
| Barracuda | 6-7-8 | Floating | 9'-12' T w/ wire | cuda fly, 4-8" long, 1-1/0 hook | 60-82; 75 best |
| Bluefish | 6-7-8-9 | F; FS; S | depends on line type. Need wire! | poppers, surf candies, other durable baitfish imitations | 50-84; 68 best |
| Bonefish | 6-7-8-9 | floating | 9'-12' tapered to 10 or 12 lb. | #4-#1 depending on depth, MOE, crab, or reverse tie | 60-93; 75 best |
| Cobia | 9-10-11 | floating | 9' tapered w/ 30-50 lb. shock | big deceivers, rabbit strip flies, other large flies 2/0-5/0 | |
| Dolphin | 8-9-10 | floating or monocore | 9' big game w/ 50-80 lb. shock | minnow imitations, 3/0- 5/0 | 70-82; 75 best |
| Jack Crevalle | from 6 to 10, depending on size of fish | F; FS; S | depends on line type- need 30 lb shock | minnow imitations and poppers #4- 5/0 depending on size of fish | 70-90; 80 best |
| King Mackerel | 9-10-11 | floating | 9' tapered w/wire | minnow imitation or chum fly- match size of chum | 70-88; 78 best |
| Permit | 9-10-11 | floating | 10'-15' tapered to 12- 16 lb. | crab flies or Clouser minnows #1- 2/0 | 65-92; 72 best |

| SPECIES | ROD WEIGHT | LINE | LEADER | FLY TYPE AND SIZE | WATER TEMP. |
|---|---|---|---|---|---|
| Redfish | 6-7-8-9 | floating | 9'-12' tapered w/ 20 lb. shock | wide variety- minnow imitations crab flies, poppers. #4- 3/0 | 52-90; 71 best |
| Seatrout | 7-8 | floating | 9'-12' tapered | minnow or shrimp imitations, poppers #2- 1/0 | 50- 81;72 best |
| Snook | 7-8-9-10 | floating | 9'-12' tapered w/ 30- 50 lb. shock | poppers or minnows, #2- 3/0 | 60-90, 70- 75 best |
| Tarpon, baby (5-30 lbs) | 5-6-7 | floating | 9' tapered w/ 20-30 lb. shock | minnows or poppers, #4- 1 | 74-100, 76 best |
| Tarpon (30-70 lbs) | 8-9-10 | floating or monocore | 9'-12' tapered or big game, 50- 80 lb. shock | primarily minnow patterns (standard tarpon streamers) 1/0- 3/0 | same |
| BIGTarpon (over 80 lbs.) | 11-12-13 | floating or monocore | 10'-14' big game w/ 80-120 lb. shock | standard tarpon streamers 2/0- 5/0 | same |
| Tuna, blackfin | 9-10 | intermediate or full sink | 8'-10' w/ 30 lb. 4' w/ 30 lb. | minnow imitations or chum flies to match chum 1/0- 2/0 | 70-82; 74 best |

# SECTION 2
# WHERE TO GO

# Introduction to the Second Section

Florida is a big state. Vast may be a better word. Starting from Orlando in the middle of the state, Key West requires about an eight hour drive on excellent modern highways. Similarly, Panama City lies about eight hours in the opposite direction, and there's plenty of space between Panama City and Pensacola.

Since Florida is a peninsula, that creates a tremendously long coastline. No one individual can possibly know it all. So when putting this section together I called saltwater fishing guides from around the state, guides who specialize in fly fishing, and interviewed them in order to learn about readily available opportunities for fly fishers in their areas. They freely gave information, and that information is shared with you here. Where guides were not available for interview, I spoke with local fly fishermen, most of whom produce custom fishing flies or fly fishing tackle, or whose names were gleaned from the roles of the Federation of Fly Fishers.

I must admit, I missed a few areas. On the east coast the coverage in the Vero Beach region and between Ft. Lauderdale and Miami is light. On the west coast Marco Island and Steinhatchee have been missed, and finally in the Panhandle Apalachicola Bay was omitted. Reasons? Vero has much the same fishing as the areas north and south of it. No reason to be redundant! Ditto for the urban areas of Ft. Lauderdale south. Similarly, Marco is sandwiched between Everglades City and Naples and those areas have excellent coverage. Fishing opportunities in the Marco area are identical. Steinhatchee is way off the beaten track. There are apparently no fly fishers in Apalachicola. If you're out there and you see this, please get in touch with me. I'd love to have you in the next printing of <u>Flyrodding Florida Salt</u>!

How is this information arranged? If you were to start at the northeast side of the state at Jacksonville, drive south along the east coast to the Keys, and then proceeded north up the Gulf coast to Pensacola, you would be following the same sequence as the fishing areas that are presented here.

Line maps have been included to make visualization of the areas easier. I cannot recommend highly enough DeLorme Publishing Company's <u>Florida Atlas and Gazetteer</u>. The <u>Gazetteer</u> contains detailed maps of every area of the state. I used it extensively in preparing this section. See the Resource Catalog in the back of this book for information on how to order the <u>Gazetteer</u>.

# FLORIDA

0   15   30        60

APPROX SCALE IN MILES

1" = Approx. 60 Miles

Not for Navigational Use

## JACKSONVILLE

Not usually thought of as an angling destination, the Jacksonville area offers some of the finest saltwater fly fishing opportunities in the state of Florida. You'll find seatrout, redfish, flounder, bluefish, cobia, and Spanish and king mackerel as the primary species, and of course other fishes are available. Anglers without boats will find some excellent fishing while those with boats will be hard pressed to decide what to do.

Warren Hinrichs grew up in his family's home on the banks of the St. John's River in Jacksonville and has fished the area his entire life. One of the finest fly casters in the state, Warren gives fly fishing instruction through the Salty Feather Fly Shop. He graciously supplied most of the following information.

### OPPORTUNITIES FOR DO-IT-YOURSELF FLY FISHERS

**-Inshore Wading**: Fly fishers can fish for redfish, seatrout, and flounder in Simpson Creek (north of Jacksonville in the Talbot Island State Parks), and in some areas in Sister's Creek (the Intracoastal Waterway north of Jacksonville) and Clapboard Creek. Best fishing for reds happens at low tide when fish come into very shallow water to feed. They can be seen splashing in the shallows then, and flies can be presented to individual fish. Also, when extreme high tides occur (5.5 feet or more) reds get up into marsh grass and feed on fiddler crabs. These fish tail and can be cast to. Access these creeks from SR 105 north of Jacksonville.

Whether wading or fishing from a boat, tides are very important to an angler's success in Jacksonville's backcountry creeks. John Bottko at the Salty Feather Fly Shop can supply you with the necessary tide information.

**-Inshore Boat**: Sister's and Clapboard Creeks provide excellent fishing for redfish and are really better fished from a small boat. The Intracoastal north and south of town provides many fly fishing opportunities. In the Intracoastal and in all the tidal creeks, best fishing happens on a low outgoing tide. The reds get in very shallow water feeding on shrimp, crabs and minnows. Their backs are often in the air as their bellies rub the bottom! As the water comes up they get harder to catch, and when the oysters are covered and the water gets up to the grass it's time to do something else.

In Guana River State Park south of Jacksonville some excellent angling for redfish is available for fishermen with canoes or other small boats. You'll find the same type of fishing below the dam as what's described above. Above the dam it's more like a saltwater impoundment, with tides no longer an influence.

With good weather fish along the jetties at the mouth of the St. John's River for jacks, Spanish mackerel, and bluefish. Look for congregations of anglers, or for fish busting bait on the surface, or just blind cast to the jetties.

Another good idea is to cruise along the beaches looking for cobia. They'll be found around floating debris, weed lines, rays, or other objects in the water.

**-From the Beach**: Little Talbot Island State Park, north of Jacksonville, offers a unique beach sight-fishing opportunity for redfish. The fish usually hold up by Nassau Sound, about a two mile walk up the beach from the parking lot. You walk along the beach looking for fish in knee-deep water, either holding their positions or cruising along looking for groceries. You may see singles or schools of 50 to 100 individual fish. You'll find the same fishing at the southern end of Amelia Island.

You'll see many sharks here and you can also try to catch them. I have yet to catch one with a fly myself (I visit Jacksonville as often as I can) but then again I don't try every time I go. John Bottko told me about a big redfish he hooked off the beach which was attacked and eaten by a shark as he was fighting it. John got only the head, which weighed between eight and nine pounds.

**-Offshore**: Fish in shrimp boat bycatch lines or chum lines you may catch jacks, barracuda, tarpon, kingfish, cobia, sharks, and other species that come into the chum. A buoy line out from the mouth of the St. John's River serves as a built-in fish attractor.

## FLIES AND TECHNIQUES

Warren recommends dark Clouser minnows for fish in the creeks. This creek fishing is best started on a low outgoing tide. The fish move into very shallow water, so much so their backs are exposed to the air. Catching these fish requires pinpoint casting accuracy- too far away and they'll never see the fly, but too close and they spook and bolt for deeper water. Look for splashing and thrashing right along the water's edge.

Along the beaches, Popovics' Surf Candy or the Surfin' Wooly, a fly by John Bottko, work well. Clouser minnows or crab patterns are also favorites. Walk the beach, alternately blind casting and looking for individuals, pods, or schools of fish.

Large Deceivers work well offshore, especially if the fish have been chummed in close. Poppers also garner strikes from feeding fish.

## ACCESS
For Waders- as detailed above.
For Boaters- There are boat ramps, some of which charge a fee for use, at the following places:
-on the east side of Sister's Creek off SR 105
-on the east side of the Ft. George River on SR 105 ($)
-on the east side of Clapboard Creek on SR 105 ($)
-on the north side of Nassau Sound off SR A1A/105.

A canoe or small boat can be launched at the dam on the Guana River in Guana River State Park off SR A1A. There is also a boat ramp at the Pine Island Fish Camp ($) off of US 1 south of Jacksonville which allow access to the Intracoastal Waterway.

## FLY SHOPS
The Salty Feather Fly Shop, 3733 Southside Blvd., Unit #9, Jacksonville, FL 32216 (904)645-8998. A full service shop.

## GUIDES
Guides are available through the Salty Feather Fly Shop.

## STATE PARKS AND OTHER ATTRACTIONS
Little Talbot Island State Park (camping) off SR 105, (904)251-3231.
Guana River State Park off SR A1A (904)825-5071

## ACCOMMODATIONS
There are plenty of motels in the greater Jacksonville area. The phone number of the Jacksonville Chamber of Commerce is (904) 366- 6600. Camping is available at Little Talbot Island State Park.

Not for Navigational Use

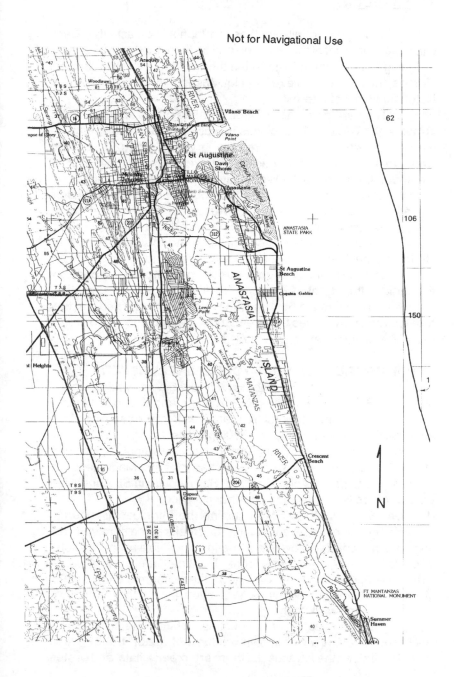

## ST. AUGUSTINE

St. Augustine bills itself as the "nation's oldest city". Certainly there are a lot of things to see and do there for the non-angler, including (but not limited to) visiting the venerable Castillo de San Marcos, the Ripley's Believe It or Not Museum, and other assorted historical points of interest.

The hard-core angler cares for none of this, though. Fishermen want to know about places to wet a line, and this stretch of the Florida coast provides more than its share. From Casa Cola Creek to the north of St. Augustine to the canals of Palm Coast to the south, the Intracoastal Waterway offers excellent angling in a wide variety of habitats for redfish, seatrout, flounder, bluefish, jack crevalle, and tarpon. Two inlets, St. Augustine Inlet and Matanzas Inlet, give access to the ocean. Splendid, fast-sloping coquina beaches here offer excellent surf fishing. The rock pile along this stretch of beach is the only one on the northeast Florida coast.

Captain Frank Bolin grew up fishing for largemouth bass on the banks of the St. Johns River. An "old-timer" took Frank under his wing when he moved to St. Augustine in 1981 and showed him the ropes. Frank now guides this area, and was good enough to share the following information with me.

## OPPORTUNITIES FOR DO-IT-YOURSELF FLYFISHERS
**-Inshore Wading**: The Summer Haven River, south of St. Augustine off of SR A1A, offers seatrout, redfish, and flounder all year long, and bluefish in the winter. At Matanzas Inlet the same species are available, as well as tarpon to 100 pounds during the fall mullet run (but good luck landing a fish like that while wading!). Anywhere in the Matanzas River between Matanzas Inlet and Marineland off of SR A1A can provide good angling. Salt Run, up in St. Augustine proper, offers limited wading opportunities, too.

**-Inshore Boat**: North of St. Augustine the Intracoastal runs up through the Tolomato River. Fishing the creeks along here you can find backing redfish on low tide sometimes, just like up in Jacksonville. Casa Cola Creek, East Creek, Moultrie Creek, and Pellicer Creek all offer good fishing. Simply cut the motor and drift with the current while working the banks. When you find a concentration of fish, anchor and work them.

Salt Run, up in St. Augustine behind Anastasia State Recreation Area, is a well known producer of "gator" trout.

All along the Intracoastal there are creeks, flats, and oyster reefs, all of which can and do produce fish.

The canals of Palm Coast offer some excellent angling during the winter months.

Lastly, Frank says the Vilano jetties at St. Augustine Inlet are good producers of tarpon during the fall mullet run.

**-From the Beach:** Fly fishers can catch whiting and pompano from the beach all year long, weather permitting. Bluefish appear during the winter months. Big bull redfish could show up at anytime, fish approaching forty pounds in size. Spanish mackerel are another possibility, as are jack crevalle. An excellent place for the surf caster to try is at Washington Oaks, where a natural rock pile on the beach attracts many species of fish.

**-Offshore:** Spanish mackerel, bluefish (during winter), cobia, especially around rays in the spring and fall, all these are possibilities. Tarpon and kingfish can be caught off the beach by setting up a chum line. Frank hardly ever goes more than a mile off the beach.

## FLIES AND TECHNIQUES

Frank only likes three patterns in different sizes and colors. The first is the saltwater popper in black and white or red and white. He throws these in water less than three feet deep, along grass edges or shorelines, or when fish are obviously feeding on the surface.

He also has excellent success with the Seaducer pattern in water up to about four feet deep. He likes these in chartreuse & yellow and red & white.

Lastly, he also likes the Deceiver pattern in a shrimp color.

Frank says they blind cast a lot for their fish in his area. He believes in covering water fast, not wasting much time in unproductive areas. The speed you work the fly depends on the speed of the current- the faster the current moves, the slower you work the fly.

He also says one unique thing about this area is that the best time to fish the flats is at low tide. The fish concentrate in deeper depressions on the flat so that they become easier to find. This is an excellent time to get out of the boat and wade, using a stealthy approach to avoid spooking the fish.

## ACCESS

For Waders-There is access to Salt Run through Anastasia State Recreation Area, but the best access to the Intracoastal is south of St. Augustine along SR A1A in the vicinity of Matanzas Inlet. You'll find the best beach fishing north of St. Augustine Inlet along Vilano Beach from SR A1A (excellent access) and south of Matanzas Inlet along SR A1A as far south as Ormond Beach (excellent access). The beach between the two inlets (including the State Park) slopes slowly and usually offers poor angling.

-For Boaters: This area has an excellent system of boat ramps. In St. Augustine there is a ramp on the west side of the Vilano Bridge. Another ramp is found at Salt Run, off Anastasia Boulevard. Still another is located at Lighthouse Park.

South of St. Augustine, there is a boat ramp at Butler Beach Park on the Intracoastal side. Frank warns that if you use this ramp be sure to go north to the Intracoastal. Do not try to run south across the flat.

Another ramp accessing the Intracoastal is found off of A1A at Devil's Elbow, south of SR 206. Still another is located at Bing's Landing, south of Marineland again on the Intracoastal.

There are many more small private ramps located at fish camps throughout this area.

## FLY SHOPS
East Coast Outdoors in Ormond Beach carries some fly tackle. The person to talk to in Brent. Their phone number is (904)672-5003.

## GUIDES
Captain Frank Bolin has been fishing this area since 1981. He has kept detailed log books of every trip he's taken in this time, and uses them to predict the location and movements of the fish. He says if he can't find the fish, he'll sure keep you entertained anyway! Frank can be reached at 1-800-Lets Fish.

## STATE PARKS AND OTHER ATTRACTIONS
St. Augustine is loaded with attractions, many historical in nature.
-Anastasia State Recreation Area (904)471-3033. Off of SR A1A in St. Augustine (camping).
-Gamble-Rogers State Memorial Park (904)439-2474. Off of SR A1A in Flagler Beach (camping).
-Faver-Dykes State Park (904)794-0997. Fifteen miles south of St. Augustine at the intersection of I-95 and US 1, this park has 752 acres on Pellicer Creek (camping).

## ACCOMMODATIONS
There are many, many places to stay in this area. The phone number at the St. Augustine Chamber of Commerce is (904)829-6477.

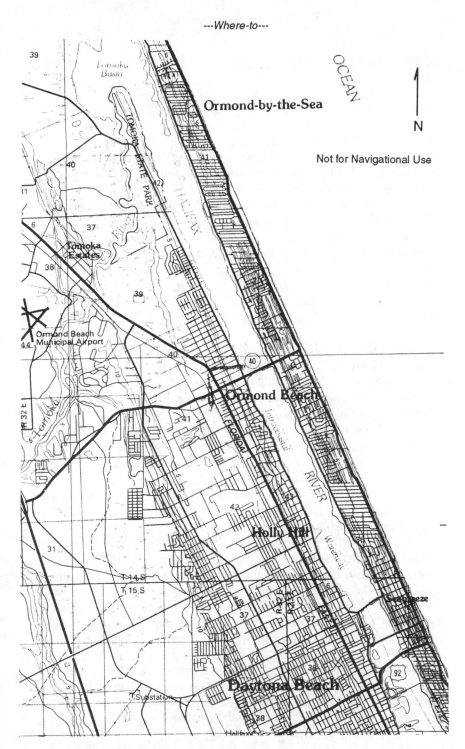

Not for Navigational Use

## DAYTONA/NEW SMYRNA AREA

Daytona calls itself, "the World's Most Famous Beach." Speed Week, Bike Week, Spring Break, and other promotional events bring tens of thousands of visitors to the condo-lined beach every year. This famous beach stuff doesn't have anything to do with fishing, though. Daytona Beach slopes very gently and consequently it, and neighboring New Smyrna Beach, usually have poor fishing except in the vicinity of the inlet.

Locales in this vicinity which do attract and hold fish include the Intracoastal Waterway behind the beach areas, Ponce Inlet, which separates Daytona from New Smyrna, the creeks feeding into the Intracoastal Waterway, the northern end of the Mosquito Lagoon, and the Apollo Beach area of the Canaveral National Seashore. All offer good fly fishing opportunities. Captain Ron Rebeck, who fishes the Intracoastal and the associated waterways from his Maverick 18, shared the following information with me.

## OPPORTUNITIES FOR DO-IT-YOURSELF FLY FISHERS
**-Inshore Wading**: Good opportunities exist for redfish and seatrout at the north end of the Mosquito Lagoon in the Canaveral National Seashore, especially around Turtle Mound and parking lot 5. Find this at the south end of SR A1A south of New Smyrna.

Between Daytona and New Smyrna along US 1, Spruce Creek is wadable all the way up to the railroad bridge. Snook, redfish, seatrout, small tarpon, and jack crevalle can all be caught around islands and oyster bars.

Both sides of Ponce Inlet can be waded. There are parks along both sides, too. You'll find the fishing best during the fall mullet run, when bluefish and jack crevalle are the primary species.

Behind the bowling alley in Port Orange is a wadable flat where tarpon to 50 pounds hold during the summer months. These fish are tough to take on flies, although it can and does does happen.

In Ormond Beach, Tomoka Basin is wadable and produces seatrout, redfish, snook, jacks, and small tarpon for the fly rodder.
**-Inshore Boat**: Excellent night fishing opportunities exist for fly rodders under lighted docks all the way from J.B.'s Fish Camp in New Smyrna to Tomoka State Park in Ormond Beach. Moonfish (near the inlet), snook, seatrout, and ladyfish are all likely catches.

During the summer tarpon can be taken between the two bridges in New Smyrna on a rising tide, after the clean seawater comes in. Try using standard tarpon streamers.

Fishing the jetties can be productive for jacks and bluefish, especially during the fall mullet run.

In the Tomoka Basin fish the mosquito ditches on the high outgoing tide. Small tarpon, redfish, snook, jacks, and seatrout all wait at the run-outs for bait to wash out.

All of the creeks on the west side of the Intracoastal Waterway from Port Orange down south into New Smyrna will produce fish on the outgoing tides. Again, predators wait in the run-out for baitfish to wash down to them. These creeks include Spruce Creek, Ten Mile Creek, Rose Bay, and others.

The docks along the Intracoastal from Edgewater north to Ormond Beach will hold such fish as snook, seatrout, and redfish.

Small tarpon to about 50 pounds can consistently be found behind the high school in New Smyrna Beach all summer long.

Lastly, the north end of the Mosquito Lagoon, including all of the islands in the Canaveral National Seashore, can produce fish during any time of the year.

**-From the Beach**: The only beach in the area with consistently good fishing is Apollo Beach in the Canaveral National Seashore south of New Smyrna. Pompano can be caught during the summer, and whiting can be caught all year long. Jacks and bluefish can be taken during the fall mullet run. Although winter and spring offer surf conditions which are usually too rough for fly casters, redfish are another possibility any time of the year. Again, the jetties at Ponce Inlet can sometimes provide good angling, but fall usually provides the most consistent fishing.

**Offshore**: Ron doesn't go offshore much. He suggests calling First Strike Marine and Tackle in New Smyrna Beach for up to the minute reports on conditions offshore. The number there is (904)427-3587.

## FLIES AND TECHNIQUES

Ron likes the following flies: Clouser minnows, especially for deeper water around docks. Big poppers and sliders work well when cast against seawalls or around docks, and produce explosive surface strikes. He ties a Crystal Flash moonfish fly that he likes to use under lights at night. Poppers and white surf candies work well in surf for bluefish. He likes the Wobbler flies when fishing in the Tomoka basin for redfish.

Ron finds it important to use sink-tip lines here due to the depth of the water. Using flies that make noise and/or push water is recommended. Try Whistlers, Siliclones, rattle flies, and similar patterns for sub-surface use, and big, noisy popping bugs when a topwater fly is needed. Bigger patterns work better in the discolored water found in this area.

## ACCESS

For Waders- Waders can access the grass flats at the north end of the Mosquito Lagoon and the best fish producing beaches in this entire area at the south end of SR A1A in the Canaveral National Seashore south of New Smyrna. Go all the way to Parking Lot 5 for the Mosquito Lagoon. Waders can also find easy access at Turtle Mound and the Eldora House to the channels and sloughs of the Indian River North, also in the National Seashore.

There are parks on either side of Ponce Inlet where a wading fly fisher can park and get easy access to the inlet.

Waders wanting to fish Spruce Creek can park along U.S.1 between Daytona and New Smyrna where it crosses the creek.

Tomoka State Park, north of SR 40 in Ormond Beach, gives the wader access to the Tomoka Basin and Halifax River.

In Port Orange, waders can park in the lot of the bowling alley and access the flat directly behind this building.

-For Boaters- There are a lot of boat ramps in the area. In the National Seashore there is one at the Visitor's Center and another at Turtle Mound. On the way down there is another at J.B.'s Fish Camp (J.B.'s is a popular weekend attraction with live music and the whole deal. Don't use this ramp on weekends if you're allergic to crowds of party-goers!)

There is a ramp in Edgewater, about two and a half miles south of SR 44. Take a left on Riverside Drive and the ramp is at Kennedy Park. There is a ramp about a mile west of the North Causeway in New Smyrna Beach.

If you have a SMALL boat, you can launch it in Spruce Creek on the southeast side of the US 1 bridge. This is a poor excuse for a ramp, however.

In Port Orange on Dunlawton Street there is a nice ramp.

Daytona has ramps at Lighthouse Park and also at the Sea Love Marina.

There is a ramp at the Brigadoon Fish Camp on Rose Bay off of US 1.

And finally in Ormond Beach there are ramps at Tomoka State Park and at the Grenada Bridge.

## FLY SHOPS

There are no fly shops in this area.

## GUIDES

Captain Ron Rebeck guides this area from his Maverick. He says that hiring a guide is a good idea since they have local knowledge. Ron knows the tides, knows which docks are usually productive, and knows where the plentiful oyster bars lie. I've fished with Ron many times and it has always been an enjoyable experience. Furthermore, few people fly fish in his area.

Ron can be reached at 31 Cunningham Road, Debary, FL 32713; 1-800-932-7335.

## STATE PARKS AND OTHER ATTRACTIONS

-Canaveral National Seashore, (904)867-0634. Camping is allowed on the beach south of parking lot 5 during the winter months.
-Tomoka State Park is located three miles north of Ormond Beach on North Beach Street. 2009 North Beach Street, Ormond Beach 32174. (904)677-3931. Camping is possible here and there's a nice boat ramp. They also rent canoes.

## ACCOMMODATIONS

Not hard to find in this area! Daytona Beach Chamber of Commerce PO Box 2475, Daytona Beach 32115. (904)761-7163.
New Smyrna Beach Chamber of Commerce, 115 Canal Street, New Smyrna, 32168. (904)996-5522.

Not for Navigational Use

## TITUSVILLE/ THE SPACE COAST

The Space Coast includes the area around Titusville, between Oak Hill and Cocoa. Included within this area lie the Mosquito Lagoon, the northern end of the Indian River, the northern end of the Banana River, and Playalinda Beach, basically all the waters surrounding the Kennedy Space Center. Obviously, you find a wide variety of angling opportunities available here, and the season lasts all year long.

Since I guide in this area, I didn't interview anyone for this section. I was fortunately able to answer all of my own questions!

### OPPORTUNITIES FOR DO-IT-YOURSELF FLY FISHERS

**-Inshore Wading**: Wading fly fishers can enjoy some fantastic sight fishing for redfish on the shallow grass flats of both the Mosquito Lagoon and the Indian River. Dike roads allow access to these many of these flats, and you can sometimes spot fish waking or tailing from your vehicle. There are no tides at all in these places, so fishing can be good at any time.

**-Inshore Boat**: With a boat, more of the flats in the Mosquito Lagoon and Indian River are available. The entire south end of the Lagoon is ringed by grass flats, and there is also a middle flat extending north from Pelican Island, at the south end of the Lagoon. North of the Haulover Canal, flats extend along the east shoreline of the lagoon all the way to Oak Hill. There are a lot of flats in the Mosquito Lagoon, and all of them hold fish at one time or another.

In the Indian River, flats ring the entire river north of the railroad trestle in Titusville. Flats extend southward along the west side of the Indian River to the NASA Causeway and beyond. The spoil islands along the Intracoastal Waterway can be reached, too, both in the Indian River and north of the Haulover Canal on the west side of the Mosquito Lagoon.

Additionally, flats on both sides of the Banana River between SR 520 and SR 404 can be fished. Some of the largest redfish in the state are caught here. For anglers who enjoy paddling, the Banana River Manatee Sanctuary, north of SR 528, provides some of the finest angling in the entire state. Redfish, seatrout, baby tarpon, snook, jack crevalle, and black drum are all found on the flats here. Since no motors are allowed, the area gets less fishing pressure than other areas.

Finally, the power stations off of US 1 south of Titusville can provide non-stop action for jacks and big ladyfish all winter long.

**-From the Beach**: Playalinda Beach has good fishing when the weather allows. During the summer months, anglers using light tackle with sinking lines and small weighted flies can catch pompano, whiting, and the occasional redfish. During the fall mullet run, jacks, Spanish mackerel, bluefish, and sometimes other species can be added to the catch.

Satellite Beach, south of Cocoa, has excellent summer catch and release snook fishing. Tarpon are also sometimes hooked but seldom landed. Spanish mackerel, jacks, and bluefish are also common catches during the fall months.

**-Offshore**: Offshore access is through Port Canaveral. Some days there are so many fish in the Port itself it's hard to make it outside. In the Port you may find snook, bluefish, jacks, seatrout, and many other species. Night fishing under the lights is also possible, and can be extremely rewarding.

The buoy line out of the Port attracts many types of fish. Cobia and tripletail love to lounge under the buoys and other flotsam. The buoy line also attracts king mackerel which can be chummed up. Expect bonito and jacks to appear in the chum line! Spanish mackerel appear during the fall and can be found fairly consistently all winter when the weather allows.

## FLIES AND TECHNIQUES

For fishing the flats in the lagoon systems floating lines are a must. A selection of flies should be carried that includes Clouser minnows in chartreuse and white and brown, crab patterns for tailing fish, seaducers in yellow and grizzly and red and white, and surface flies such as deer hair poppers and sliders.

The surface flies are used mostly when blind casting, especially by waders. The sound of the fly attracts fish which cannot be seen. Use other patterns for sighted fish, depending on water depth, the amount of floating and bottom grasses, and what the fish are doing. For example, tailing redfish are usually suckers for a well presented crab pattern.

Since there are no tides in the lagoons, fish tend to move a lot. The most successful anglers have good hunting skills which they use to locate fish. Fish in the lagoon system could be scattered about in singles or pairs, or may be in schools of hundreds of fish.

Beach flies depend on the target species. For whiting and pompano a small mole crab fly works best when delivered with a sinking line. For snook along Satellite Beach; large Deceivers or Blanton's Sar-Mul-Mac pattern tethered to a monocore line works best. Jacks and bluefish will slam poppers cast along the beach.

Offshore, Clouser deep minnows work well for Spanish mackerel and tripletail. The 'tails also like seaducers. Cobia and kings want a bigger mouthful, and large Deceivers in white and/or chartreuse work well. Anytime you fish in a chum line the fly should reasonably imitate the chum.

## ACCESS

**For Waders:** several points allow access to the Mosquito Lagoon. On the southeast side of the lagoon try the boat ramp between parking lots 7 and 8 at Playalinda Beach. The flat to the north of Eddy Creek is often productive.

On the west side there is a dike road which runs along the bank, and can be accessed from the south end off the beach road. Go past the entrance to the national seashore. About a mile after the entrance you will come to a gate which is usually open. On the left side of the road next to this gate is a dirt road. Follow this north and you will find yourself on the dike road with the Mosquito Lagoon to your right. At the north end of this same road access is from SR 3 at a small sign which says "NASA Atmospheric Sciences". This road is about six miles north of the intersection with SR 402.

There are other access points to the north of the Haulover Canal along SR 3. These are dirt roads which are marked with small brown boat ramp signs. These roads will put you on the inside of the spoil islands on the west side of the lagoon along the Intracoastal Waterway.

Indian River Access- 100 yards south of the "NASA Atmospheric Sciences" sign which marks the entrance to the Mosquito Lagoon dike road is an unmarked road on the opposite side of SR 3. This road accesses Dummit Cove, an excellent wade fishing spot off the Indian River. The road twists and turns its way around for a few miles before coming to what looks like a parking area, further identified by the culverts under the road. You'll find the bottom here is kind of soft.

Another excellent access to the east Indian River flats lies 1-2 miles north of the Haulover Canal off of US 3. A dirt road on the west side of the road leads into a citrus grove and immediately turns and heads north along the east shore of the Indian River. The flats all along this road are both wadable and productive.

On the west side of the Indian River are access points off of US 1 in both Scottsmoor and Mims. The <u>Florida Gazetteer</u> clearly shows both of these access points as boat ramps.

Lastly, to the south of SR 406 on Merritt Island is a dike road which gives waders access to Catfish Creek and Peacock Pocket. One word of warning, though- never try to cross the ditches which often separate the dike roads from the main river. The bottom of these ditches is soft and treacherous and could easily trap an unwary wader.

**For boaters:** Boat ramps can be found at the following places:

-Eddy Creek, between parking lots 7 and 8 at Playalinda Beach, giving access to the Mosquito Lagoon;

-at the Haulover Canal off of SR 3, giving access to both the Mosquito Lagoon and the Indian River;

-on SR 402 just east of Titusville, giving access to the Indian River;

-off of US 1 in Port St. John south of Titusville, giving access to the Indian River and the excellent cold weather fishing at the power station discharges ( this ramp gets extremely crowded, though);

-at Kelly Park on Banana River Drive just south of SR 528, giving access to the Banana River;

-at Port Canaveral, which accesses the Port and the Atlantic Ocean.

Canoeists can get into the Banana River Manatee Refuge on the east  side just south of the Canaveral Air Force Station entrance on SR 401, and on the west side at the north end of Banana River Drive, just north of SR 528. Paddling north about two miles will bring you to the refuge. Don't get tunnel vision about reaching the refuge, you may see fish all along the flats here.

**Beach access:** Playalinda Beach has superb access. Take SR 406 east from Titusville, then bear right onto SR 402. Obey the posted speed limits- rangers love to set up radar on this road!

Satellite Beach has access from SR A1A. You'll see parking areas on the east side of A1A south of Patrick Air Force Base. Any of these can provide excellent fishing.

Keep in mind these are all public beaches and they can get mighty crowded on summer weekends. Try to get your fishing done early in the day.

## FLY SHOPS

The Fly Fisherman, 1400 S. Washington Avenue, Titusville, FL 32780. (407)267-0348 A full service fly shop.

## GUIDES

-Captain John Kumiski, (407) 834-2954. I can custom design various trips in this area: sightfishing for reds in the Mosquito Lagoon, Indian River, or Banana River; canoeing in the Manatee Refuge for reds, snook, seatrout, and baby tarpon; night fishing

under the lights in Port Canaveral; fishing off the beach for cobia, tripletail, and Spanish mackerel; and more!
-Captain Rodney Smith (407)777-2773. Banana River, Port Canaveral.
-Captain Eric Ersch (407) 779-9054 Indian River, Banana River.

## STATE PARKS AND OTHER ATTRACTIONS
-Merritt Island National Wildlife Refuge, PO Box 6504, Titusville 32782. (407)861-0667
-Canaveral National Seashore, 308 Julia Street, Titusville, 32796. (407)267-1110.

These two natural areas, administered by the National Park Service, lie next to each other and provide thousands of acres of wildlife habitat. Birding here is especially rewarding. There are nature trails and wildlife drives, and you may see dolphins, manatees, alligators, wild hogs, bobcats, otters, raccoons- any number of wild creatures.

## ACCOMMODATIONS
There are lots of motels in Titusville and in Cocoa. The phone number of the Titusville Chamber of Commerce is (407) 267-3036. The phone number of the Cocoa Chamber of Commerce is (407) 459-2200.

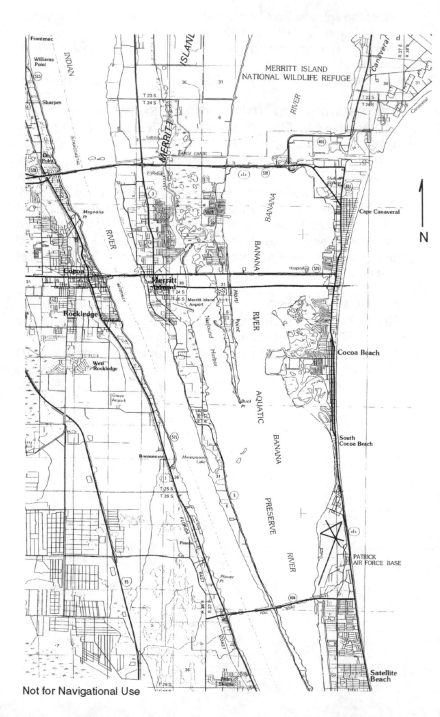

Not for Navigational Use

## COCOA/MELBOURNE

The coastline between Cocoa (Patrick Air Force Base, actually) and Melbourne boasts a terrific fishing beach with good access and big, strong fish, especially snook. The Indian River Lagoon system, behind the barrier islands, provides excellent shallow water sight fishing for many different species; as a matter of fact this lagoon is the most biologically diverse estuary in North America, with over 700 different species of fish having been catalogued from its waters.

The lagoon has the largest population of shallow water brood stock redfish anywhere in the country, with many fish reaching weights between 20 and 40 pounds. Since these fish are essentially landlocked, the fishery for them is not seasonal, but rather exists all year long.

This area definitely deserves a visit by the visitor anxious to see a relatively untapped fishery in an area not usually frequented by tourists.

Captain Rodney Smith lives in Satellite Beach, and from his home fishes along and offshore from the beaches, as well as in the Banana River Lagoon. He supplied the information that follows.

## OPPORTUNITIES FOR DO-IT-YOURSELF FLY FISHERS

**-Inshore Wading:** Lots of good access to shallow water flats awaits those wanting to wade for seatrout and redfish. Some of these areas include the following causeways: The Pinedas Causeway (SR 404), the Eau Gallie Causeway (SR 518), and the SR 520 Causeway. Additional access is supplied by Tropical Trail on Merritt Island, and US 1 which runs along the west side of the lagoon system. Rodney says that access to the water from these roads is easy to find.

**-Inshore Boat:** In the lagoon system the top four gamefish targeted by most anglers include redfish, snook, seatrout, and small tarpon. You'll find other species of fish. Extensive grassflats along both shorelines (especially the west side of the Banana River) and the Thousand Islands area behind Cocoa Beach are good places to try. Additionally, an extensive system of canals behind Cocoa Beach holds tarpon during the summer and seatrout during the winter.

**-From the Beach:** Excellent surfcasting opportunities exist from the beach here, possibly the best in the state. Snook patrol the beaches from spring through fall, averaging from 8 to 15 pounds and sometimes topping thirty. Ladyfish, jack crevalle, barracuda, tarpon, Spanish mackerel, and other species also find their way to the rock reefs found along this stretch of beach.

-**Offshore**: In Port Canaveral itself there is sometimes excellent fishing for a variety of fish, including snook, jack crevalle, and bluefish. Fishing the lights at night in the Port is becoming increasingly popular, and with good reason. Out of Port Canaveral it's possible to catch multiple species in one day along the buoy line, under debris and weed lines, along the beaches, or well offshore, including cobia, tripletail, tarpon, large jack crevalle, blacktip sharks, Spanish and king mackerel, bonito, blackfin tuna, and dolphin.

## FLIES AND TECHNIQUES

Rodney says his favorite fly is whatever worked the day before. I guess we've all felt that way! He develops new patterns constantly, including the Schroach, the Last Chance Fly, and the Whitebait Fly. He also like Ron Winn's Finger Mullet, the Glass Minnow pattern, Blanton's Sar-Mul-Mac, and the Siliclone.

The technique used depends on the fishing being done, of course. Along the beach Rodney likes to look for activity from birds, or baitfish, or best of all from the targeted gamefish themselves. He likes the Sar-Mul-Mac in white and green for snook fishing here. He says that using a fast sinking line from these beaches is a bad idea, since you snag on the rocks all the time. A floating or intermediate sinking line performs better.

Start at daybreak. You can cast from shore, or wade out to the first, second, or third reef (depending on the height of the tide) and fan cast around your position. Ordinarily you blind cast. Don't forget to cast toward the beach sometimes, since the fish will cruise along right in the wash. As in most beach fishing, a stripping basket comes in very handy, especially with some surf.

Fishing out of Port Canaveral, it's vital to start with a full tank of gasoline. Oftentimes a lot of water will need to be covered while you look for debris or weed lines. Work the buoys along the buoy line first, looking for tripletail and cobia. You need to start early in the morning in order to beat competitors to the buoys. If the buoys don't produce, you need to cruise along the beaches from one to ten miles out, searching for pieces of wood, plastic bags, or any other type of debris in the water. We've even seen tripletail lying under dead jack crevalle that had been discarded by mackerel netters.

Weed lines often have cobia working through them, searching for crabs and small fish. The weeds shelter barracuda and tripletail, too. Usually you will cruise slowly along the weeds, looking for fish. When you see them you cast to them. Very straightforward.

The other technique out of the Port is so obvious it barely deserves a mention. In the fall, especially in October, look for excited terns working. They are usually over Spanish mackerel. The fish get so thick sometimes you literally get tired of catching them since it's too easy. Glass minnows or Clouser minnows work well for this. Use a 30 pound mono shock leader. You'll lose a lot of fish and flies but will get so many more strikes than if you used a wire trace.

In the lagoon system looking for redfish is done in much the same way as it's done elsewhere in the state. Waders blindcast while looking for signs of fish, preferably over a bottom with mixed sand and grass. Boaters pole (or electric motor) along the flats, looking for fish in groups as small as singles or in schools as large as hundreds of individuals. Bigger fish will generally be on the deeper flats, between 3 and 4 feet deep. Smaller fish will go in closer to shore, sometimes right against the bank if they're looking for crabs. Check the flat from edge to edge.

## ACCESS
For Waders- see wading opportunities, above.
For Boaters- Boat ramps can be found at the following locations-
-on Banana River Drive, just south of SR 528. Access to Banana River.
-at Port Canaveral there is an excellent ramp, accessing the Port and the Atlantic Ocean.
-at both ends of the Pineda Causeways over both the Indian and Banana Rivers.
-at the Eau Gallie Causeway, on the east side. Access to both the Banana and Indian Rivers.
-off Ramp Road in Cocoa Beach, access to the Banana River.
-off of US 1 in Grant, access to the Indian River.
-at Sebastian Inlet- access to both the Indian River and the Atlantic Ocean through Sebastian Inlet.

## FLY SHOPS
The Fly Fisherman in Titusville on US 1 south of town (407)267-0348.
Harry Goode's in Melbourne, (407) 723-4751.
## GUIDES
Captain Rodney Smith, 265 South Robert Way, Satellite Beach, FL 32937. (407)777-2773
Captain Eric Ersch, PO Box 372865, Satellite Beach. FL 32937. (407)779-9054

## STATE PARKS AND OTHER ATTRACTIONS
The Banana River Manatee Refuge is part of the Merritt Island National Wildlife Refuge.
Cocoa Beach has plenty to see and do for any non-anglers in the party, including "World Famous" Ron Jon's Surf Shop.

## ACCOMMODATIONS
There are lots and lots of hotels and motels along the beach on SR A1A. The Cocoa Beach Chamber of Commerce at (407)459-2200 will be able to recommend some.

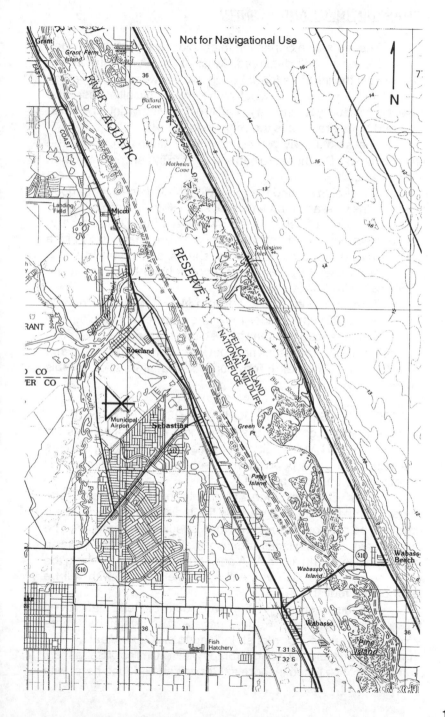

## SEBASTIAN INLET AND VICINITY

The reputation Sebastian Inlet holds as the premier snook hole in Florida is well deserved. Most of the successful snook fishermen at the inlet use (dare I even use the word in a fly fishing book?) BAIT. Fly fishing for snook at the inlet is difficult at best . The currents are usually too strong to easily get a fly down into the strike zone and there are always too many people!

That's not to say you couldn't catch snook on flies at the inlet. People do. But there are better places to fly fish for snook than in the inlet itself.

The region around the inlet, with the Indian River Lagoon system to the west and the Atlantic Ocean to the east, probably has as large a variety of fish species available as any other area in Florida. Seatrout, redfish, snook, tarpon, jacks, snapper, Spanish and king mackerel, barracuda, cobia, sharks, and more all call this area home. Several fly rod world records have been set in the vicinity of the inlet on various species.

Terry Parsons, displaced from New Jersey and now in Florida for over 20 years, guides the entire area between Melbourne and Ft. Pierce, specializing in the Sebastian area. Tom Pierce is another guide who shares his time between living in Sebastian and Key West. Both Terry and Tom supplied the information for this section of the book.

### OPPORTUNITIES FOR THE DO-IT-YOURSELF FLY FISHER
**-Inshore Wading:** good access to the Indian River for waders will be found along SR A1A south of Sebastian Inlet. Healthy grassflats here support a good population of seatrout. Other species will sometimes be encountered too.

North of the inlet along A1A about a mile is Long Point Park. Waders can park here and wade in the Indian River. The primary target will be seatrout but again, other species will sometimes be encountered, including jacks, ladyfish, redfish, and snook. You can continue driving north along A1A and find river access all along the way. The species of fish you will most likely tangle with will be seatrout and redfish.

On the west side of the river south of Sebastian River, Indian River Drive gives waders access. The oyster bars here provide good hunting for redfish looking to pick up a meal.
**-Inshore Boat:** there are 14 boat ramps within 10 miles of Sebastian. Every kind of fish found inshore in Florida can be found here, with

the exception of bonefish. Also, a good part of this area is posted as slow speed manatee zones. Marine Patrol officers work this area on a regular basis and the fine for speeding is almost $300.00. Learn the manatee areas and obey the law.

In the inlet itself you can find schools of crevalle tearing up mullet, especially during the mullet migrations. The flats adjacent to the inlet can provide a wide variety of different species, including snook, reds, and trout. The flats to the north of the inlet are especially productive.

South of the inlet by Sebastian the docks and canals on the western shoreline can provide good action for seatrout. The spoil islands produce trout too. As is the case all through this area, other species could show up at any time. On the opposite side of the river the points and islands produce trout and reds on a regular basis, and deserve exploration.

North of the inlet the area around Long Point Park often produces trout, reds, and snook. If you go a little further north, the canal system known as the Honest John Canals support a well-known winter trout fishery which has produced several world record seatrout. Snook and reds in addition to trout can be found in this area all year long.

Drop-offs on the west side of the river around the spoil islands often produce trout.

Finally, Sebastian River provides an interesting fishery for small tarpon and jack crevalle out in the river itself, and snook under the many docks. Fishing is good during all but the coldest months. The tarpon here are about as ornery a critter as you'll find anywhere. You can literally be surrounded by rolling fish and cast for hours without a strike. My best luck (I love Sebastian River) has been late in the day. Fish range from about 10 to 40 pounds, with bigger fish seen rarely. All of Sebastian River is a slow speed manatee zone. There are quite a few manatees in it most of the time.

**-Along the Beach:** the fishing along the beach here is arguably the best in the state. North of the inlet the beach is sandy, but has a fast slope. South of the inlet rock reefs run parallel to the beach. With clean water both beaches will attract fish.

Snook and to a lesser degree tarpon can be caught off the beach all summer long. Other species, especially jacks, will crash the party from time to time. If you like pompano, you can sightfish them from the beach when conditions are right.

During the fall Spanish mackerel will show up and can be caught all winter long. Bluefish are a common winter catch, too.

Whiting can be caught year round.

Undoubtedly the highlight of any surf fisherman's year is the annual mullet run in the fall. As mullet move along the beach every other fish that eats them follows. Fishing for snook, jack crevalle, bluefish, and other species can be spectacular. It is quite possible to hook tarpon in excess of a hundred pounds from the beach. Good luck landing them!

-**Offshore:** All of the same species mentioned in the section on Port Canaveral can be caught here, by exactly the same techniques. Please refer to that section for offshore fishing information.

## FLIES AND TECHNIQUES

Parsons has very definite ideas about fly selection. His number one selection for potluck fishing is a Clouser minnow on a #1 hook. However, he prefers using surface flies and will, if conditions allow it. His favorite fishing is snook on fly, and he strongly believes that most folks use flies which are much too small. Using 9- or 10-weight rods he'll throw 3-D or slab flies tied on 4/0 and 5/0 hooks, flies which are seven or eight inches long. Most of this is casting to docks or other structure rather than sight fishing, since the water is usually too murky to see fish.

Pierce approaches the problem with a little more delicacy. Those tough Sebastian River tarpon are fished with small (#4) brown flies on a slow sinking line like a monocore. Pierce likes to sightfish for reds whenever possible. He'll hunt for tailing fish, or fish pushing wakes, or even try to see them if the water is clear. He likes Merkins for his redfishing.

Pierce also likes snook fishing. He uses large Deceivers or deerhair sliders, again fishing around docks or other structure. He made an excellent point when he said not to do this if you value your fly line!

## ACCESS

For waders- see the section on wading opportunities.

For Boaters- You can find ramps at the following locations along the east side of the Indian River:

-at Sebastian Inlet State Park.

-Honest John's Fish Camp, off of A1A north of the inlet ($).

-south of the SR 510 Causeway in Wabasso.

On the west side of the river you can find more ramps at:

-Grant, off of US 1.

-Sand Point Marina, just west of US 1 and north of the Sebastian River Bridge on Sand Point Road. ($)
-At both Dale Wimbrow Park and Donald McDonald Park on the south fork of the Sebastian River, off of CR 505.
-at the town landing in Sebastian, off of US 1.

## FLY SHOPS
The closest is the Backcountry Fly Shop in Vero Beach. (407)231-9894.
-Wabasso Bait and Tackle. Call Terry Parsons- it's his shop!

## GUIDES
-Captain Terry Parsons says in his modest way that he's the guy to fish with because he knows all the spots! Terry is Orvis endorsed, and can be reached at (407)589-7782 or 589-8518.
-Captain Tom Pierce alternates his time between Sebastian and Key West, so is not always available. However he can be reached at (407)388-0911.
-Captain Charlie Fornabio also guides this area. (407)388-9773.
-Captain Rodney Smith knows the inlet as well as anyone. (407) 777-2773.

## STATE PARKS AND OTHER ATTRACTIONS
Sebastian Inlet State Recreation Area- the focal point for snook fishing on Florida's east coast. 9700 South A1A, Melbourne Beach, 32951. (407) 984-4852. Camping sites are available here.

## ACCOMMODATIONS
The phone number for the Melbourne-Palm Bay Chamber of Commerce is (407)724-5200. For the Sebastian River Area Chamber of Commerce the number is (407)589-5969.

Not for Navigational Use

## STUART

Any angler visiting Florida to fish owes it to himself to visit Stuart. There is great fishing here, much of it easily accessible by the uninitiated. The great variety of fish and fishing makes the area even more interesting.

Stuart offers what guide Gregg Gentile calls the best summer snooking in Florida. No chumming is needed to get these fish to eat, either! Tarpon are also available all summer long. A boat ride out through the St. Lucie inlet puts the angler in some heated action along the beaches- snook, tarpon, barracuda, bonito, big jack crevalle.

During the winter the tarpon and snook calm down. Their places are taken by big jack crevalle and ladyfish. Seatrout are always a possibility, and redfish have started staging a comeback in this area, too.

Gregg Gentile answered most of my questions about this area. Mark Nichols of DOA Lures and Captain Mike Holliday helped out as well. For a complete guide to fishing spots in this area, I strongly recommend Robin Smillie's book, A Fisherman's Guide to Martin and St. Lucie Counties (see the Resource Catalog in the back of this book for ordering information). It accurately pinpoints most of the best places to fish.

## OPPORTUNITIES FOR THE DO-IT-YOURSELF FLY FISHER

**-Inshore Wading**: Along the Stuart Causeway you'll find grassflats where an angler can fish for snook and seatrout. The best fishing happens early or late in the day. Along SR A1A on Hutchison Island there are really a lot of places to park and fish. The best thing to do is look for the local's cars, and follow the leaders. Having said that, try fishing both Little Mud Creek and Herman's Bay. In Little Mud Creek you cast along mangrove shorelines (bring your insect repellant). Herman's Bay has lush grassflats to wade on.

**-Inshore Boat**: From the Fort Pierce Inlet to the St. Lucie Inlet the boater has the entire Indian River and St. Lucie River to explore. Snook and tarpon of all sizes are available all summer long. Try Big Mud Creek for tarpon. The inlets produce exceptional snook action- as a matter of fact, the 20 pound tippet IGFA world record snook was caught at the St. Lucie Inlet. Grassflats along the river produce snook, reds, and seatrout. The St. Lucie's North Fork harbors many big snook and tarpon. It is a very fishy looking and productive area. It's safe, too, with very few rocks around.

**-Along the Beach**: Again, the fly fisher can have superb angling on the beach. At the House of Refuge and Bathtub Beach, rock reefs attract and hold fish all summer long. The ambitious angler can walk the beach a mile and a half to the St. Lucie Inlet. Access for fly fishers is also available at Ft. Pierce Inlet. Both Martin and St. Lucie counties have purchased beach access. The Hobe Sound National Wildlife Refuge offers six miles of undeveloped beach on the south side of St. Lucie Inlet. During the mullet run it's possible to hook hundred pound tarpon from the beach. There's also a strong run of bluefish in the fall and winter most years.

**-Offshore Boat**: For the fisherman who knows how, you can get so sick of catching big fish out here that you cut the hook off your flies. This fishing is done by chumming with live pilchards or mullet. Giant jack crevalle, snook, barracuda, and bonito move into the chum line and will make up the majority of the catch.

Those who don't like chumming can still catch fish (not so many though) around bait pods. Cobia will be found in addition to cuda and tarpon. The mackerel and bluefish show up in the fall.

Finally, the Gulf Stream awaits those with big enough boats, with its blue water species such as dolphin.

## FLIES AND TECHNIQUES

Gregg likes poppers. Like most of us, he loves surface strikes. The poppers are used around structure, especially for what Gregg calls "urban fish"; that is, fish working around seawalls, docks, pilings, and other man-made fish attractors.

Unfortunately, poppers don't always work. Gregg then falls back on the old reliable- the Clouser deep minnow. His favorite colors include chartreuse and white, red and white, green and white, and just plain white.

He'll use these flies wherever moving water passes by some type of fish-holding structure, for current brings food to the fish. Whether working a mangrove shoreline, casting along a grass flat, or fishing docks and seawalls, try to let the current carry your fly to where the fish are. You'll catch more and bigger fish this way.

Along the beach poppers will work when the water is reasonably calm, but if the water is too rough or if the fish aren't coming up for them, bigger flies are needed. Deceivers will usually do the trick, but during the mullet run woolheads and siliclones provide ample size and bulk for the fish to zero in on. As in most beach fishing,use a monocore line for best results.

## ACCESS

For Waders- see opportunities for waders.

Along the Beach- it depends which beach you want to fish. For Bathtub Beach and the House of Refuge, take the causeway (SR A1A) from Stuart over to Hutchinson Island. Take a right on MacArthur Boulevard. As you head south toward St. Lucie Inlet you will see periodically small parking lots that allow beach access, then the House of Refuge (great place to fish!) and finally the parking lot at Bathtub Beach. From here it's all walking if you want to fish the inlet- this is the southernmost access point on Hutchinson Island.

If you go north on A1A on Hutchinson, you'll find beach access intermittently all the way to the south jetty in Ft. Pierce.

For Boaters- there are lots of boat ramps in this area. For example:

-Stuart Causeway ramp. This ramp is located on the east side of the Stuart Causeway (SR A1A) and allows access to the grassflats of the Indian River, the St. Lucie River, and St. Lucie Inlet. It is nasty with a south or southeast wind.

-Jensen Causeway ramps. There are ramps on both sides of the Jensen Beach Causeway (SR 732) on the west end. The north facing one is normally the better one to use. If the wind is from the north, though...

-Little Mud Creek. This isn't really a ramp, just a little beach where you can put a small boat in and park the car and trailer. It is the ramp to use though if you want to fish this part of the Indian River, or Big Mud Creek. Coming from Stuart, Little Mud Creek is the third bridge after the power station. The ramp is on the left, just before the bridge.

-Shepard Park in downtown Stuart boasts an excellent ramp, at the intersection of US 1 and West Ocean Boulevard. Access to the north fork of the St. Lucie River.

-In Ft. Pierce you can find boat ramps at the both the North and South Causeways.

## FLY SHOPS

-Southern Angler, 3385 SE St. Lucie Blvd, Stuart, 34997. (407) 692-4359. This store is located in the Topside Marina.

-Tropical Outfitters, 2163 South US Highway 1, Jupiter 33477. (407)243-2600.

## GUIDES
Captain Gregg Gentile- Indian and St. Lucie Rivers (407)878-0475
Captain Mike Holliday- Indian River, offshore fly fishing (407)229-1565
Captain Butch Constable- Indian River, offshore fly fishing (407)744-6665
Captain Scott Hofmeister- offshore fly fishing (407) 747-2101.

## STATE PARKS AND OTHER ATTRACTIONS
-Hobe Sound National Wildlife Refuge, c/o US Fish and Wildlife Service, PO Box 645, Hobe Sound 33475-6141. (407)546-2067. Three miles of beach with reef formations offer excellent fishing for snook and other species during the summer months.
-Jonathan Dickinson State Park is over 10,000 acres on the Loxahatchee River, 12 miles south of Stuart on US 1. There are two camping areas, as well as cabins for rent. Jonathan Dickinson State Park, 16450 SE Federal Highway, Hobe Sound 33455. (407)546-2771.
-St. Lucie Inlet State Park, accessible only by boat. Three miles of beach adjacent to the Hobe Sound National Wildlife Refuge. St. Lucie State Park, c/o Jonathan Dickinson State Park, (407)744-7603.
-Fort Pierce Inlet State Recreation Area, four miles east of Ft. Pierce on the Atlantic Ocean. (407)468-3985.

## ACCOMMODATIONS
The Stuart/Martin County Chamber of Commerce can be reached at 800-524-9704.
The Greater Port St. Lucie Chamber of Commerce can be reached at (407)335-4422.

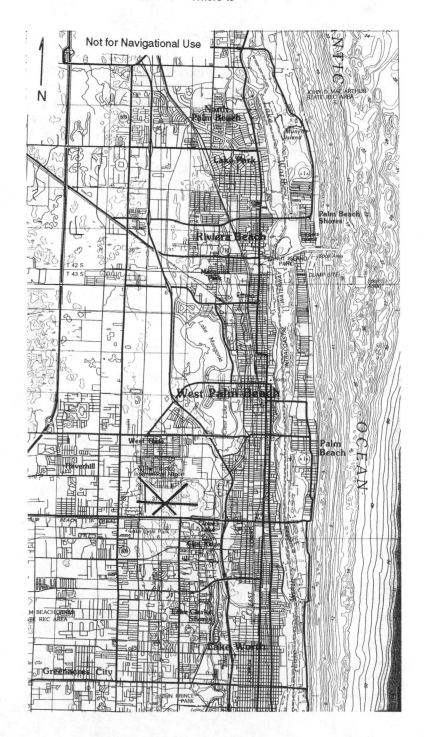

## FORT LAUDERDALE/PALM BEACH

Most people don't think of the Ft. Lauderdale/Palm Beach area as a light tackle fly rod mecca, and frankly, it isn't. But fly fishing opportunities exist for the fly rodder willing to look for them. "Look" is definitely the operative word here, too. The fishing spots aren't obvious, and sometimes are located in housing developments or other unusual areas.

Interviewees for this section were Captain J.R. Fairbanks and the "Land Captain", Steve Kantner. They offered widely different perspectives on fishing opportunities around Fort Lauderdale and the Palm Beaches.

## OPPORTUNITIES FOR THE DO-IT-YOURSELF FLY FISHER

**-Inshore Wading**: Wading opportunities as we usually think of them do not exist. However the entire region is criss-crossed with drainage and flood control canals. Most of these canals hold fish. Some of them hold freshwater species, some hold saltwater species, and some have both.

The C-14 canal in Palm Aire Condominium on Powerline Road in Pompano Beach provides fishing, especially at the locks after a rain. Baitfish wash over the locks, and snook, tarpon, and bass, both largemouths and peacock bass, lurk below waiting for an easy meal. Tarpon merit the most attention, although the peacocks are pursued by some.

A similar situation occurs at the C-13 Canal. Several other other easily accessed canals lie along I-75 and SR 84. The Tamiami Trail in Dade and Collier Counties has a canal along its entire length which has been written about for forty years. It offers sight fishing for snook and tarpon. Griffin Road parallels the C-11 canal down in Davie. You can actually drive along this road on the stretch between SR 441 and Holiday Park and look for rolling tarpon as you go. The best fishing has been east of 90th Avenue or west of Interstate 75.

Up in Palm Beach Lake Worth offers some opportunities, especially at the north end. There's a spillway which attracts the attention of jacks and snook. Get there by taking I-95 to the 10th Avenue exit, then going north on Dixie Highway until you reach the spillway. If you can't find it, ask someone for the locks on the Palm Beach Canal. In downtown Palm Beach the seawalls along Lake Worth attract some huge crevalle, usually in the winter and spring.

**-Inshore Boat**: J.R. Fairbanks does 40-50 charters a year along the Intracoastal in the Lauderdale area. The water is deep here, but snook, tarpon, big jacks, and barracuda are all possibilities.

Lake Worth has quite a bit of fishing in its 20 plus mile length. Some places for the fly rodder to try include the flats at the north end of the lake, the tip of Munyon Island on the east side of the lake, Lake Worth Inlet, the discharge pipes from the Florida Power and Light plant, the grassflats just south of the A1A Causeway across the lake in West Palm Beach, the mouths of any canals emptying in on the west side of the lake, the eastern end of the Ocean Avenue Bridge in Lantana, and around the inside of Boynton Inlet. At this location some surprising catches can be made.

The canals where Kantner does much of his fishing can be fished from a canoe, which can be launched almost anywhere.

**-Along the Beach**: There is plenty of beach access and there are fish to be caught here, but the prevailing winds are from the east. This tends to make fishing tough. Snook are the primary targets, with jacks available anytime and bluefish possible in the fall.

Any of the inlets between Palm Beach and Ft. Lauderdale provide an obvious fish attraction and consequently an angling opportunity for the adventurous fly fisher.

**-Offshore**: The same species can be caught here as anywhere else along the east coast. Cobia, jack crevalle, Spanish and king mackerel, and bonito are all fairly common. Since the Gulf Stream is so close, dolphin are always a distinct possibility, especially during the summer.

## FLIES AND TECHNIQUES

For canal fishing Kantner likes floating lines combined with streamers, although poppers are useful at times. Flies should be matched to the available baitfish. Below spillways shad imitations work best. At other times flies which imitate the tiny mosquitofish work better. Deerhair minnows often work well if no baitfish concentrations are obvious. He prefers black and yellow for colors.

In the Intracoastal, Fairbanks uses a #4 Wet-Cel shooting head along with weighted flies. J.R. likes Blanton's Sar-Mul-Mac and a non-buoyant version of the Dahlberg Diver.

It's also possible to fish floating lines in the Intracoastal and still meet with success. The trick? Fish lighted docks, seawalls, or ships at night.

In the shallow area of Lake Worth, you can sometimes sight fish. Floating lines and baitfish imitations work well. In deeper areas sinktips or sinking shooting heads are recommended. Flies should be weighted. You never know what kind of fish you'll come up with in these areas, especially around the inlets.

Fishing along the beach or offshore is done the same way as elsewhere along the east coast, and has been described earlier.

## ACCESS
For waders/shore fishing- see **wading opportunities**.
For boaters- along the west side of Lake Worth there are three excellent ramps:
-Boat Ramp Park in Boynton Beach, off of US 1.
-Bryant Park in Lake Worth, off of Lucerne Avenue.
-Phil Foster Park in Riviera Beach, on the east end of Blue Heron Boulevard on Singer Island.

By Port Everglades Inlet there is a ramp just north of John Lloyd State Park.

## FLY SHOPS
The Fly Shop of Fort Lauderdale, 5130 North Federal Hwy, Ft. Lauderdale 33308 (305)772-5822.
LMR Fly Shop, 1495 SE 17th St., Ft. Lauderdale 33316 (305)525-0728.

## GUIDES
-Captain J.R. Fairbanks is the only fly fishing guide along this stretch of the Intracoastal. He can be reached through the LMR Fly Shop.
-Land Captain Steve Kantner can be reached at (305)761-3570.

## STATE PARKS AND OTHER ATTRACTIONS
Yes, there are state parks here in the concrete jungle.
-John D. MacArthur Beach State Park, 2.8 miles south of the intersection of US 1 and PGA Boulevard in North Palm Beach, 10900 SR 703, North Palm Beach. (407)627-6097.
-Hugh Taylor Birch State Recreation Area, 3109 East Sunrise Blvd., Ft. Lauderdale 33304. (305)564-4521. This 180 acre park lies between the beach and the Intracoastal. Canoe rentals available.
-John U. Lloyd State Recreation Area, 6503 N. Ocean Drive, Dania, 33004. (305)923-2833. This park allows fishermen access to both the Atlantic and the Intracoastal.

## ACCOMMODATIONS
The Ft. Lauderdale Chamber of Commerce can be reached at (305)462-6000. The Palm Beach County Chamber of Commerce is at (407)642-4260.

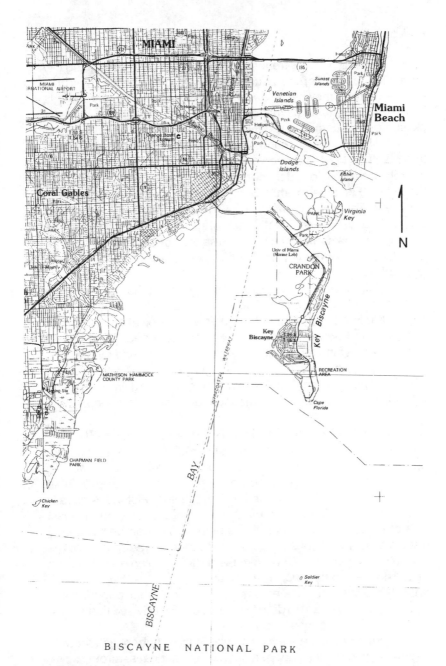

Not for Navigational Use

## MIAMI

Miami! This metropolitan area has all of the usual big city amenities, and all of the usual big city problems. One thing that makes Miami somewhat unique among America's big cities, though, is the fantastic fishing available almost within the shadows of the skyscrapers. Miami is a great place to fish!

Unfortunately, much of Miami's fishing is available only to those with a boat. You can find wadable water though, and it's entirely possible to catch bonefish by wading right off of Key Biscayne. For those with a boat, bonefish and permit fishing is excellent. Tarpon and snook are widely available. Jack crevalle, seatrout, ladyfish, and the other usual inshore species fill Biscayne Bay. Barracuda sometimes make nuisances of themselves. A short run offshore can put you in dolphin, bonito, mackerel, and other types of fishes.

Miami boasts many excellent guides who can help the visitor find fish. I interviewed two for the information here. Captain Lee Baker is a highly respected guide who specializes in tarpon, bonefish, and permit fishing. Lee was the featured guide in Billy Pate's "Fly Fishing for Giant Tarpon" video, produced by 3M.

Captain Jim Weber is a younger guide, not as well known or established as Lee. But Jim is a very good, hard working guide who will no doubt earn some measure of fame before long.

## OPPORTUNITIES FOR THE DO-IT-YOURSELF FLY FISHER

**-Inshore Wading**: As stated above, not much wading is available. Both Lee and Jim gave me identical information about wading locations. On the northeast corner of Key Biscayne are wadable flats where bonefish can often be found tailing. Fishing is usually best early or late in the day. By Matheson Hammock, on the west side of Biscayne Bay south of Miami, bonefish can be caught by wading on lower tide phases. Jim told me there's wading around the old Cutler Power Plant/Chapman Field Park area south to Chicken Key. And that pretty much wraps it up.

**-Inshore Boat**: The boater has so many different opportunities available it will be hard to decide what to do. Be advised that the list given here is by no means complete.

First of all, the species available include bonefish, permit, tarpon, snook, mutton snapper, sharks, barracuda, seatrout, jacks, ladyfish, and more.

Next, from Key Biscayne south to the Ocean Reef Club on

Key Largo you'll find more or less continuous flats covered with lush grassbeds. These flats support vast numbers of large bonefish and seatrout, as well as permit and mutton snapper. Tarpon cruise along the edges of oceanside flats during May and June.

The flat on the southwest side of Key Biscayne often has numbers of large tailing bonefish when a low tide coincides with early morning or late afternoon. These fish average about seven pounds with larger ones being common.

You can find excellent snook fishing at night by fishing around lighted docks and bridges. The 36th Street Causeway has excellent night fishing for snook and small tarpon. You can actually see the fish cruising along the shadow line, and cast to the ones you want. Many anglers tie up their boats to the bridge, then climb up on the bridge abutments and cast from there.

The oceanside flats of Elliott Key in Biscayne National Park are excellent producers of bonefish and permit when the weather allows. You need to have a west wind to fish here.

Permit love the hard bottom found around the Ragged Keys, also in Biscayne National Park. You'll see bonefish and other species here, too.

**-From the Beach**: In spite of having a lot of waterfront area, Miami Beach has notoriously little fishing. For a few days or maybe a few weeks during the fall mullet run, the beach will produce fish following the mullet. The rest of the year the beach is best left to vacationers who have activities other than fishing on their minds.

**-Offshore**: The waters off Miami will produce dolphin around weed lines or floating debris. All three species of mackerel can be caught sometimes. Bonito and blackfin tuna can also be caught by fly rodders, but they usually need to be chummed up.

## FLIES AND TECHNIQUES

Lee Baker was rather noncommittal on the topic of favorite flies, saying emphatically that presentation is much more important than the pattern whenever sight fishing. If the presentation is good, and the fish refuses the fly, change flies! He did say that he likes brown epoxy flies in sizes 1 and 2. He likes to use a fly that is big enough for both the fish and the angler to see.

Jim Weber likes Bonefish Charlies and other standard bonefish patterns. He likes flies with lead or bead chain eyes when fishing in deeper water (2-3 feet), and unweighted flies for tailing fish. For permit he likes crab flies, with the Merkin being a particularly good one. For Biscayne area tarpon he likes smaller sizes of the standard Keys tarpon streamers, from size 1/0 to 3/0.

Both guides said that they chum bonefish up with live shrimp, especially with first time bonefishermen. The idea is to find a flat with both the wind and current going in the same direction. The boat is staked out 30 feet or so from a white sand patch. A dozen or so live shrimp are cut into pieces and tossed out over the sand. When the bones respond to the chum, they are easily spotted. The angler then presents the fly.

If the wind is blowing the wrong way, or if there are a lot of small chum-stealing types of fish around, they use a chum tube made out of a short section of PVC pipe with a lot of holes drilled in it and a cap at both ends. The shrimp pieces are placed in the tube, and the tube (with a tether attached, of course) is tossed over the sand patch. After that everything else is the same.

## ACCESS
For Waders- see above.
For Boaters- you can find boat ramps at the following locations:
-at Oleta River State Park, off of SR 826 in North Miami;
-Crandon Park, at the north end of Key Biscayne;
-Matheson Hammock, off of Old Cutler Road south of Coral Gables;
-at Black Point Park, off of Palm Drive south of Miami, and;
-at Homestead Bayfront Park, off of Canal Drive on the east side of Homestead.

## FLY SHOPS
The only purely fly tackle shop in Miami is Charlie Richter's Fly Shop, 472 NE 125th Street, North Miami, 33161. (800)866-0763.
-Captain Harry's Fishing Supply sells fly tackle along with the rest of their inventory. 100 NE 11th St, Miami 33132. (305)374-4661.

## GUIDES
-Captain Lee Baker, (305)448-1447. Bonefish, permit, and tarpon in Biscayne Bay and the Florida Keys. Also, fishing for snook, tarpon, and redfish in Everglades National Park, and giant tarpon in Homosassa.
-Captain Jim Weber, (800)982-3110. Fishing for bonefish, permit, and tarpon in Biscayne Bay, and giant tarpon in Homosassa.
-There are many, many excellent guides in Miami.

## STATE PARKS AND OTHER ATTRACTIONS
-Biscayne National Park, PO Box 1369, Homestead, FL 33090. (305)247-2044. The only national park in the US with most of its acreage under water. Camping is available on Elliott Key.
-Oleta River State Park is located at 3400 NE 163rd St., North Miami. The mailing address is PO Box 601305, North Miami, 33160. (305)947-6357.
-Cape Florida State Recreation Area, at the southern tip of Key Biscayne. 1200 S. Crandon Blvd., Key Biscayne 33149. (305)361-5811.

## ACCOMMODATIONS
World class accommodations with world class prices can be found all through Miami. Of course there are lower priced accommodations too, usually in the more questionable neighborhoods. The phone number of the Greater Miami Chamber of Commerce is (305)350-7700.

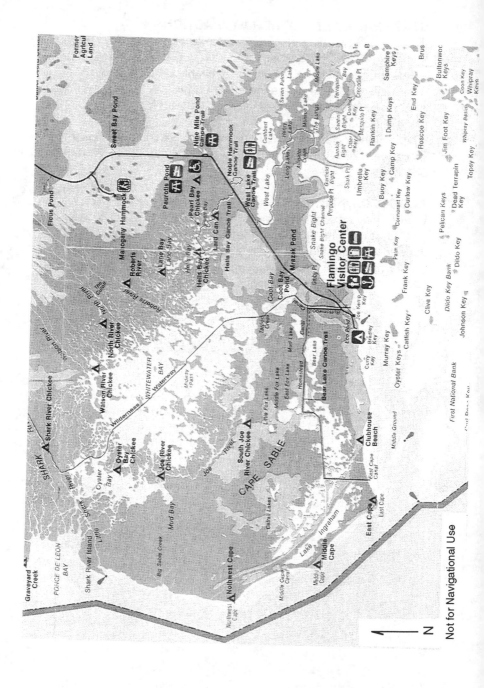

Not for Navigational Use

N

## FLAMINGO

How can I do justice to Flamingo in just a few pages in this book? I put this question to Flip Pallot, one of the best known and most respected names in saltwater fly fishing today. His answers were a little surprising and very insightful. They appear below.

Flamingo allows access to the southern portion of Everglades National Park. There is enough fly fishing there to keep anyone busy for the rest of their lives. Quite frankly, you'd need a lifetime to explore it all and take advantage of it. Most of us just don't have that much time. But even if you only have a few days, most of the time you can find some fish, and you might even catch the fish of a lifetime. They're certainly there.

For the angler hauling a family with non-fishermen, there are plenty of other things to do and see besides fishing. EVERYONE should visit Flamingo before they die!

**OPPORTUNITIES FOR THE DO-IT-YOURSELF FLY FISHER**
**-Inshore Wading**: There is absolutely no wading that can be done here. Don't even think about it.
**-Inshore Boat**: Flip suggested that the first time fly fisher to Flamingo avoid the flats until he learns his way around. You'll find plenty of fishing in channels around Flamingo. You need a Wet-Cel shooting head to maximize your success doing this, either a #2 or #3. You want the fly to be right on the bottom. What can you catch this way? Seatrout, redfish, jack crevalle, ladyfish, snook, tarpon, mangrove snapper and many others.

Why not fish the flats? It's easy to get into trouble on the flats, since you can go from several feet of water to absolutely none in less time than it takes to read this sentence. Also, the flats are large, and many flats are piscatorial deserts. Even productive flats have areas that seldom hold fish. Certainly, anyone wanting to try flats fishing for the first time could work the edges of flats from the safety of deeper waters, learning where it's safe to go and also how to find and see fish.

Why not fish back up in Whitewater Bay and the rest of the backcountry? Backcountry fishing requires knowledge and skill. The area is so large that the chance of just stumbling into fish is unlikely. So Flip recommends the channels and "lakes" in Florida Bay as the best area to start.

That being said, on a rising tide it's quite easy to explore the flats in Snake Bight, only a couple minutes east of Flamingo, especially in a small aluminum boat or a canoe. It is NOT a good idea to get way up on this huge flat. The tide or wind or both can push the water out quickly, leaving you high and dry. A strong wind can keep the water out for days- not a pleasant prospect. Stay close to the edge of the flat, looking for redfish waking or tailing, or moving behind stingrays.

Another close in and easy place to fish for crevalle, baby tarpon, and seatrout is in the dredge hole right behind the Flamingo Campground, next to the two spoil banks there. This hole often holds fish and is easy to fish. Again, flats around the hole can be explored from a small boat fairly easily on a rising tide.

Finally, for those with a thirst for adventure, and who like paddling, you can canoe down the Bear Lake Canoe Trail to Bear Lake and blindcast around the snags (east and north sides best) for baby tarpon, snook, and redfish, or go sight fishing around the margins of Mud Lake for redfish. You might find a load of fish there, or nothing at all. I've hit it both ways.

**-From the Beach**: In order to get to the beach, you must have a boat. The beach is out on Cape Sable (about 12 miles west of Flamingo), and is as magnificent a stretch of sand as you will ever see. Snook, jack crevalle, redfish, seatrout, sharks, even tarpon, and other species all come within easy fly rod casting distance of the shoreline out here.

**-Offshore**: Trout, Spanish mackerel, sometimes bluefish, can be found offshore. These latter two species can usually be found by watching birds. Out around the park's boundary markers tripletail and sometimes cobia can be found. Tripletail will also stay under the buoys along the crab trap lines outside of the park boundaries.

## FLIES AND TECHNIQUES

Flip's favorite fly is a Clouser minnow. These work especially well on the shooting heads in the channels. Remember to keep the leader short! This channel fishing is essentially blindcasting, although muds, skipping mullet, birds, current rips, and other obvious evidence of fish or locations that attract fish should be thoroughly checked out.

Another favorite is a modified Deceiver, used along the beach (and many other places) at Cape Sable. Called a Glades Deceiver, it features a body weighted with fuse wire and covered with silver Mylar, and a grizzly and white neck hackle tail, and a white kiptail collar. This fly is blindcast along the beach while the angler keeps an alert eye peeled for visible fish.

He also likes a fly called the Prince of Tides, which resembles a cichlid minnow, one of the many exotic species of fish now living in the park. This fly is especially good for snook up in the backcountry, where the majority of these exotic fishes are found.

## ACCESS
For Waders- there is none.
For Boaters- there are two ramps in Flamingo. One is on the Buttonwood Canal and gives access to Coot Bay, Whitewater Bay, the Shark River system, and the rest of the Flamingo backcountry. The other is on the small harbor on the Florida Bay side, and gives access to Florida Bay and the Gulf of Mexico.

## FLY SHOPS
There are none. The Flamingo Marina sells some fishing tackle, but nothing for the fly fisher. The closest true fly shop is Charlie Richter's in Miami.

## GUIDES
Guides are available through the Flamingo Marina.
Captains Nat Ragland, Lee Baker, Ben Taylor, and J.R. Fairbanks are four guides recommended elsewhere in this book who will guide this area and who are familiar with the needs of fly fishers.

## STATE PARKS AND OTHER ATTRACTIONS
Flamingo lies smack dab in the middle of Everglades National Park, the most magnificent wild area east of the Rocky Mountains. What else could you want? The address and phone number for more information is Everglades National Park Information, P.O. Box 279, Homestead, FL 33030, (305)247-6211.

## ACCOMMODATIONS
Flamingo Lodge offers both standard motel rooms and efficiency cabins. The phone number at the Lodge is (305)253-2241. There is also a restaurant, bar, gift shop, and the Marina Store.
        The National Park Service operates a campground here. See address and phone number above.

        For more in-depth information on fishing and exploring this area read <u>Fishing the Everglades- A Complete Guide for the Small Boater</u>, by John A. Kumiski. See the Resource Catalog in the back of this book for ordering information.

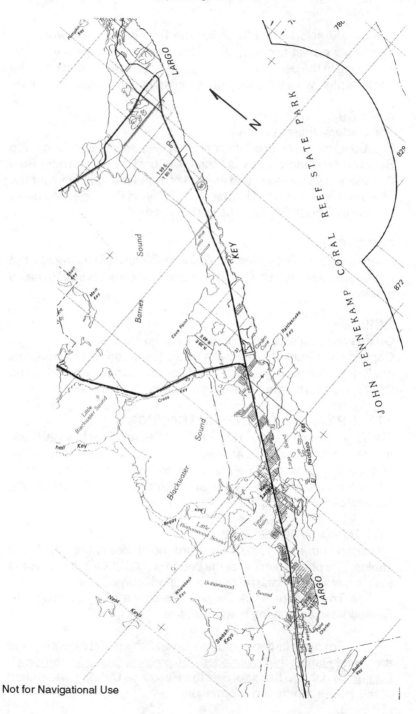

Not for Navigational Use

## UPPER KEYS

The Florida Keys hold a long and distinguished history as an angling destination. From Key Largo to Key West, crystal clear water shelters bonefish, tarpon, permit, and many other species of fish. Tackle stores and fly shops abound. Motels and restaurants are plentiful. Sometimes it seems like angling is the only reason for the existence of the Keys.

Captain Ben Taylor lives on Plantation Key and trailers his boat all through the upper Keys to fish the Keys waters as well as Florida Bay. He says that "Islamorada offers the world's most consistent fishing for big bonefish and the best shallow water sight fishing for giant tarpon in the world." Ben was kind enough to share the following information with you.

## OPPORTUNITIES FOR THE DO-IT-YOURSELF FLY FISHER

**-Inshore Wading:** Many ocean side hotels have bonefish on appropriate tides on their beaches. With work access can be found from Key Largo to Marathon to decent bonefish flats for waders. Good spots with easy access include Harry Harris Park on Key Largo and the oceanside flats at Long Key State Park. County and state parks are surest bets. An open stretch on lower Matecumbe offers good early morning and late evening bonefishing.

**-Inshore boat**: You can fulfill your life's dreams in the upper Keys for bonefish or tarpon. At Pennekamp State Park both canoes and outboard skiffs are available for rent. With the canoes you can fish for bonefish along the east side of Largo Sound. A motorboat can get you out to the east side of Key Largo to the oceanside flats, which are firm and very wadable. Both bonefish and permit use these flats. Oceanside flats near Whale Harbor Channel and Tavernier Creek by Tavernier Key will produce bonefish. On the bay side, the flats around Cotton Key and the Crane Keys are good.

During the summer and fall every flat on the bay side of the Keys from Plantation Key to Long Key with a direct connection to the populated keys has bonefish and some permit. During the winter the oceanside generally provides better opportunities, weather permitting.

In the Islamorada area try the bridges from Channel Two to Tom's Harbor. Lots of Tarpon hang out at Indian Key Channel and Tom's Harbor, while Channel Two is good for snook.

There is excellent fishing for barracuda and sharks all through this area. Additionally, a short trip will put you in excellent position to catch redfish, snook, and an assortment of fun back-country critters around Flamingo.

**-From beach**: You won't find many beaches in this area except at hotels where sand has been trucked in. Some folks ladder fish in the Grassy Key and Marathon area for tarpon and permit from the shoreline!! Bring binoculars and a ladder if you want to try this.

**-Offshore:** Dolphin and kingfish would be the species most available to fly rodders and many Keys charter boats are adept at matching angler to fish. Carysfort and Elbow Reefs are easily accessed from Key Largo, and Tavernier Creek allows access to Molasses and Crocker Reefs.

## FLIES AND TECHNIQUES

Captain Ben said this about his favorite flies and when he uses them: "We tend to throw much heavier bonefish flies than anyone else because our fish are big and use more water than most. I fish a lot of size 2 crazy Charlies for bonefish when they are up on the flats, preferring a copper sparkle braid body and brown bucktail. I am not afraid to use the same fly with lots of weight for spot tailers or edge mudders tied on a 1 with a bunch more weight.

The Merkin is quickly proving itself for bonefish in appropriate weights and offers the advantage of being the right fly to toss at the occasional permit.

For tarpon all black early and late in the day and an Apte 2 the rest of the time will feed plenty of fish though they will occasionally get pickier than that."

He suggests that anyone wanting to fish tarpon who doesn't have much experience start early in the day. The fish roll more then and can be seen more easily.

Regardless of where you go, fishing for bonefish, tarpon, and permit on your own often calls for a long hunt and can be quite frustrating. Be prepared to fish for 'cuda, sharks, snapper, jacks, or other species if your primary target plays hard to get.

## ACCESS

For Waders- as described earlier.

For Boaters- On Islamorada try Matecumbe Marina at about mile marker 80 bayside as out of the way and safe. For ocean side fishing in the Key Largo area Harry Harris park has a nice ramp though it can be hectic on weekends. There is also a ramp in John Pennekamp State Park on Key Largo. Most of the motels have ramps, but you can only use a motel ramp if you're staying there.

## FLY SHOPS
-Florida Keys Outfitters is the shop of choice for up to the minute info. (305)664-5423.
-H.T. Chittum's, MM 82.7 Islamorada. (305) 664-4421.
-World Wide Sportsman, MM 82.5, Islamorada. (305) 664-4615.

## GUIDES
There are LOADS.
Captain Ben Taylor (305)852-1775
Captain Mike Guerin (305)743-8702
Captain Bruce Stagg (305)664-8213

## STATE PARKS AND OTHER ATTRACTIONS
-John Pennekamp Coral Reef State Park, PO Box 487, Key Largo 33037. (305)451-1202. This park covers over 53,000 acres of water and over 2000 acres of dry land. It is a mecca for both anglers and divers. Canoes and motor skiffs are available for rent, and campsites (bring a good sleeping pad!) are available.
-Long Key State Recreation Area, PO Box 776, Long Key, 33001. (305)664-4815. Swimming and some of the best wade fishing in the Keys are right off of your campsite.
-Lignumvitae Key State Botanical Site, PO Box 1052, Islamorada 33036. (305)664-4815. You need a boat to get out to this wonderful, quiet island. It's a fine place to have a picnic lunch if you're in the area.
-Indian Key State Historic Site, c/o Lignumvitae Key State Botanical Site, PO Box 1052, Islamorada 33036. (305)664-4815. You'll need a boat to get here, but a ferry runs to the key from Indian Fill Key several times on the weekends. As the name implies, lots of history here.
A highlight is the wild bird hospital on Key Largo just south of the Sheraton or Theater of the Sea for non-anglers to view our quarry.

## ACCOMMODATIONS
There are a lot of motels. The phone number at the Key Largo Chamber of Commerce is 1-800-822-1088. At the Islamorada C of C it's 1-800-FAB-KEYS. Lastly, the phone number for the Florida Keys Visitor's Bureau is 1-800-FLA-KEYS.
Camping available at the Pennekamp and Long Key State Parks. There are also private campgrounds available.

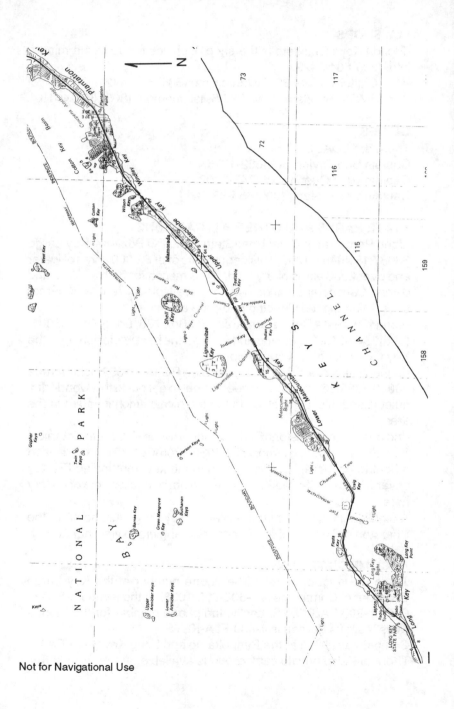

Not for Navigational Use

## THE MIDDLE KEYS

This area has some of the world's finest fly fishing. Bonefish, permit, tarpon, and barracuda are widely available inshore. Dolphin, cobia, and amberjack can be sight fished offshore. Many other species of fish can be found here, too.

Waders can find happiness, and boaters have a wide variety of options. There are many, many motels and a state park with a campground on Long Key. Guiding fishermen is perhaps the number one industry (actually this is an exaggeration, but only a small one) and many good guides are available here.

Captain Nat Ragland is a long time resident and guide who works out of Marathon, a guide who has a reputation for knowledge and innovation unmatched anywhere. Nat was featured as a guide in the video "Fly Fishing for Tarpon", with world record holder Billy Pate, produced and marketed by 3M/Scientific Anglers.

Captain Steve Huff is widely regarded, even by other Keys guides, as the best damn guide in the Keys. Both of these men supplied most of the information in this section.

### OPPORTUNITIES FOR THE DO-IT-YOURSELF FLY FISHER

**-Inshore Wading**: There are quite a few opportunities for waders along oceanside flats through this area. Long Key State Park has excellent flats. Although bonefish are the primary species, permit can also be caught out on the deeper part of the flat. I have personally seen big tarpon within easy casting range during tarpon season while I was there wading for bonefish. Other easily waded flats are found on Grassy Key, Missouri Key, and Little Duck Key.

**-Inshore Boat**: I was not sure if Nat was being vague or telling the truth when he said "anywhere you can get to by boat is a place you can find some fish!" Steve Huff backed him up when he told me that every piece of water in the Keys which is dry land at low tide gets fish on it at some time or another when the water is up. Nat did specify however that the flat in front of the Seven Mile Bridge oceanside and some Gulf flats in the same area usually hold bonefish.

The Florida Sportsman fishing chart of this area recommends oceanside flats in front of Grassy Key, Fat Deer Key, and Bahia Honda Key, and Gulfside flats behind Little Duck Key for bones. Stu Apte, in his book "Fishing the Florida Keys and Flamingo" (highly recommended, by the way) suggests that the area around the Content Keys may have the best bonefishing in the Keys. Permit and barracuda are other frequent visitors, and tarpon show sometimes, too. Stu also says (and I quote), "THE BACK-COUNTRY AREAS OF THE FLORIDA KEYS CAN BE TREACH-EROUS TO THE INDISCRETE ANGLER WHO BELIEVES THAT ALL HE NEEDS IS A CHART AND A BIT OF BOLDNESS."

**-From the Beach**: There aren't many beaches in this area. You'll find one on Grassy Key where bonefish can be found. Long Key State Park has what could be called a beach. There is a large and very pretty beach in the state park on Bahia Honda Key on the oceanside which also provides good bonefishing.

These beaches are popular with bathers, and need to be fished early or late in the day.

**-Offshore Boat**: Find weed lines and search them for dolphin. Trolling is another way to find these magnificent fish. Another way to take fish offshore here is to chum over "humps", reefs which rise above the bottom and attract many species of fish, including barracuda, amberjack, king mackerel, wahoo, sailfish, and others. This technique has been raised to an art form by several guides working out of Key West, including Jose Wejebe, Ken Harris, and Bob Trosset. Perhaps the most important factor in this type of fishing is a plentiful supply of live baitfish for use as chum.

Finally, in the Gulf backcountry you can sightfish cobia, amberjack, barracuda, permit, and tripletail around markers or under debris. The fish will also be found over wrecks, if you can locate one. See Stebbins' <u>Coastal Loran & GPS Coordinates</u>.

## FLIES AND TECHNIQUES

Which flies are Nat's favorites depends on what he's fishing for. He likes bonefish flies that "breathe", with a bucktail or marabou wing or a combination of these two materials. He also prefers fairly large flies for bonefish (#2), feeling that it's easier for both the fish and the angler to see. He likes these flies in yellow, orange, and brown, or combinations of these colors. Again, the color helps the angler to see the fly.

Steve Huff likes epoxy flies for bones, the MOE style. For tarpon he has gone to a very SIMPLE fly- he simply ties a rabbit strip in at the bend of an appropriately sized hook, and that's that.

Nat says for tarpon any of the standard Keys style tarpon streamers work well. Actually, any type of saltwater streamer will take Keys tarpon. The Keys style streamer was designed to prevent the fly from fouling on the cast, not because the fish wouldn't eat anything else. Nat has originated several well known tarpon patterns including the Dirty Nellie and the Orange Quindillon. He also likes the Black Death and almost any color combined with grizzly.

Nat was one of the pioneers of permit on fly. He originated one of the first permit patterns, the Puff. Nowadays, crab patterns take fish better than does the Puff. The Merkin is one of the best crab imitations currently available.

Sight fishing for barracuda on the fly is an exciting pastime, especially during the winter months. Long barracuda flies which imitate needlefish are used. These are usually tied with synthetic materials. Needless to say, a short wire trace is needed.

The Keys offer an excellent place to chum for bonefish with shrimp, as was described in the section on Miami. The boat is anchored 30-40 feet upcurrent of a white sand patch. Live shrimp are broken or cut up and thrown out over the sand, either by itself or in a PVC chum tube. When bonefish move over the sand, they are easily seen and cast to.

Steve Huff says his most important technique is to keep poling the boat, hunting for fish. He rarely runs his outboard after he reaches the fishing grounds. He believes that if you pole your boat far enough you will find fish, or fish will find you.

## ACCESS

For Waders- Long Key State Park offers excellent access to excellent, easily wadable oceanside bonefish flats. Others are available on Grassy Key, Missouri Key, and Little Duck Key.

For Boaters- Monroe County maintains many ramps along and off of US 1. Vehicle security is somewhat of a problem in the more secluded areas. Most motels, especially on the Gulfside, have boat ramps. There are also several private ramps whose use if available for a fee. Finally, there is a boat ramp at Bahia Honda State Park.

## FLY SHOPS

World Class Angler on Marathon. (305)743-6139.

There are other "tackle" shops along US 1, especially in Marathon.

## GUIDES

-Captain Nat Ragland lives on Marathon and guides primarily for bonefish, permit, and tarpon. His phone number is (305) 743-5806.

-Captain Steve Huff can be reached at (305) 743-4361. Steve has so many people who want to fish with him that he has the luxury of calling his clients and offering them available days.

-Captain Tommy Busciglio, the "Mayor of Marathon", is another excellent guide. (305)743-7225.

## STATE PARKS AND OTHER ATTRACTIONS
-Long Key State Park- see upper Keys section.
-Bahia Honda State Recreation Area, Route 1 Box 782, Big Pine Key 33043. (305)872-2353. This park has one of the few natural beaches in the Keys. It also has campsites and cabins for rent, two boat ramps, and great fishing for all of the Keys species close by.

## ACCOMMODATIONS
Camping is available on both Long Key and Bahia Honda Key at the state parks. The are also many private campgrounds.

Many, many motels are available. The Marathon Chamber of Commerce phone number is 1-800-842-9580. The Florida Keys Visitor's Bureau number is 1-800-FLA-KEYS.

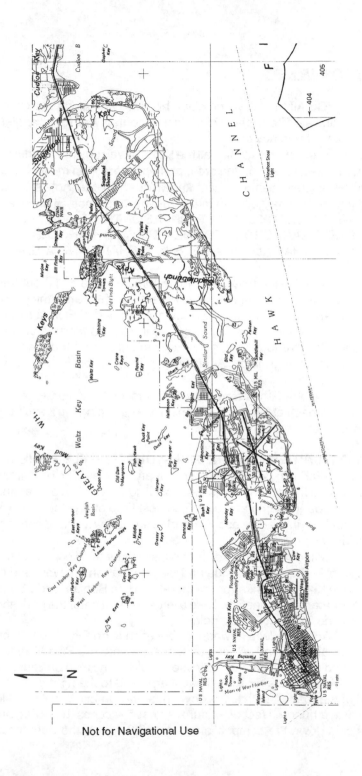

Not for Navigational Use

## THE LOWER KEYS

"Go All the Way!" proclaim billboards all along the Overseas Highway. They refer to Key West, of course. And for an angler, it's really not bad advice.

The Lower Keys, like all the Keys, have some great angling opportunities. However, the area, perhaps more than most others, requires a great deal of "local knowledge". In Stu Apte's book, Fishing the Florida Keys (an indispensable reference, by the way) he says, "THE BACK COUNTRY AREAS OF THE FLORIDA KEYS CAN BE TREACHEROUS TO THE INDISCREET ANGLER WHO BELIEVES THAT ALL HE NEEDS IS A CHART AND A BIT OF BOLDNESS."

Jose Wejebe was the guide I interviewed to fill out this section of the book, and he said essentially the same thing. He advises anyone trailering a boat down to this part of Florida to hire a guide for at least one day so you can start to learn your way around. Be sure to tell the guide your intentions so there are no misunderstandings later. Actually, this is excellent advice anywhere you go.

Wejebe fishes from Key Largo to the Dry Tortugas. He shared a wealth of information with me about fishing the Keys from Marathon on down to Key West.

## OPPORTUNITIES FOR THE DO-IT-YOURSELF FLY FISHER

**Inshore Wading:** Bonefish are the primary species. The best times of year for fishing for bones is between August and November and again between March and July. The best time of day for bones is early and late in the day, especially if the tide is low to mid-incoming, or mid-outgoing.

Some places to wade for bones include the west end of the Seven Mile Bridge oceanside and the rock bar on the west end of Missouri Key oceanside (permit here, too!). In Bahia Honda State Park you can also bonefish. Take a left when you enter the park and fish on the west side of the point.

Another place to wade for bonefish is on Big Pine Key off of Long Beach Road. When you first drive onto Big Pine from the mainland side, you immediately see Long Beach Road on your left. Take this left and after it makes a sharp bend to the right go to the end of the road. A path leads down near the water. You'll need to traverse a hundred feet of mangrove trees to access the water, but this cuts down the competition, doesn't it? Again, the best times of day are early in the morning and late in the afternoon.

You can also target barracuda in any of these spots.

Tarpon can be caught around and off most of the bridges at night between September and November and again during tarpon season, April, May, and June in this part of the Keys. Wejebe said he is continually surprised at the lack of popularity of this fishery. During the fall they are "fun fish", up to about fifty pounds or so. During tarpon season a boat is necessary, not to hook up, but to land them. The fish are too big to be landed from a bridge!

Some of the best bridges to look for these fish include the Seven Mile Bridge, the Spanish Harbor Bridge, and the Bahia Honda Bridge. Wejebe says that by using standard tarpon streamers or especially popping bugs you can have excellent sport on these bridges at night, and few people do it. Give it a try!

**Inshore Boat**: There are fish everywhere. Wejebe says (and it's already been mentioned) you will break off your lower unit if you do not know your way around, and so he was unwilling to answer this question. Extreme care is needed to fish flats in this region. Having said all of that, here are some places to try.

The Bahia Honda Channel loads up with tarpon during season, April, May, and June. The Spanish Harbor Channel also holds tarpon. Another place to fish for tarpon is at the Tarpon Belly Keys, on the gulfside north of Cudjoe Key. Tarpon can be found in most of the channels on the gulfside during tarpon season, and oceanside around all the bridges mentioned earlier, as well as the deeper flats in front of Spanish Harbor Key, Loggerhead Key, Boca Chica Channel, and west of Key West.

Key West Harbor is known for its winter tarpon fishery. Most anglers use bait for these fish. Fly fishers can take them if they run out into the Gulf, find a shrimp boat, load up with chum, and then use the chum to lure the tarpon behind the anchored boat, where they might be convinced to take a fly. Again, most visitors won't know how to do this- a guide will be needed the first time or two.

Bonefish can be found on oceanside flats along literally all of the keys between Bahia Honda and Boca Chica. Big Pine and Saddlebunch Keys have excellent oceanside fishing for bones. On the gulfside, the Content Keys have long been known for producing bonefish and permit. Most of the keys to the southwest of the Contents also produce both bones and permit until you reach the Mud Keys. Bonefishing peters out further to the west.

**Offshore**: There can be superb offshore fly fishing in the Lower Keys. You usually must chum with live pilchards to see it, though.

Finding the bait takes local knowledge, so again a guide is the best way to go.

The reef is out on the oceanside, and there are a number of wrecks to fish. Over these wrecks all different types of fish can be caught, including cudas, amberjack, jack crevalle, and various species of tuna. Coastal LORAN & GPS Coordinates by Captain Rodney Stebbins pinpoints many of the wrecks all through the Keys and throughout the rest of the state (see ordering information in the catalog in the back of this book), and can help you find many wrecks if your boat has a LORAN-C or GPS unit.

## FLIES AND TECHNIQUES

Wejebe likes epoxy flies for bonefishing. He says that typically when he bonefishes he looks for tailers and he's only in ankle deep water. The epoxy flies land softly and resist getting hung up. Another important point is that the fish take them quite readily.

For permit Wejebe likes the McCrab fly. This is a heavily weighted spun deerhair crab imitation.

Standard hackle Keys style tarpon streamers are what he prefers for tarpon. I had to laugh when he said, "When they're eating they'd hit a piece of s---." He prefers subdued, earth tone colors for both his tarpon flies and his bonefish flies.

Finally for fishing offshore he likes large white Deceivers or large poppers. Again, to get the fish offshore to come up near the boat you'll have to chum them up.

Wejebe, along with Ken Harris and Bob Trosset, helped develop the offshore live bait chumming technique which is now becoming so popular all around the state. In order to use it you must know how and where to use a cast net.

## ACCESS

Access for waders has already been discussed.
Boaters will find ramps at the following places:
-at the west end of the Seven Mile Bridge on Money Key.
-at the Big Pine Key Fishing Lodge on Big Pine (fee required).
-at the Old Wooden Bridge Fish Camp on Big Pine (fee required).
-at the Sugarloaf Key Marina on Sugarloaf Key (fee required).
-at the King's Point Marina on the east side of Key West (fee required).
-at the public ramp at Garrison Bight on Key West.

## FLY SHOPS
-Jeffrey Cardenas' Saltwater Angler, 219 Simonton Street, Key West 33040. (305)294-3248, or (800)223-1629. A full service shop with a stable of fine fly fishing guides.
-Sea Boots Outfitters on Big Pine Key. 1-800-238-1746.

## GUIDES
Many excellent guides are available here. Wejebe has so much work he asked that his number not be listed! Here are some others:
-Capt. Ken Harris (305)294-8843
-Capt. Bob Trossett (305)294-5801
-Capt. Tom Pierce (305) 294-6098 (March through June)
-Capt. Mark Schmidt (305) 745-2800
-Capt. Michael Vaughn (305)745-2800
-Capt. Marshall Cutcheons (305) 296-0252
-Capt. Ray Fecher (305) 872-2487

## STATE PARKS AND OTHER ATTRACTIONS
Key West is an attraction unto itself. Fort Zachary Taylor State Historic Site is on Southard Street on Truman Annex in Key West. (305)292-6713.
-Big Pine Key National Wildlife Refuge is the home of the endangered Key deer.
-Bahia Honda State Park- see section on middle Keys.
-Dry Tortugas National Historical Monument is fifty miles west of Key West and is accessible only by boat or seaplane. If you go bring everything you need, including water. There's nothing out there.

## ACCOMMODATIONS
The phone number for the Key West Chamber of Commerce is 1-800-LAST-KEY, for the Lower Keys Chamber of Commerce it's 1-800-USA-ESCAPE, and for the Florida Keys Visitors Bureau it's 1-800-FLA-KEYS.
      The Saltwater Angler provides bed and breakfast accommodations for fly fishers. Their number (again) is 800-223-1629.

Not for Navigational Use

## THE TEN THOUSAND ISLANDS

You can consider the Ten Thousand Islands as the northern gateway to Everglades National Park. This mangrove labyrinth provides excellent angling for snook, redfish, tarpon, seatrout, and many other species, too.

Waders will find themselves out of luck. A boat is mandatory here. You can rent boats, from canoes to motor skiffs, at the Everglades City Ranger Station and on Chokoloskee Island. Many guides also work here, but only a few specialize in fly fishing.

Captain Joe McNichols charters in this area and specializes in sight fishing with a fly rod for all the species found here. Joe supplied most of the information below.

### OPPORTUNITIES FOR THE DO-IT-YOURSELF FLY FISHER

**-Inshore Wading:** None available without a boat. Boaters can get out and wade at some of the outside islands, including Rabbit Key, Pavilion and Little Pavilion Keys, and New Turkey Key. Oyster bars at the mouths of the Chatham, Huston, Broad, and Lostman's Rivers offer some difficult but productive wading.

**-Inshore Boat:** Limitless. Thousands of miles of mangrove shorelines offer superb fly fishing opportunities for snook, tarpon, redfish, and mangrove snapper. River mouths on the outside (along the Gulf of Mexico) attract tarpon in the spring and early summer and big snook all summer long. Snook move into backcountry bays during the winter and spring months. Shallow flats produce the above species as well as seatrout, sheepshead, and pompano. Redfish could be found anywhere, at any time.

**-Along the Beach:** with the exception of a few outside islands in the national park there are no beaches available.

**-Offshore Boat:** Out beyond the islands and beyond the park boundary you may find tripletail under stone crab trap floats, cobia around the markers or under floating debris, or Spanish mackerel and bonito busting minnows on the surface. There are a couple of wrecks not too far out (see Stebbins' Coastal LORAN & GPS Coordinates) with snapper, grouper, pompano, sheepshead, snook and other species which can be chummed up and enticed to hit a fly.

### FLIES AND TECHNIQUES

Joe's favorite fly is a deerhair popper. He loves tossing a bug with a 1/0 hook and a weedguard up into the mangrove roots for snook. He also loves a chartreuse Deceiver for EVERYTHING-snook, tarpon, redfish, everything.

As so many other guides have stated, a Clouser minnow is another favorite fly. Joe's favorite colors are white, chartreuse and white, and smoke color (grey) for clear water.

This area provides superb sight fishing for laid-up tarpon in the spring. These fish are just sitting there not moving, very unlike the fishing in the Keys or Homosassa. All the conditions need to be perfect, but when they are... LOOK OUT!!!

Snook can be sight fished around the mangroves on lower tide phases. Use the chartreuse Deceiver or Clouser minnows for this. On higher tide phases use the deerhair bugs to blindcast in the same locations. Watch out for the heart stopping strikes!

## ACCESS
For Waders- none.
For Boaters- You'll find boat ramps in the following places:
-Glades Haven Marina and Campground, across the street from the Ranger Station in Everglades City, (813)695-2746;
-the public boat ramp next to the Outdoor Resort on Chokoloskee Island;
-at the Barron River Marina and Villas & RV in Everglades City, (813)695-3591, and;
-at the Captain's Table Motel in Everglades City.

## FLY SHOPS
Carlisle's Tackle (813)695-2244 on Chokoloskee carries some fly tackle. The nearest "fly shops" are in Naples- the Everglades Angler, (813)262-8228, and Mangrove Outfitters, (813)793-3370. Naples Sporting Goods also has a good selection of flies and fly tackle.

## GUIDES
Captain Joe McNichols has been fishing out of Glades Haven for the past eight years. Before that he guided out of Naples. He says the quality of the angling experience is incomparable. You really feel removed from the "modern world" and its stresses. He thinks that the angling experience should be fun first and foremost, then everything else will follow naturally. Joe can be reached at (813) 262-4132.

## STATE PARKS AND OTHER ATTRACTIONS
Everglades National Park, 2,000,000 acres of mangrove and

sawgrass wilderness. For information call (813)615-3311.

## ACCOMMODATIONS
Everglades Area Chamber of Commerce (813)695-3941.
Outdoor Resort, Chokoloskee (813)695-2881.
The Captain's Table, Everglades City (813)695-4211.

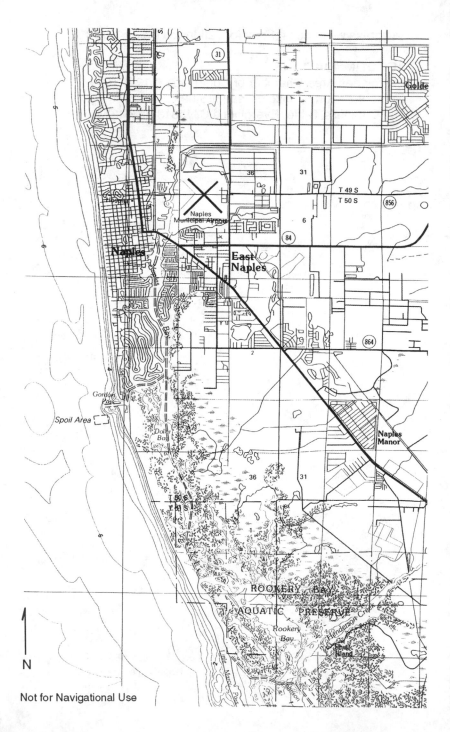

Not for Navigational Use

## NAPLES

Naples holds the reputation of being the high rent district in southwest Florida. Expensive homes face the beach, and line the waterfront of Naples Bay. The fish care about none of this though.

Naples boasts of good fishing opportunities all year 'round. It's quite possible to catch a dozen or more different species of fish in the Intracoastal in a single day. In spite of the close proximity to a populated area, anglers can get away from it all and on weekdays not see another boat all day.

I interviewed Todd Geroy to get my information for this area. Todd has fished Naples and the surrounding backcountry for 20 years. He has been a full-time guide for the past 14 years, starting at the tender age of 18.

**OPPORTUNITIES FOR THE DO-IT-YOURSELF FLY FISHER**
**-Inshore wading**: Todd says the bottom here is too soft for wading, and there aren't any wading opportunities available.
**-Inshore boat:** There are 18 species of fish available to fly fishers with boats. Tarpon, snook, seatrout, and redfish are only the most popular fishes available. The Intracoastal Waterway (Naples Bay) behind Naples to the east offers excellent opportunities for all of these species. Night fishing for snook around residential docks in Naples Bay is a summertime institution.

From March through October Gordon Pass is the local snook hotspot. Although most fish are taken with bait, fly fishers can score here by fishing at either end of the day, or by trying it at night. Tarpon also feed at night on the outgoing tide, especially on the full and new moons.

The residential canals north of Gordon Pass hold big tarpon all summer. You'll find these fish very difficult to fool with flies. Try it if you're looking for a challenge.

South of Gordon Pass in Dollar Bay seatrout work the grass flats just to the east of the Intracoastal. Either tide works, especially early in the day. Ladyfish will be found there, too.

Lots of good fishing can be found all along the Intracoastal between Naples and Marco. Those with a taste for adventure will want to explore around Rookery Bay and Johnson Bay. The many oyster beds in this area will quickly tear up the boat of the incautious navigator, so proceed with caution. The treasure chest of piscatorial rewards available here can definitely make the time and effort involved seem worthwhile.

**-From the Beach**: jetties and groins right along Naples Beach will attract fish, especially early and late in the day. If you drive north on North Gulf Shore Boulevard towards North Naples you can park your car and hike north a mile or so to Clam Pass, a small unnavigable pass which opens up to a series of brackish lagoons. Snook use the pass and the lagoons, and fly fishing here can be quite rewarding. Look for fish along the beach as you walk, too.

South of Gordon Pass, Kee Island (Keewaydin Island locally) offers excellent beach fishing for snook from April until October. This is an essentially undeveloped 11 mile stretch of beach. The only problem is you can't drive or walk- you need a boat to get access.

**-Offshore:** Todd doesn't get into true offshore fishing much, but there are fish available. Close to the beach you can find tripletail under crab trap buoys from November until March. In April the tarpon start showing up. They usually swim in about 15 to 20 feet of water, one half to one mile off the beach. These are big fish averaging over 100 pounds.

There are wrecks off of Naples which hold large numbers of barracuda and permit as well as other species all summer long. LORAN/GPS numbers are found in Stebbins' Coastal LORAN & GPS Coordinates. See the catalog in the rear of this book to order.

## FLIES AND TECHNIQUES

Like any experienced angler, Todd has definite preferences when it comes to flies. For snook he likes what's known locally as a mangrove snook fly. This is basically a white Deceiver topped with peacock herl. The whole fly is tied at the bend of the hook like a tarpon fly to prevent the wing from fouling. Fitted with a wire weedguard, it eases through the branches without hanging up on those inevitable shots into the trees.

For inshore tarpon a woolhead mullet is preferred. This fly has a wool head in grey and white, with big eyes. The tail hackles are natural grizzly. Cast it to rolling, cruising, or laid-up fish.

Todd says reds aren't usually very fussy eaters. He prefers fishing them on a low tide when they are more easily sight fished. For this fishing he likes a fly that settles slowly. Seaducers work well.

Finally, in the colder months he likes the Clouser deep minnow, and says they work on everything. Since he fishes in the backcountry a lot this time of the year, and since the water back there is discolored, he prefers darker colors for this pattern. His current favorite is purple.

## ACCESS
-For waders- except as detailed in the section on fishing from the beach, there is no access for waders.
-For boaters- In Naples itself there are two public ramps. The most popular is at Naples Landing on 9th Street, giving access to Naples Bay and the Intracoastal. The other is at Bay View Park on Bay Shore Drive in East Naples. There are several private marinas, all of which have ramps available for a nominal fee.

South of Naples you can get access to Rookery Bay by using the gravel ramp at Shell Island. Take US 41 south to SR 951, then go west on Shell Island Road. The ramp is at the end of the road. This area is loaded with oysters- be very careful.

## FLY SHOPS
-Everglades Angler, 810 12th Avenue South, Naples 33940. (813) 262-8228. An Orvis shop.
-Mangrove Outfitters, 4111 E. Tamiami Trail, Naples 33962. (813)793-3370.

## GUIDES
-Captain Todd Geroy, (813) 793-7141 or 450-7314.
-Captain Glenn Puopolo, (813)353-4807.
-Other fly fishing guides can be recommended by either of the shops listed above.

## STATE PARKS AND OTHER ATTRACTIONS
-Rookery Bay National Estuarine Research Reserve occupies most of the land between Naples and Marco. All kinds of scientific inquiry about estuaries is conducted here. The interpretive facility is known as the Briggs Nature Center, 401 Shell Island Road, Naples 33962. (813)775-8569.
-Collier Seminole State Park, 20200 E. Tamiami Trail, Naples 33961. (813)394-3397. Over 6000 acres of mangrove swamp. Canoes are excellent craft with which to explore and fish. Camping is available.

## ACCOMMODATION
The Naples Area Chamber of Commerce can be reached at (813) 262-6141. Their address is 3620 Tamiami Trail North, Naples 33940.

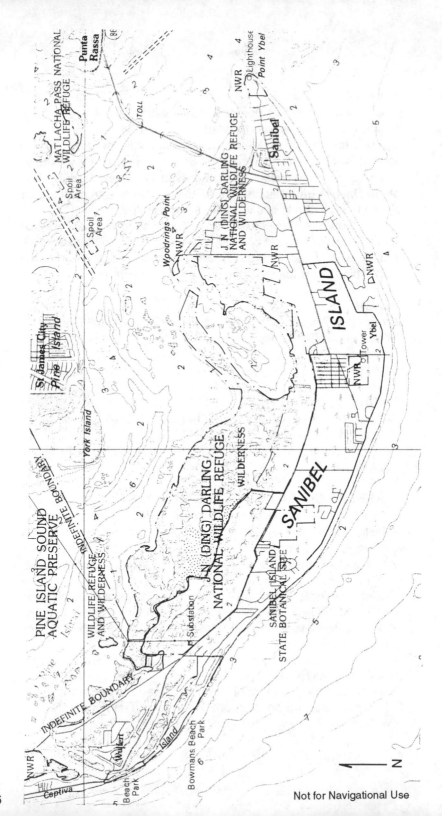

Not for Navigational Use

## SANIBEL/CAPTIVA ISLANDS

Excellent fishing awaits visitors to these islands. The Gulf of Mexico lies to the south and west of Sanibel, and to the west of Captiva. San Carlos Bay lies to the north of Sanibel, and the rich seagrass beds and flats of Pine Island Sound lie to the east of Captiva. With all the water around, the most difficult decision may well be where to fish on any given day!

Captain Mike Rehr lives on Sanibel Island and guides these waters over 250 days a year from his Silver King flats skiff. He kindly shared with me the following information.

### OPPORTUNITIES FOR THE DO-IT-YOURSELF FLY FISHER

**-Inshore Wading:** Most of the prime fishing areas in Pine Island Sound are accessible only by boat. However, good fishing is available in the vicinity of the east side of the Sanibel Causeway. Grass flats pocked with sand hole produce all kinds of fish- snook, redfish, seatrout, and flounder (yes, on flies!). Also, by walking the beaches in the morning during the summer months you can see and cast to snook lying in the trough. These fish will take plain white feather streamers, especially if they have lots of silver flash.

**-Inshore Boat**: There are miles of flats on the east side of Pine Island Sound. Lush grass beds with sand holes, mangrove islands, oyster reefs, sand beaches, and other habitat types support huge numbers of redfish, as well as snook, seatrout, and many other species, depending on the season.

Mike says Pine Island Sound is the best place in the state for a novice fly fisher to hook tarpon. This fishing peaks during May and June. There is also a spring cobia run. If conditions are perfect the cobia can be sight fished over rays the same way they are fished in Homosassa.

Since the area is so large, it helps to know what to look for. Drop-offs or other ways a fish can escape to deeper water often have fish near them. Broken bottoms of mixed sand and grass make it easier to find fish. Oyster bars will often attract fish, especially on an incoming tide. Healthy grass in good condition attracts more fish, especially with a current flowing. Finally, look for activity in the area in the form of stingrays, baitfish, and most importantly birds such as cormorants, terns, or pelicans.

**-From the Beach:** All summer long snook can be caught from Sanibel and Captiva beaches. Get out in the morning as soon as the sun throws enough light to enable you to see into the water. Walk along the beach, taking care to stay out of the water! The snook lie right at the water's edge, and are (sometimes) suckers for a well presented white streamer fly. It's possible to catch snook into double digit weights this way, too.

**Offshore**: Mike does not do much fishing offshore; however, he does know that tripletail are available in the fall around markers, floating debris, and crab trap buoys. This fishing can last from October into May if the weather is good.

## FLIES AND TECHNIQUES

Mike recommends experimenting with various flies to see what the fish want, and then sticking with it until it no longer works. However, a chartreuse Clouser minnow is his number 1 choice for most fishing. He also uses the same chartreuse Clouser with a pair of grizzly hackle feathers tied in, and yet another Clouser variation with marabou, flies he calls his "joy" flies, since they bring joy to the anglers using them.

He says sometimes you can find redfish feeding over stingrays. A small Merkin crab is deadly in these situations.

He also likes epoxy flies in tan and brown.

All Mike's flies have two-prong monofilament weedguards tied in. He prefers 20 pound hard Mason mono for this purpose. Mike can get exactly what he wants in his flies, since his wife does all his tying for him!

As already mentioned, Mike feels his most important technique is to use activity in an area to locate feeding fish. He says if there's not much life on the flat, and if the birds are lounging in the trees, he knows he's probably in for a slow day.

Mike's favorite type of fishing is for tarpon. He uses two stern mounted electric motors as well as a bow mounted electric to chase strings of fish and get his anglers in position to cast to them. He says there lots of schools of tarpon during season, and many daisy-chaining situations.

## ACCESS

For Waders-Along the Sanibel Causeway waders can park and access the flats along the east side. There is beach access all along Sanibel and Captiva. Blind Pass on Sanibel also has access. Finally, canoe rentals are available at Ding Darling National Wildlife Refuge on Sanibel which allow the canoeist to get out into Tarpon Bay, and if they're real adventurous to San Carlos Bay.

For Boaters- Boat ramps are fairly plentiful, and found in the following locations: in Punta Rassa at the east end of the Sanibel Causeway; at Pineland Marina off of SR 767 toward the northern end of Pine Island (private); on Sanibel Island proper on the east side of the causeway; at the Burnt Store Marina off of SR 765 north of Fort Myers; and in downtown Fort Myers between the Edison Bridges. Other ramps are available at fish camps and waterfront motels throughout the area.

## FLY SHOPS
Lehr's Economy Tackle in Fort Myers carries a full line of fly tackle and may have the finest flies in the entire state, all tied locally. The phone number there is (813) 995-2280. The person to speak with is Dave Westra.

## GUIDES
Captain Mike Rehr is available for charter. He knows his area extremely well. His boat, a Silver King, is clean and in excellent condition. He supplies top-quality tackle- Sage rods and Abel reels. He offers an educational experience in addition to a day on the water. He can be reached at P.O. Box 152, Sanibel Island, FL 33957; (813)472-3308.

## STATE PARKS AND OTHER ATTRACTIONS
On Sanibel Island is the Ding Darling National Wildlife Refuge, a bird watcher's paradise. (813) 472-1100.

## ACCOMMODATIONS
There are many motels on both Sanibel and Captiva. The phone number at the Chamber of Commerce there is (813)472-1080.

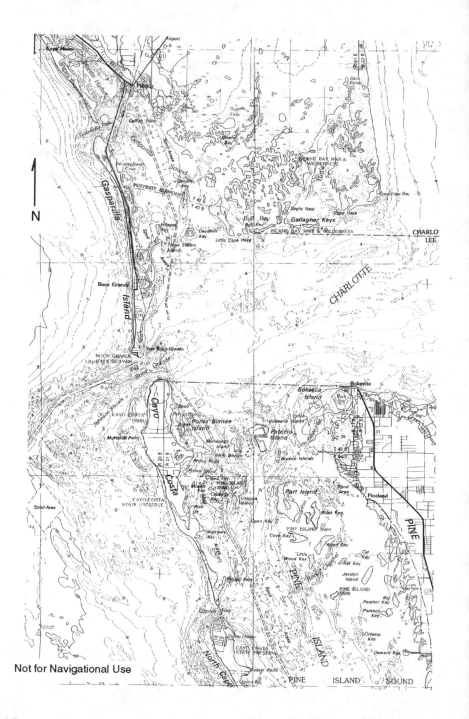

Not for Navigational Use

## BOCA GRANDE

Boca Grande Pass holds a national reputation as the world's best tarpon fishing hole. It is a hole, too- about 70 feet deep. Needless to say, fly fishers aren't terribly welcome in the pass itself, where most fishermen either use live bait or use fairly heavy jigs.

Tarpon live in places other than the pass though, and many guides target these fish, especially along the beaches. A few guides specialize in fly fishing for tarpon during season, mostly during May and June.

When the tarpon leave Boca Grande, lots of other fishing remains. The Peace and Myakka Rivers pour their waters into Charlotte Harbor, creating a huge fishing area. Pine Island Sound stretches off to the south, to San Carlos Bay and the Caloosahatchee River. Countless small islands, a few large ones separated by passes, many smaller bays and rivers, extensive grass flats and oyster reefs, and miles of beach make this as fishy an area as you'll find anywhere in Florida.

Some of the state's top guides work this area. Two were interviewed for the information in this section. Captain Phil O'Bannon has a national reputation for excellence. He grew up in this area in a family that made its living by fishing commercially. Phil knows the area like the back of his hand, and has fished such well-known anglers as former President George Bush.

Tommy Locke grew up near Homosassa. A relative newcomer in the Boca Grande area, he's only been there a few years. Nonetheless, he's quickly learned the area and is an excellent, hard working young guide.

## OPPORTUNITIES FOR THE DO-IT-YOURSELF FLY FISHER
**-Inshore Wading**: Although there are literally miles of wadable flats, a boat is needed to reach most of them. However, good opportunities for waders can be found near bridges throughout the area. For example, the SR 775 Causeway out to Gasparilla Island offers waders some access at its northern end. There is some access for waders along the bay side of Gasparilla Island, too. Another place you can wade is at the north end of Pine Island, in Bokeelia. Folks without a boat who want to fish can catch fish along the beach in the summer months. See below.
**-Inshore Boat**: The entire area of Charlotte Harbor and Pine Island Sound offers superb opportunities for redfish, snook, and seatrout all year long. Tarpon are available in season, as well as cobia.

The snook here, as well as the rest of southeast Florida, exhibit seasonal movements, moving into the backcountry creeks in the fall and back out through the passes and along the beaches in the late spring.

Miles of grass flats await exploration. Oyster reefs litter the seascape, and mangrove islands dot the area. Large barrier islands are separated from each other by cuts or passes through which enormous volumes of water move as tides change. Small creeks and the large rivers lie off to the east. There's plenty to do!

**-From the Beach**: All summer long snook patrol the beaches, oftentimes lying right in the wash at the edge of the shore. Sight fish these fish! This fishing starts in April and continues into October, although the best fishing happens during the summer months. Use a white streamer, cast about two feet in front of the fish, and stay out of the water!

Tarpon also work along the beaches during May and June. These fish are usually out of range of an angler standing on the beach, though. During the summer redfish sometimes work along the beach as they go through the passes. This is very much a hit or miss fishery though. Snook provide the most consistent fishing.

**-Offshore:** Off the beaches tarpon are available in early summer, as mentioned above. Farther out, kings run by every spring (March through May, mostly) and fall (October to mid-December). Using live pilchards you can chum the kings into an absolute frenzy, then easily entice a strike on a fly. Cobia remain around markers all year long. Tripletail show during the fall and stay into the spring months. You'll find them if you look under crab buoys, markers, weed lines, and floating debris.

## FLIES AND TECHNIQUES

Season has a lot to do with how you fish for some species here. For example, (and as already been mentioned), snook fishing is widely available along the beaches and in the passes during the summer. In the fall those fish start moving into backcountry bays and creeks, where they can be sight fished over white sand holes in grass flats all winter long.

Small schools of reds are here all year long, but the big schools (50-500 fish) arrive in July and are gone by October. Redfish tail more frequently during the winter months. Of course if you see tailers, start casting to them!

The main run of big tarpon begins in April and tapers off in

July. These fish are usually fished from skiffs along the beaches. The boat is positioned in front of the school with an electric motor, and then the angler throws a standard tarpon streamer fly in front of them. Smaller fish (and the occasional big one) can be found all year long. These fish frequent the mouths of the Peace and Myakka Rivers, where they are very difficult fly rod targets, and many of the canals on the east side of Charlotte Harbor, where they are easier to catch.

Seatrout used to be very easy to catch in three to five feet of water over grass flats. Their numbers have declined precipitously in recent years due to overharvest. Now that the net ban has passed, expect to see seatrout numbers quickly rebound.

Kingfish can be taken in 20 to 40 feet of water along the buoy line out of Boca Grande, most easily during the spring run. A livewell full of pilchards is a necessity for this. The fish are chummed up behind the boat and can become so ravenous they will strike anything remotely resembling a pilchard. Not much casting skill is required, since casts are only 30 feet long or so. You'd better have tackle up to the task and adequate fish-fighting skills, though!

Phil and Tommy both like chartreuse Clouser minnows for a lot of their fishing, saying that they are good for all types of fish. They also both like surface strikes, and so like to use poppers. Phil says he loves throwing a big popper in the middle of a school of redfish and watching several fish struggling to eat it before one finally does!

He also likes using a Dahlberg diver type of fly for tailing reds. Finally, since pilchards are such an important baitfish in the area, Deceivers in white or green and white should be carried. This is the fly of choice for beach snook and also for kingfish.

## ACCESS

For Waders- Most of this was already discussed in the section on wading opportunities. One thing I didn't mention was the ferry out of Pineland Marina on Pine Island. This ferry carries passengers over to Cayo Costa State Park on La Costa Island. Here anglers can walk the beach while searching for snook. You can camp near the beach, and the park also has some (ugly) cabins for rent which have bunks in them for those allergic to sleeping on the ground. Of course anglers who own boats can also take advantage of this opportunity. For Boaters- Boat ramps can be found at the following places:
-in Placida, just before the Boca Grande Causeway on CR 775;
-in Englewood off of CR 775;

-at the Pineland Marina on Pine Island, off of SR 767;
-at the Burnt Store Marina, on the east side of Charlotte Harbor, off of SR 765.

## FLY SHOPS

Kokomon's Tackle Outlet, at 1182-C Tamiami Trail in Port Charlotte. 800-895-FISH
Fishing Unlimited, an Orvis Shop on Boca Grande. (813)964-0907.
Angler's Image in Sarasota. (813)925-1206.
Shallow Water Outfitters in Punta Gorda. (813)637-9989.

## GUIDES

There a lot of good guides in this area; however, not all of them fly fish or understand fly fishing. Here is a list of a few who do:
-Captain Phil O'Bannon (813)964-0359
-Captain Tommy Locke (813)766-9070
-Captain Pete Greenan (813)923-6095
Captain Mike Rehr (813)472-3308 will come up and work this area.
-Captain Ray Moss (813)423-0125

## STATE PARKS AND OTHER ATTRACTIONS

-Cayo Costa State Park, PO Box 1150, Boca Grande, 33921. (813)964-0375. Accessible only by boat, but a ferry runs out to the island from the Pineland Marina. Camping right on the Gulf of Mexico is the main attraction here. Fishing is literally at your doorstep.
-Gasparilla Island State Recreation Area, c/o Cayo Costa State Park. Access is via the Boca Grande Causeway (CR775).
-There is a restaurant on Cabbage Key in Pine Island Sound which is famous for its excellent lunches, and was the inspiration for the Jimmy Buffet song, "Hamburger in Paradise". It's an unusual and interesting place which is worth a visit.
-The beaches in this area are famous for their shelling opportunities.

## ACCOMMODATIONS

Lee County Visitor & Convention Bureau, 800-338-6444.

Not for Navigational Use

## SARASOTA

Sarasota Bay presents one of Florida's delightful para-doxes- a highly urbanized area surrounded by a bay full of fish. Divided somewhat arbitrarily into a north bay and a south bay, it provides excellent fishing for snook, redfish, and seatrout, much of it very accessible to the wading fly fisher. Captain Pete Greenan lives in Sarasota. Although he now guides out of Boca Grande, he used to guide in Sarasota Bay and and still fishes there, and knows the area well. He supplied the information that follows.

**OPPORTUNITIES FOR THE DO-IT-YOURSELF FLY FISHER**
**-Inshore Wading**: Many opportunities await waders in Sarasota, Bradenton, and Venice. Side roads west of US 41 invite exploration. For some specific examples, though, read on.

The Ringling Causeway, SR 789, connects Sarasota to Lido Key. Between the twin bridges a flat on the north side of the causeway produces redfish, seatrout, and snook. The best times to fish are early in the morning and late in the evening.

On Lido Key go south until you run out of beach. A long grass flat extends out to the left, into the bay, and often produces excellent angling for the above named species.

Siesta Drive intersects US 41 on the south side of Sarasota and leads out to Siesta Key. On the southeast side of the Siesta Drive Causeway a flat produces (on occaision) excellent fishing for snook, reds, and seatrout.

Out on Siesta Key you'll find beach access on Midnight Pass Road (SR 72). You'll find good fishing along the beach during the summer for snook, especially around the Point O' Rocks.

On US 41 south of Sarasota look for the Sarasota Square Mall. Across US 41 from the mall you'll see Vamo Road. Take Vamo Road to Vamo Drive, then go right. You can park at the end of Vamo Drive, and the oyster bars and islands on the flat before you usually hold snook and redfish, especially on the higher tide phases.
**-Inshore Boat**: The flats and oyster bars at the north end of Sarasota Bay in the vicinity of Longboat Pass provide excellent fishing for redfish and seatrout, along with the occasional snook. Between Stickney Point and Point Crisp is another good area to try.

The keys along the west side of the bay, especially Whale Key and White Key, usually attract and hold fish.

Down in the south bay, the grass flats between markers 5 and 7 consistently produce excellent fishing for jack crevalle, ladyfish, and seatrout.

During the winter months, Zwick's Channel and the adjacent boat turning basins provide a deep thermal refuge for many species of fish, including snook, black drum, seatrout, jacks, and others. This channel runs from just inside of New Pass north almost the entire length of Longboat Key, ending between Buttonwood Harbor and Longboat Pass. Fish with a sinktip or sinking shooting head with fast sinking flies.

When the current is flowing over or past them, the oyster bars and the docks along the shoreline of Roberts Bay are consistent producers, too.

**-From the Beach**: Snook lay along the trough of the beach all summer, just as they do on the Gulf beaches farther south. Cast a white streamer, such as Deceiver, making sure that you do not walk in the water and spook the fish. Additionally, schools of redfish work along the beach. One of these schools may appear at in front of the fly fisher any time.

**-Offshore**: Beach fishing for tarpon gets more popular every year. Electric motors put the fly fisher in front of a cruising string of fish, and when they're in range, you deliver the fly. If things go according to plan, the fireworks start immediately after this.

Also in season, you can find Spanish mackerel and bluefish. Tripletail and cobia can be found around markers, and cobia can also be chummed in close to the boat. Sarasota county has an excellent system of artificial reefs which will hold cobia, kingfish, permit, and other species.

## FLIES AND TECHNIQUES

Pete supplied the following list of fly patterns for specific types of fish, and hook sizes:

Tarpon: Black Death.... AM       4/0
    Cockroach.......AM        "
    Orange/ Grizzly.AM        "
    Blue/Grizzly Gold..All day      "
    Chartreuse/yellow.......Back country 1/0
    Purple/Black....Back country   1/0
Snook: Red/White finger mullet       1/0
    Greenback finger mullet     1/0
    Greenback Deceiver (no weed guard for beach) #1
    Chartreuse/White or Yellow deceiver (tannic water)
    Clouser (grey, chartreuse, pink, etc.)
    Pearl Glass minnow #2 (under lights)

Reds:  Greenan Redfish #1
          Popper (red/white) #1
          Clouser (Chartreuse, Black, Grey)
          Brown/ Olive crab #1
          Tan shrimp #1
    Trout:  Purple/black
          Clouser (grey, Chartreuse, Pink)
      Jacks: anything
      Ladyfish: anything
Use a weed guard for back country fish and around mangroves. Seatrout don't require one usually though. Baby tarpon are in canals and boat basins with at least 6 feet of water and access to a river, the Intracoastal Waterway or other egress.

You must be able to adjust and adapt to rapidly changing conditions!

## ACCESS
For Waders: see above information about wading opportunities
For Boaters: Boat ramps are available at the following locations:
-on 10th Street in Sarasota;
-at City Island on Lido Key;
-at Turtle Beach on Siesta Key;
-at Blackman Point in Nokomis;
-at Nokomis Beach in Venice.

## FLY SHOPS
Angler's Image, 5714 Clark Road, Sarasota. (813)925-1206
Mr. CB's Bait and Tackle (813)349-4400
Economy Tackle (813)922-9671

## GUIDES
Captain Roy String, Jr. (813)925-9134
Captain Brandon Naeve (813)966-4978

## STATE PARKS AND OTHER ATTRACTIONS
Oscar Scherer State Recreation Area off of US 41 in Venice. (813)966-3154. You can camp here, and a boat ramp is about a mile away on the Intracoastal Waterway.

## ACCOMMODATIONS
The Sarasota Chamber of Commerce will happily recommend places to stay. (813)955-8187.

Not for Navigational Use

## TAMPA/ST. PETE

The Tampa/St. Pete area again offers anglers one of those delightful paradoxes- a major metropolitan area surrounded by clean water full of fish. What more could a fisherman want?

Tampa Bay extends inland for over 30 miles, all the way up into Lake Tarpon in Tarpon Springs. A series of barrier islands stretch down the coast from Honeymoon Island off of Dunedin south to Anna Marie Island off of Bradenton and beyond, offering beach anglers countless opportunities. Pass after pass cut through the barriers, offering fish and fishermen easy access from the Intracoastal Waterway out to the Gulf of Mexico. Literally thousands upon thousands of acres of fishable water await the visiting angler. Many rivers enter Tampa Bay, including the Hillsborough, Alafia, Little Manatee, and Big Manatee. You'll find good fishing around all of these river mouths, as well as around the docks and seawalls in downtown Tampa. Obtaining a copy of the Florida Sportsman Fishing Chart #707 for Tampa Bay is highly recommended. See the catalog at back of this book to order.

My informants for the section on Tampa were Captain Paul Hawkins and Captain Bill Miller. Paul, born and raised in St. Petersburg, has fished the bay his entire life. He's been fly fishing longer than he cared to think about and has been guiding full time for the past 11 years. Bill is a nationally known light tackle and fly fishing guide.

## OPPORTUNITIES FOR THE DO-IT-YOURSELF FLY FISHER

**Inshore wading:** The entire perimeter of Tampa Bay is ringed with flats, the only exception being the dredge and fill areas. All these flats are wadable, and if there's seagrass and/or mangroves there will be fish there at one time or another. Some of the easier places to get access include (but are not limited to):
-Fort DeSoto Park, on Mullet Key at the entrance to Tampa Bay, offers both beach fishing and wading;
-either end of the Sunshine Skyway at the fishing piers;
-Pinellas Point, off 4th Street in St. Pete;
-North Shore Park;
-Weedon Island Park, on the east side of St. Pete just south of the Gandy Causeway, offers miles of grass flats interspersed with oyster beds;
-at the north end of 4th Street in St. Pete, just before I-275, potholes in grass flats offer targets for the wading fly fisher. Also, some deep

dredge holes in this areas will hold fish during winter's cold snaps;
-at both ends of the Gandy Bridge waders can get access to good flats;
-Picnic Island Park, south of Port Tampa of the west side of the Interbay Peninsula;
-Ballast Point Park on the east side of the Interbay peninsula;
-north of the Howard Frankland Bridge on the Tampa end.

**-Inshore boat:** the opportunities are truly unlimited. Boaters can fish all the same areas that waders can, and have so many more options. They can sightfish for reds, trout, and snook along the relatively undeveloped south shoreline of the bay where waders have very little access. Obvious places to try are grass flats, bars, points, mangrove shorelines, and creek or river mouths.

Boaters can fish for tarpon all summer long on deeper flats (from three to ten feet deep) and the edges of those flats. Sight fishing for tarpon in Tampa Bay isn't as publicized as it is in other parts of the state, but it's done the same way and it's just as good.

Channel markers along the main shipping channel in the bay offer the investigative angler shots at cobia and tripletail. Kingfish also hang around these buoys and can be chummed up and caught on flies. Spanish mackerel, bonito, jacks, and bluefish are other species which could show up at any time, depending on the season. Look for surface activity or working birds in the open waters of the bay.

All the lighted bridges provide good fishing at night. During the summer you can have heart-attack fishing for tarpon here.

Folks with canoes can fish the no motors areas around Weedon Island on the east side of the Pinellas peninsula, or in Cockroach Bay on the south side of Tampa Bay. Both of these areas have excellent fishing, and receive less angling pressure because of the use restriction.

**-From the beach:** the beach runs from Honeymoon Island all the way down to Mullet Key. Jacks, bluefish, Spanish mackerel, pompano, seatrout, snook (summertime), and various other species can all be caught from the beach. Structure along the beaches always attracts fish, and it's no different here. Jetties and passes are the two most obvious places to check. Some of the better known passes, from north to south, are Hurricane Pass, Dunedin Pas, Clearwater Pass, Johns Pass, Blind Pass, and Pass-a-Grille. Possibly the prime beach fishing site in the entire metro area is Fort DeSoto Park on the tip of Mullet Key.

**-Offshore:** Captain Hawkins doesn't often leave the bay. He tells me there are plenty of tarpon along the beach in the early summer. The buoy line marking the channel out of the bay attracts the same species as it does in the bay itself- cobia and tripletail on top and kingfish down below. You can sightfish the first two species, but kings will usually need to be chummed up. There are wrecks off the coast over which, in addition to the cobia and king mackerel, amberjacks and barracuda will also be found.

## FLIES AND TECHNIQUES

The flies to use depend on what species you're targeting. Hawkins is fond of the bonefish fly known as the Crazy Charlie, which has an inverted hair wing with bead chain eyes. He ties these on number 1 and 1/0 hooks for use on the bay's seatrout, redfish, and snook. He likes red and white or brown and orange color combinations.

The Clouser deep minnow is a favorite all along Florida's coast. Paul likes them primarily for ladyfish and Spanish mackerel.

For fishing the bay's abundant tarpon Paul uses the standard Keys-style tarpon streamer. His favorite colors are orange and grizzly (good anywhere tarpon swim, by the way) and blue and white. These are tied on 2/0 or 3/0 hooks.

As far as techniques go, Paul greatly prefers hunting, stalking, and casting to fish on the flats above all else. He looks for an area with clean water, healthy grass, and bait or other signs of life, and then starts hunting. When the fish are spotted then the stalk begins, which culminates in the cast and presentation. Hopefully the fish eats and a hookup results!

In dark water or deeper areas he says the best thing to do is to blind-cast, working the shoreline or structure in the water.

## ACCESS

For waders- as described earlier.
For boaters- The metro Tampa area has a lot of good boat ramps. In St. Petersburg you can find ramps at the following locations:
-Bay Vista, at 4th St. and Pinellas Point Dr. S.;
-at 1st St. and 31st Ave., NE;
-at Poplar St. and 35th Ave. NE;
-at Bayshore Dr. and 2nd Ave. S;
-6th St. and 39th Ave.;
-Park St. and Elbow Lane N;
-Pinellas Point Dr. and 34th Dr. S;
-and at Sunlit Cove Dr. and Bay St. NE.

In Tampa boat ramps will be found at:
-Ballast Point on Bayshore Boulevard;
-Marjorie Park, on Davis Island Boulevard, and;
-on Picnic Island.
Elsewhere in the Tampa Bay region you will find ramps at:
-Baycrest, on Baycrest Boulevard off Memorial Highway;
-Cockroach Bay, on Cockroach Bay Road, east of US 41;
-Courtney Campbell, on the north side of the Courtney Campbell Causeway;
-on Davis Island, on the south end of Davis Island Boulevard;
-Domino, on the south end of 22nd Avenue and 8th Avenue in Ruskin;
-E.G. Simmons, 2401 19th Avenue NW, two miles west of US 41;
-Ruskin Commongood, 121st Street and 2nd Street, Ruskin;
-Salty Sol Fleishman, on Gandy Boulevard west of Tampa;
-Williams, 6401 Riverview Drive, west of US 41.

## FLY SHOPS
Sporting Classics
1702 Dale Mabry South
Tampa, FL 33609
(813)254-5627

## GUIDES
Captain Paul Hawkins, PO Box 7005, St. Petersburg 33734. (813)894-7345
Captain Bill Miller, PO Box 17397, Tampa 33682. (813)935-3141
Captain Denis Quilligan, (813)210-4996

## STATE PARKS AND OTHER ATTRACTIONS
-Weedon Island State Preserve, 1500 Weedon Island Drive, St. Petersburg 33702. (813) 570-5146. This preserve has 1250 acres for hiking, picnicking, and fishing, The waters around Weedon Island are a no motors allowed zone.
-Little Manatee River State Recreation Area, 215 Lightfoot Road, Wimauma, 33598. (813) 634-4781. This park, over 1600 acres, allows canoeing and fishing among the recreational opportunities offered. The Little Manatee River, which flows for four and one-half miles through this park, is a designated Outstanding Florida Waterway and is part of the Cockroach Bay Aquatic Preserve.
-Honeymoon Island State Recreation Area, #1 Causeway Boulevard, Dunedin 34698. (813)734-4255. Beach fishing here can be

awesome, especially during the summer when snook prowl the near-shore waters. A ferry here takes visitors to Caladesi Island, another state park which is not accessible by road.

-Caledesi Island State Park, #1 Causeway Boulevard, Dunedin 34698. (813)443-5903. One of the last undeveloped islands on the Gulf Coast of Florida, it offers the same fishing opportunities as Honeymoon Island.

Of course you can always visit Busch Gardens, and probably should if you've never done that sort of thing before. If you have, once is probably enough. Let's face it- the fish need catching!

## ACCOMMODATIONS

A huge number of accommodations are available all through the metro Tampa area. Call the St. Petersburg Area Chamber of Commerce at (813)821-4049 or the Greater Tampa Area Chamber of Commerce at (813) 228-7777.

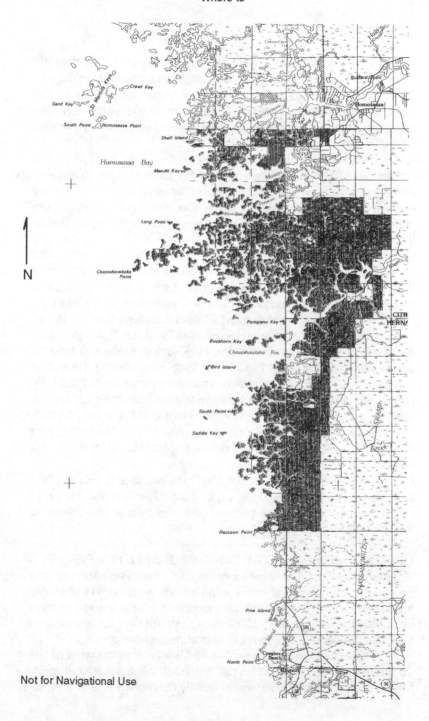

Not for Navigational Use

## HOMOSASSA

Florida's coastline is divided into sections. There's the First Coast, the Space Coast, the Gold Coast, and others. Homosassa sits smack dab in the center of what's called the Nature Coast. With extensive salt marshes and very little shoreline development, the coastline here is as beautiful and wild as any coastline anywhere, with lots of birds and other wildlife.

The widest Continental Shelf on the Gulf Coast lies off of Homosassa. This wide shelf makes for extensive shallow flats. Lush grass beds, which anchor the bottom sediments and quickly trap any suspended material, cover the bottom. As a result, the water here is as clear as what you are used to drinking, adding to the aesthetics of fishing here.

Most fishermen who visit Homosassa are not looking to see birds, though. The serene nature of the coastline is less important than the fact that those extensive grass beds in that crystal clear water support what is possibly the finest redfishery in the state.

Homosassa has lots to offer besides redfish, too. Cobia and seatrout are other well known Homosassa fisheries. Spanish mackerel and bluefish are available, and large jack crevalle and ladyfish live in the headwaters of the Homosassa River during the winter months. But Homosassa is best known for, and what draws fly fishermen here in droves year after year after year, the giant tarpon that come through each summer, giant fish in the shallow, crystalline waters, fish that make your heart quake, your knees shake, and your breath come hard. Homosassa is the Holy Land for fly fishing tarpon anglers.

Mike Locklear grew up in the Homosassa area. He's fished it all his life, and has been guiding for a good portion of it. He and I spent a lot of time on the phone, while he related the following information to me.

## OPPORTUNITIES FOR THE DO-IT-YOURSELF FLY FISHER

**-Inshore Wading**: There isn't a great deal of wading here, but you can find some quality fishing. Taking it from the north to the south, in Crystal River SR 44 goes literally right to the water's edge, ending in a boat ramp at Fort Island Gulf Beach. Wade here for redfish and seatrout. Jacks and ladyfish will sometimes show up.

South of Crystal River, SR 494 leads off to the west of SR 19, heading to Ozello. Waders can fish back in the salt marsh in St. Martin's Aquatic Preserve, again mostly for redfish and seatrout.

South of Homosassa a ride along SR 50 west will bring you to several wading opportunities. If you take SR 595 north, you'll find extensive grass flats off the beach at Pine Island. Fishing is also possible out at Cooglers Beach. And lastly, you can park at the county park in Bayport and wade fish. In all three places the primary target will be redfish.

**-Inshore Boat**: First of all, boaters need to navigate with extreme caution in these waters. Rocks are frequently seen, and sometimes not until after they've smashed some part of the boat. Local knowledge is very important here, and even the locals hit rocks sometimes. The wise angler uses an aluminum boat.

Several seasonal fisheries exist off Homosassa. By the end of February cobia start following stingrays around on flats in about three to four feet of water. Active rays will often have cobia, and sometimes big cobia, shadowing them. These ling take a well presented fly, and put up a whale of a fight in the shallow water. This fishing ends around the beginning of May.

When May comes, though, people start thinking about tarpon. Several fly rod world records have been caught here and every season all of the biggest names in saltwater fly fishing congregate in Homosassa for eight tough weeks of searching for the Big Mamoo. This is not a type of fiching for the first-time do-it-yourselfer, due to the tackle and knowledge you need. There is no more exciting fly fishing anywhere, though. Every serious saltwater fly fisher should try this fishing at least once!

Redfish are available most of the year. Without going out into the Gulf, redfish can be found in all of the creeks feeding the Homosassa River all year long. Mason's Creek is one good one to try. All of the others are worth exploring, too.

If you want to try the Gulf for reds, the areas of the coast to the north and south of the Homosassa River offer almost unlimited opportunities. Mike says that summer (particularly July and August) provides some of the best fishing of the year for reds, but they feed all year long IF the water stays over 70 degrees. In January and February the water often becomes colder than that, though.

Anyone who cares to tow the boat up to Crystal River can be in redfish less than a mile from the boat ramp at Fort Island Gulf Beach at the end of SR 44. Oyster bars in this area almost always attract and hold redfish, and seatrout too. Once again, take care in navigating. Oysters are unforgiving creatures when you run a lower unit into them.

Trout fishing off Homosassa, as in most other places in Florida, "ain't what it used to be!" Now that the net ban has passed, expect the trout to recover fast.

**-Along the Beach**: there are no beaches to speak of along this stretch of coast.

**-Offshore**: Mike told me about a fly fishing opportunity off Homosassa of which I had never even heard, but would love to try- shallow water grouper. I mentioned above that there were rock piles which required the boater to proceed with caution. These rocks hold grouper, and are shallow enough that the fish can be reached with a fly. These rocks can be found visually just by looking, or with a LORAN unit. The numbers are published in a book called <u>Coastal LORAN & GPS Coordinates</u>, by Captain Rodney Stebbins. (See catalog for ordering information.)

Cobia hold around the markers for most of the summer, sometimes in gangs. My guess is that they would also be around the same rock piles that the grouper are. Some of these fish get to be well over 50 pounds. It's quite difficult getting them away from the marker after the hookup. It sure is fun trying, though!

Sea bass can be caught on flies over deeper grass flats. The bottom here drops only one foot per mile, so you could be ten miles offshore in only ten feet of water. The clear water allows the seagrass to grow, and catching seabass with a fly rod in this situation is easy.

During the fall and winter months Spanish mackerel can come through in miles-across schools, dimpling the surface as they feed on glass minnows and driving the birds nuts. Fly fishers can catch fish until they're sick of it. Although less likely, kingfish are another possibility, especially over the artificial reefs. The location of these reefs is again found in Stebbins' <u>LORAN & GPS</u> book.

## FLIES AND TECHNIQUES

Mike Locklear is yet another fan of fly rod poppers. He likes them for both seatrout and redfish.

Deceivers work well on everything.

He likes the Merkin for redfish, especially on an incoming tide. The fish often tail then, digging for crabs. A well placed cast is almost a sure hookup.

Mike told me of a fly I hadn't heard of, the Wakulla Wobbler, originally designed by Ted Forsgren. This "fly" is actually a gold colored spoon made from epoxy. Mike said he thought this fly would soon be marketed by Orvis. Evidently it is deadly on reds.

Large weighted flies are used over stingrays for spring cobia, especially around the markers of the Chassahowitzka National Wildlife Refuge. Eelworms and tarpon bunnies in dark colors are good. These need to be fished on a nine- or ten weight rod equipped with a monocore line. If the fish appear to be selective, or are out of range, they can be teased up with a six inch black or brown plastic worm on a 1/4 ounce jig head. Cut the hook off the jig. The cobia will strike and follow the worm right into range of the fly rodder.

For tarpon Mike keeps his fly selection simple. He wants his fly to have color contrast with the bottom. Over light sand bottom he likes purple, brown, or black. Over dark grass bottom he likes red and white or yellow and orange. Depending on the depth of the water a floating or intermediate line is used.

Most Homosassa tarpon fishermen use twelve-weight tackle. Big fish are the rule rather than the exception. Eighty and 100 pound fish are called rats and the truly serious world record seekers just break them off so when a big fish comes by the angler will be ready! Most fly fishers appreciate the lively battle provided by these smaller fish, however. Heavy tackle is needed to take the fight to the fish and whip it so it can be released in good shape.

If you're fortunate enough to hook one of these fish, fight it hard. No fish should be fought for over an hour, as doing so makes the chances for post-release survival very slim. Sharks love to eat tarpon! Do not remove it from the water- get your photos from the boat or get into the water to hold it if necessary. Let the fish give someone else the same thrill it gave you!

## ACCESS

For waders- as detailed above.

For boaters- boat ramps can be found in the following places:

-MacRae's, on the Homosassa River. Use of this ramp is free, but parking is along the road and it does get crowded.

-River Haven Marina, on the Homosassa River. There is a $5.00 charge to use this ramp, but it's the best on the river and there's plenty of room to park.

-Tradewinds Motel has a ramp on the Homosassa River. They charge $2.00 to use it.

-In Bayport on the west end of SR 50 there is a county park with a boat ramp. There is no charge to use this ramp.

-In Crystal River there is a ramp at the west end of SR 44 at Fort Island Gulf Beach. There is no charge.

## FLY SHOPS
Leisure Time Fly Shop in Crystal River. The phone number is (904)795-3474.

## GUIDES
Oh yes, there are a lot. Many guides work here seasonally during the tarpon run.
Captain Mike Locklear, (904)628-4207.
Captain Billy Hampton, (904)795-6765.
Captain Bruce Williams, (904) 795-7302.
Captain Jim Long, (904)628-0383.

## STATE PARKS AND OTHER ATTRACTIONS
-Homosassa Springs State Wildlife Park, 9225 West Fish Bowl Drive, Homosassa 32646. (904)628-5354. See manatees, bears, bobcats, fish of all kinds, and other wildlife displays.

## ACCOMMODATIONS
-McRae's of Homosassa, (904)628-2602.
-Riverside Inn, (904)628-2474.
Homosassa Springs Area Chamber of Commerce, (904) 628-2666

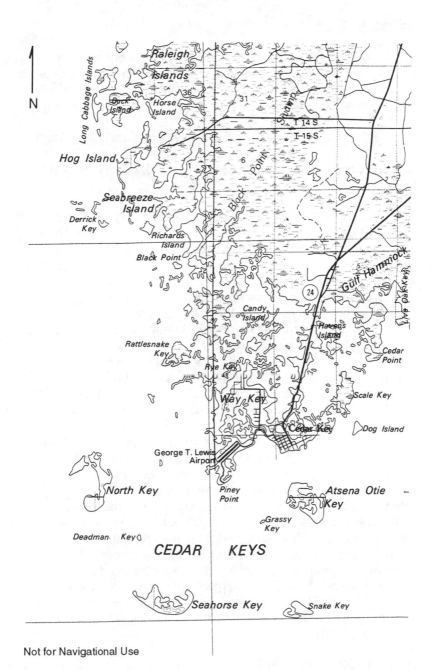

N

Not for Navigational Use

## CEDAR KEY

Many folks would argue that Cedar Key is one of the most beautiful areas in Florida. A quaint small town with a lot of artists, historic buildings, and old time Florida charm, the area around this key also attracts a lot of birds and other wildlife, fishermen, and other lovers of the outdoors.

Captain Jim Dupre has been fishing (including fly fishing) out of Cedar Key for 10 years and guiding for the past seven. He graciously answered my questions about the fly fishing opportunities in this area.

### OPPORTUNITIES FOR THE DO-IT-YOURSELF FLY FISHER

**-Inshore wading**:Jim recommends not wading in most of the Cedar Key region because of the soft, marshy bottom. If you use a canoe you can access the numerous oyster bars in the backcountry, from which it is possible to fish on foot.

**-Inshore boat**: Canoe the backcountry areas around Cedar Key to target seatrout, redfish, and in the spring and summer, big black drum. You can launch at either the SR 24 ramp by the bridge out to Cedar Key, or at the end of CR 326. You'll find lots of rocks and oyster bars in both places and the water tends to be murky. It's an easy place to bang up a motor skiff- most folks use aluminum boats. Look for moving water around the oyster bars and you're much more likely to find fish. Although you should cast to any fish you see, you'll usually blindcast around here.

On a rising tide take your skiff to the outside islands, North Key, Seahorse Key, or Snake Key. Plenty of grass flats with clean water over them allow for excellent sightfishing opportunities for seatrout, or you may stalk tailing or waking redfish.

**-Along the beach:** there are no beaches for fishermen here.

**-Offshore**: Jim doesn't usually fish offshore. He says there are Spanish and king mackerel, bonito, (called little tunny locally), bluefish, tripletail, grouper (over rock piles), sea bass, jack crevalle, cobia, and sometimes amberjack and sharks to be found around the channel markers. There is a small group of offshore fly fishers from the North Florida Fly Fishers who fish out of Cedar Key. Most of the time they use a chum line to entice mackerel, kingfish, and bonito into casting range.

### FLIES AND TECHNIQUES

Dupre has developed a couple of patterns for fishing in this area which are becoming quite well known. The most famous is probably Dupre's Spoonfly, an epoxy spoon resembling a small, lightweight Johnson Minnow. He says the flash and vibrations this lure makes enables the fish to find it from quite a distance away, even in the murky backcountry waters.

Jim uses another epoxy fly, simply a larger version of the MOE flies bonefishermen use in the Florida Keys. Dupre's version of this fly is about three inches long.

Another favorite is the seaducer in red and white or red and yellow, but Jim prefers his with lead eyes. He strongly believes redfish like picking up their meals from the bottom. The lead eyes sink the fly into the strike zone quickly, and produce an up-and-down motion when stripped that the fish find appealing.

He says folks fishing the oysters in the backcountry should blind-cast with flies that bump the bottom like the Clouser minnow, or the Spoonfly fished on a sinking line.

During the winter months try to find deep holes in the backcountry areas. These deep spots act as thermal refuges and they will quite literally fill up with fish. Use a weighted fly, such as the Clouser deep minnow.

Eight months of the year you can find reds, sometimes in big schools, waking and tailing over the grass flats on the outside. You must find clear water in order to do this, most easily done around the outside islands mentioned earlier. At lower tide phases it's quite possible to get out of the boat and wade, always an excellent strategy when the fish are spooky. Don't expect a firm bottom- you'll sink in a little.

## ACCESS

For waders: there is almost none. During the winter you can walk out on bars at low tide from the CR 326 ramp at the Shell Mound. Cast into holes and flowing current around the ends of oyster bars for trout and reds.

For boaters: The crude ramp on CR 326 north of Cedar Key is usable only by small boats. You can of course launch your canoe there. Another small ramp suitable for canoes is at the first bridge going out to Cedar Key. There are loads of oysters, and fish, in this area. Dupre suggests trying in the #4 channel. The first bridge from the mainland going out to Cedar Key crosses this channel.

In Cedar Key itself you'll easily find a good ramp at the boat basin since much of the town is built around it. Put in here to fish either outside or in the backcountry.

## FLY SHOPS
The nearest shop with fly tackle is the Tackle Box, at 1490 SE Hawthorne Road in Gainesville. (904)372-1791.

## GUIDES
Although many locals have taken fisherman out in boats through the years, Captain Jim Dupre was the first fly fishing skiff guide to work out of Cedar Key, which he's been doing for six years. He can be reached at (904) 371-6153.

## STATE PARKS AND OTHER ATTRACTIONS
Cedar Key is an attraction in and of itself. The Cedar Key State Museum is off SR 24 on Museum Drive.

-Waccasassa Bay State Preserve and the adjoining Cedar Key Scrub State Preserve account for almost 35,000 of wild lands, including extensive areas of salt marshes and tidal creeks. A primitive campsite is accessible only by canoe. This area lies nine miles east of Cedar Key on SR 24. The address and phone number: Waccasassa Bay State Preserve/Cedar Key Scrub State Reserve, PO Box 187, Cedar Key 32625. (904)543-5567.

## ACCOMMODATIONS
Contact the Cedar Key Chamber of Commerce, PO Box 610, Cedar Key 32625. (904)543-5600.

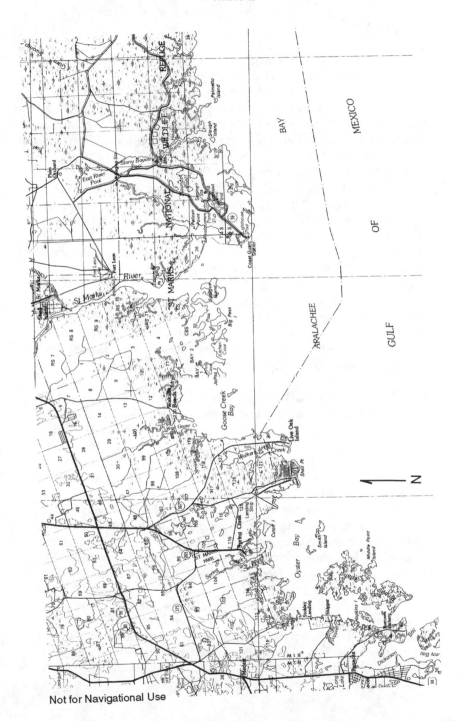

Not for Navigational Use

## ST. MARKS

Many Floridians consider Tallahassee the source of many of the state's problems. No surprise there, since the Governor and the Legislature work here, (or don't work, depending on your point of view). However, this is a fishing guidebook and not a political tome. For the fly fisher the St. Mark's area south of Tallahassee offers many excellent angling opportunities far removed from the halls of the Legislature, if not by actual distance then certainly by their laid back southern ambiance.

The St. Marks National Wildlife Refuge contains a good portion of this coast. The Refuge faces out onto Apalachee Bay and the Gulf of Mexico. The rest of the coast in this area looks as if it were part of the refuge- very little coastal development has occurred anywhere along here. Points and bays, creeks and oysters, rock piles and grass flats, and the open Gulf, all beckon the fly fisher. It's a good area.

John Underwood supplied the information for this section. Although not a licensed guide, John opened the very first fly shop in Tallahassee and now owns John's Guns and Fly Fishing Shop. He's lived and fly fished in this area for many years and is probably the most knowledgeable fly fisherman within a hundred mile radius.

### OPPORTUNITIES FOR THE DO-IT-YOURSELF FLY FISHER

**-Inshore Wading**: There aren't a great many areas for the non-boater to gain access around these parts. Wakulla Beach is one. Trout, redfish, and occasional Spanish mackerel and bluefish can be found over the grass flats here. Another wade area lies off of Lighthouse Point at the mouth of the St. Marks River, where the same species are available.

**-Inshore boat**: there are lots of opportunities for folks with boats. Even a boat as simple as a canoe will give you a lot more flexibility to fish in the creeks, sloughs, and bayous in the refuge for redfish and trout. Certainly the numerous oyster bars at the mouth of the St. Marks River usually hold redfish and seatrout. With a power boat, even more choices await.

Nine miles of grass flats extend to the east of Coast Guard Light at the mouth of the St. Marks. These are known locally as the East Flats. Five miles of flats extend to the west, known as the West Flats. On these flats, depending on the time of year, you may find any or all of the following species- cobia, redfish, seatrout, Spanish mackerel, bluefish, and some truly large tarpon.

Evidently the Air Force used the West Flats as a bombing target during World War II. The craters the bombs made are still there, sandy depressions in an otherwise lush bed of grass. These craters often hold both reds and trout.

There are many rock piles in the area. THESE PRESENT A HAZARD TO NAVIGATION- keep your eyes open and speed to a minimum until you learn your way around. Most rocks are within a mile and a half of shore. The rocks attract fish of course. Gray Mare Rock (LORAN 14507.1, 46435.2) is found about halfway between the St. Marks and Aucilla River mouths, on the east flats. This rock clears the water surface at half tide or lower.

Another well-known rock on east flat is Blacks Rock (LORAN 14496.3, 46444.5), found about four miles east of St. Marks. Although this rock has a sand patch around it, the surrounding area is all grass. This is a good one to find, because to the north of it is the Rock Garden (LORAN 14459.0, 46443.2), a number of rocks sticking up from the grass beds.

Straight out from the mouth of the Aucilla River two miles lie Cobbs Rocks (LORAN 14505.7, 46414.5). Like all the rock piles, the crabs and other creatures living on and around the rocks attract gamefish looking for a meal.

Two miles out from the light at the St. Marks River mouth is the Bird Tower. This piece of structure often attracts and holds fish, especially cobia.

**-From the Beach**: except for the areas mentioned in the wading section there are no beaches in this area.

**-Offshore**: St. Marks area has the same types of offshore fishing as other areas in the Panhandle, although you need to go out farther to find it. There are a series of 100 foot tall towers out from the lighthouse at St. Marks, the K (26 miles out, LORAN 14368.0, 46346.6), S, and O towers. These structures attract fish, including kings, cobia, barracuda, and some blackfin tuna. Small chicken dolphin will also show, especially when grass floats into the area.

At Pass Buoy #24 (12 miles south of the light house, LORAN 14443.3, 46361.8) look for balled up bait. If it's there you won't need to go any farther. The LORAN/GPS coordinates of all these structures will be found in Stebbins' book, Coastal LORAN & GPS Coordinates (see catalog at back of this book for ordering information).

Underwood chums with ground pogies or cat food for kingfish and bonito. He says this works well. He says live bait chumming is a lot more trouble and only slightly more effective.

## FLIES AND TECHNIQUES

John likes Blanton's Whistlers for dark or turbid water in red and white and red and yellow. He says these should be retrieved FAST, especially in the shallow areas.

Another effective fly in this region is a yellow epoxy minnow with doll eyes, designed by Ed Arrington, and known locally as Mr. Ed's Minnow. This fly accounts for many big seatrout, again usually when retrieved quickly.

Underwood recommends Mr. Bob's Lucky Day saltwater foam popper for all species which will take surface lures, primarily jacks, seatrout, and redfish.

Everyone likes the Clouser deep minnow, and Underwood is no exception. He prefers this fly in grey and white when fishing for mackerel of any kind.

Finally, John likes to use seaducers when he needs a fly he can retrieve slowly. These are used primarily for seatrout, redfish, and bluefish.

Those looking for redfish are advised to start at low tide. Slowly motor inshore until the boat runs aground. The fish will work in with the rising tide. Wait until you see tailing fish and work in along with them. You can do this from your boat, or you could get out and wade, as you prefer.

In the event that the reds don't show, find a rock pile and blind-cast around it with a popper. Remember to approach these rocks quietly or you'll spook all the fish before you ever get a chance to cast.

Should this not work either, try drifting and blindcasting across the west flats. Work the potholes well. You should catch some trout this way, and possibly other species as well.

John thinks most folks retrieve too slowly. He thinks a fast retrieve will elicit more strikes, especially from seatrout.

## ACCESS

For waders: Wakulla Beach is reached by taking SR 363 south from Tallahassee, then heading west on US 98-30. After crossing the bridge over the Wakulla River take the first road on the left. Follow this road to the beach.

To reach the lighthouse, take SR 363 south from Tallahassee, but head east on 98-30. Go south on CR 59 all the way to the end. It will cost you two dollars to get in.

For boaters: canoes can be launched in many different places around here, including those locations listed above for waders.

Consult DeLorme's <u>Florida Atlas and Gazetteer</u> for details, or ask at John's Gun and Fly Shop.

You can find boat ramps at the following places:

-on the Aucilla River. SMALL BOATS ONLY. Take US 98 and take a right about a mile and a half east of the bridge over the Aucilla River, then follow the signs. This river is difficult and dangerous to run because of all the rocks and oysters.

-there is a ramp for small boats at the St. Marks Refuge on CR 59.

-in St. Marks there are three ramps. One is at Shields Marina, where fuel, rest rooms, and a marina store will be found. ($)

Another ramp is at Shell Island Marina, which has similar facilities. ($)

Lastly in St. Marks you can find a ramp without facilities at San Marcos de Appalache. Keep in mind that the Wakulla River and the area around Shell Island are manatee zones- slow speed only.

## FLY SHOPS

John's Guns and Fly Fishing, 2555-4 N. Monroe Street, Tallahassee, 32303. (904)422-1553.

## GUIDES

As of this writing there are no fly fishing guides in this part of the state.

## STATE PARKS AND OTHER ATTRACTIONS

-St. Marks National Wildlife Refuge, c/o US Fish and Wildlife Service, PO Box 68, St. Marks 32355. (904)925-6121. Over 65,000 acres of wild lands, including extensive salt and brackish marshes.

-Apalachicola National Forest, Woodcrest Office Park, 325 John Knox Road, Building F-100, Tallahassee, 32303. (904)942-9300. Over 500,000 acres south and west of Tallahassee. Someplace to explore when you get sick of catching fish. Includes the Leon Sinks Geological Area, where there are more than a dozen different sinkholes. Don't fall in!

-Wakulla Springs State Park, One Spring Drive, Wakulla Springs, 32305. (904) 922-3632. Wakulla Springs is one of the world's largest, deepest, and clearest springs. This place is definitely worth a visit, especially for a refreshing swim after a hot day in the boat.

## ACCOMMODATIONS

The Leon County Tourist Development Council can be reached at (904) 681-9200 or 800-628-2866.

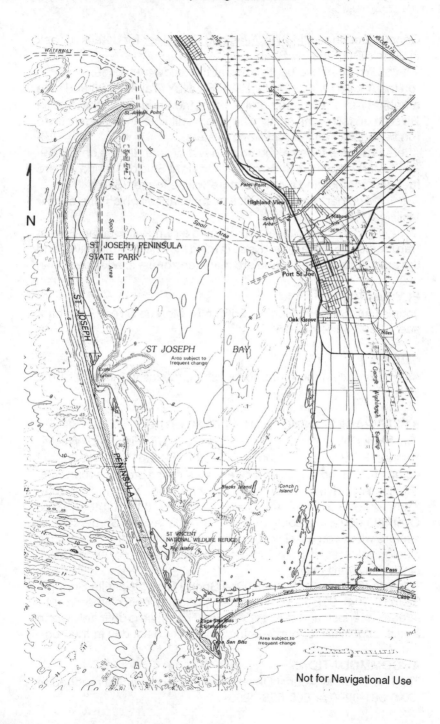

Not for Navigational Use

## ST. JOSEPH'S BAY

St. Joseph's Bay lies along the edge of the Florida pan-handle in a lightly populated area of the state between Panama City and Appalachicola. No freshwater rivers enter the bay, so it receives very little runoff from the land. The north end of the bay is wide open to the Gulf of Mexico, so it "flushes" extremely well. As a result, the water is extremely clear. This body of water just may be the most pristine bay in Florida.

St. Joseph's Bay has other unique features. Of all the bays in the panhandle, only this one runs north and south. You can usually find a fishing spot protected from the prevailing winds. St. Joe Bay is deep- over 30 feet in places. It attracts and holds big fish as a result. Rich grass flats line the entire periphery of the bay, supporting an excellent shallow water fishery.

Captain John Guinta has been fishing in St. Joe Bay for the past ten years, the only fly fishing guide to do so. John provided all of the following information.

### OPPORTUNITIES FOR THE DO-IT-YOURSELF FLY FISHER

**Inshore Wading:** You can wade on both sides of the bay. From the boat ramp in Port St. Joe south for about three miles lush grass beds parallel the easy access from SR 30. The bottom has a series of troughs which run parallel to the shoreline, and which stairstep out into deeper water. Because of the deep water access it's possible to wade fish for cobia here! Redfish and seatrout will be the usual targets, however. Some truly big sharks work this shoreline, and there are plenty of stingrays (which many species of gamefish will follow). Keep your eyes open and keep those feet shuffling.

Along the west side of the bay there are miles of wadable flats. Access these through St. Joseph Peninsula State Park. In order to get to most of the fishing spots you'll have to be willing to hike a while. Access here requires more effort.

**Inshore boat:** Many different species are available, with many individuals of each. Spanish and king mackerel, cobia, bluefish, sharks of all kinds, redfish, seatrout, flounder, jack crevalle, and tarpon (sometimes) all show up either on the flats or in the hole at St. Joseph's Point.

As has already been stated, grass flats 1/4 to 3/4 of a mile wide surround the entire bay. Sandy potholes in these flats attract trout and reds and while over the sand they can easily be seen, stalked, and cast to.

The islands at the south end of the bay sit in clear shallow water with thick grass beds carpeting the bottom. Reds and trout love this area and you can fish here on the windiest days.

A deep hole and strong currents at St. Joseph Point act as a natural fish magnet. If fish aren't seen on the surface you can often chum them up. If you get bored with the everyday ordinary kinds of fish, try chumming up sharks. Guinta will often gig a couple of stingrays and use them as chum, then throw bright orange flies made with rabbit strips at the sharks that show up. Exciting stuff!

**Along the Beach:** along the peninsula beach you'll find good fishing for pompano, whiting, and flounder. All the fish found in the bay work along the beach out toward the end of the point.

You can drive out on Cape San Blas at the south end of the peninsula. Folks frequently fish for sharks out here along the sand bar which extends for miles out into the Gulf. They use a steel cable attached to a winch on the front of their four wheel drive trucks to pull the 600-700 pound brutes in. Fly fishers will have to settle for smaller quarry, such as pompano or redfish.

Also, the stretch of sand between St. Joe Beach and Mexico Beach on the mainland side offers similar opportunities.

**Offshore:** Guinta has little experience offshore, although he believes the same type of fishing would be available as elsewhere in the Panhandle.

## FLIES AND TECHNIQUES

John loves to use poppers of any kind for as much fishing as possible- seatrout, reds, jacks, and anything else that will hit them. When he must go subsurface, he likes the following patterns:

-Whitlock's Baitfish in green and gray or chartreuse.

-Clouser deep minnows.

-crab patterns for redfish, especially the Merkin.

He says that in the clear water of this bay a poling tower gives a huge advantage, allowing the anglers to spot fish from quite a distance. He likes to fish the east side of the bay in the morning, and the west side in the afternoon. This allows him to use the sun to his advantage as he tries to spot the fish.

He also says that when the stingrays are active you should work them, as redfish, cobia, and even big seatrout will cruise over them looking for an easy meal.

John says that the seatrout here are the largest found in this part of the state, often reaching five and six pounds and sometimes reaching eight or nine.

## ACCESS
For Waders- as described earlier.

For Boaters- You can find three boat ramps on the bay:

-In Port St. Joe there a ramp downtown, just south of the paper mill.

-Six miles south of town there's a ramp at Presnel's Fish Camp, on SR 30. ($)

-On the west side of the bay there's a ramp it St. Joseph Peninsula State Park.

There is also a ramp up in Mexico Beach at Marquardt's Marine. This isn't convenient to the bay, but does give access to the Gulf.

## FLY SHOPS
The just mentioned Marquardt's Marine in Mexico Beach. The phone number is (904)648-8900.

## GUIDES
Captain John Guinta is the ONLY choice for a fly fishing guide here. (904)926-2720.

## STATE PARKS AND OTHER ATTRACTIONS
St. Joseph Peninsula State Park , Star Route 1 Box 200, Port St. Joe 32456. (904)227-1327. This park has 2,516 acres surrounded by the Gulf of Mexico and St. Joe Bay. The highest sand dunes in the state are found here along the miles of beach. Camping is available, and there are cabins for rent and a boat ramp here.

## ACCOMMODATIONS
The Gulf County Chamber of Commerce can be reached at (904)227-1223.

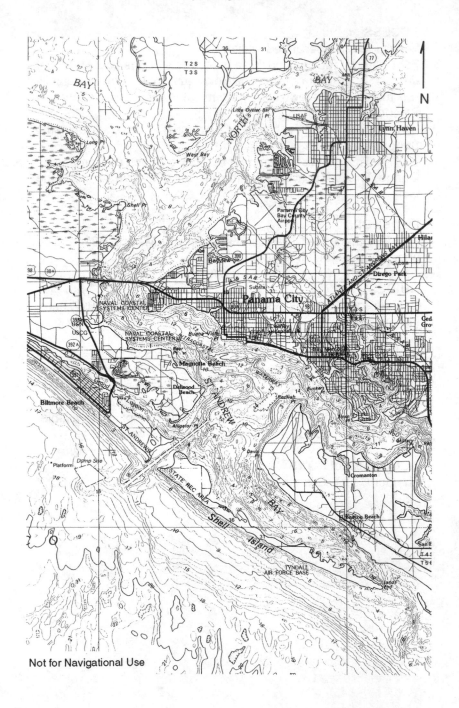

Not for Navigational Use

## PANAMA CITY

Panama City reminds me of a beach resort town from the 60's, kind of a refreshing change from Palm Beach and Fort Lauderdale. Things move more slowly here, and the people are friendlier, and there's less traffic and congestion. It's nice!

Panama City boasts of lots of attractions for the angler. The St. Andrew Bay system covers a lot of area. It's an extensive, sprawling body of water which reaches well inland, and exceeds 30 miles from east to west. Panama City Beach faces the Gulf of Mexico, with all of its piscatorial attractions. Plenty of places to stay, and eat, and lots to do make it a great place to visit for any non-anglers in the family. The beaches are among the finest in Florida.

My informant for this section was "Captain Blood"- Mike Ware. Mike doesn't have a lot of accidents, he just loves the color red. His boat is red, his clothing is red- it's his trademark. He's a colorful character! He grew up in Panama City and has fished and guided other fishermen in this area all his life, primarily in St. Andrew Bay and inshore on the Gulf.

## OPPORTUNITIES FOR THE DO-IT-YOURSELF FLY FISHER

**-Inshore Wading:** Much of the extensive shoreline of St. Andrew Bay is wadable and accessible. Most of the bay has a hard bottom, which waders always like. Some easy places for wader access to the bay include Beach Drive (US BR 98) on the south side of Panama City proper; at the east (Panama City) side of the Hathaway Bridge (US 98); and at the north end of the Dupont Bridge (US 98) across East Bay. You can also drive to St. Andrews State Recreation Area and wade in Grand Lagoon and cast for trout and reds, or walk out to the point and try for some Spanish mackerel.

**-Inshore Boat:** The large and fairly deep bay has no dangerous shoals, making it an excellent place to explore. Exploration is heartily recommended. It's divided somewhat arbitrarily into sections- St. Andrew Bay, West Bay, East Bay, and North Bay. Salt marshes and bayous surround every section of the system. These and points of land are good places to look for fish. Healthy beds of grass surround the edges of the bay.

On the southeast side of St. Andrew Bay, directly south of Panama City, the bay extends out to the Gulf behind Shell Island. This old St. Andrew Pass (now locally known as Old Pass), used before the present pass was dredged out, still allows Gulf access for shallow draft boats. You'll find many sandy shoals here, excellent places to fish for cobia, jack crevalle, redfish, seatrout, bonito, sharks, and many other species. Camelback Shoal, located about five miles northwest of the old pass, is the first of these. Located in the middle of the southern side of St. Andrew Bay between Shell Island and the main shipping channel, the water surrounding this shoal is 25-30 feet deep and attracts bluefish, ladyfish, Spanish mackerel, and sharks.

-**From the Beach:** From St. Andrews State Park west there is almost unlimited beach access all the way to Phillips Inlet and beyond. You'll find all the typical beach species available during the warmer months- pompano, whiting, Spanish mackerel, ladyfish, bluefish, jack crevalle, redfish sometimes, and blacktips and other species of sharks. The water typically is so clear that this is pure sight fishing- you walk along the beach looking for fish and do not cast until you spot them.

Another excellent trip possibility is to take the ferry boat from St. Andrews State Park over to Shell Island. Use the same technique- sight fishing from the beach. There are a lot fewer people over there so the chance of hooking up with Charles Atlas or his girlfriend is much less than it might be on Panama City Beach.

-**Offshore:** Offshore in Panama City during the spring means one thing- COBIA! Not just any cobia, either- BIG COBIA! No one around here raises an eyebrow at a 50 pound fish and triple digit specimens are caught every year. Again, most fish are caught with conventional tackle only because a directed fly rod fishery is just now beginning to form. Future fly rod world records from this region are only a matter of time.

These cobia always head west, sometimes travelling just yards off the beach in two to twenty feet of water. You'll find BIG jack crevalle cruising along the coast at this time of year, too.

During the summer months cobia will still use flotsam and weed lines, markers and buoys, or the artificial reefs. Many other fish make the reefs their home, too. Chum, either dead or alive, will pull these reef dwellers up to the surface where the fly rodder can tangle with them. Small 20 to 30 inch amberjack in particular are plentiful and aggressive. Kingfish and bonito are other common catches. Schoolie dolphin may show up in a chum line at any time from June on through September.

## FLIES AND TECHNIQUES

Captain Mike likes Clouser deep minnows in chartreuse and white for much of his inshore fishing, although when he finds bluefish he'll switch to a pink and chartreuse deep minnow. He also likes small versions of the Keys-style tarpon streamer for seatrout in various color combinations.

When fishing offshore he makes a white Deceiver with either a green of blue back his first choice, although for fishing for dolphin along the Sargassum weed he likes yellow and brown flies that match the color of the baitfish and crabs found in the weed.

Mike sight fishes the shallow areas in the bay for redfish. Jack crevalle are also sight fished, primarily when they churn into baitfish. They're not terribly difficult to find then! Jacks school according to size, and most of these flats jacks run 25-30 pounds.

Anchoring in the bay and chumming often proves effective for Spanish mackerel and bluefish. Mike likes menhaden (pogies to you Northerners), either fresh or frozen. Most of these will be ground up, but he'll throw chunks in too. He anchors off of points, or over shoals, or by drop-offs or channels and tries to chum the fish in close. Ask at the local tackle store or call Mike and ask him where the fish have been holding recently before wasting time chumming where no fish are present.

Finally, and has already been mentioned, chumming over wrecks and artificial reefs offshore is a great way to have plenty of action. While the best chum is undoubtedly live baitfish, oftentimes the fish aren't very fussy. Ground chum or frozen minnows often work just as well.

## ACCESS
For waders- as described above.
For boaters- in Panama City proper the Municipal Marina is on Harrison Avenue (US 231), downtown behind the Civic Center.
-at Carl Gray Park on the east side of the Hathaway Bridge.
-at St. Andrews State Recreation Area (closest ramp to the pass).
-in Calloway Bayou on East Bay by the Calloway Men's Club.
-on US 98 at the north end of the Dupont Bridge (under the old bridge).
-on SR 77 at the Bailey Bridge, on the south side of North Bay.
-on SR 79 over the Intracoastal Waterway on West Bay.
-at the Bayside Trailer Park off Wildwood Road on the west side of the Hathaway Bridge ($).
-on Dolphin Drive, on the south side of Grand Lagoon.
-on the west side of Pretty Bayou on Danley Avenue (turn right off of Michigan Avenue).
-for military personnel only, on Tyndal AFB.

## FLY SHOPS
-Cogburn's Clothing Company, 437 Harrison Avenue in Panama City. (904)769-7634
-Captain Joe's Ultimate Angler, 1025 Harrison Avenue, also a Hewes dealer. (904)785-0017
-Half Hitch Tackle, 2206 Thomas Drive. (904)234-2621

## GUIDES
-"Captain Blood", Captain Mike Ware, PO Box 16021, Panama City, 32406. (904)785-6216
-Captain Joe Smith III, Box 1821, Panama City 32402. (904)785-0017
-Captain Buddy Dortch, (904)769-8370 or 832-0793.
Other light tackle guides are available.

## STATE PARKS AND OTHER ATTRACTIONS
St. Andrews State Recreation Area, 4415 Thomas Drive, Panama City 32408. (904)234-2522. The park is right on St. Andrews Pass and offers waterfront campsites, a boat ramp, two fishing piers, and a jetty.

## ACCOMMODATIONS
There are loads of motels in Panama City and on Panama City Beach. The phone number at the Panama City Beach Chamber of Commerce is (904)235-1159.

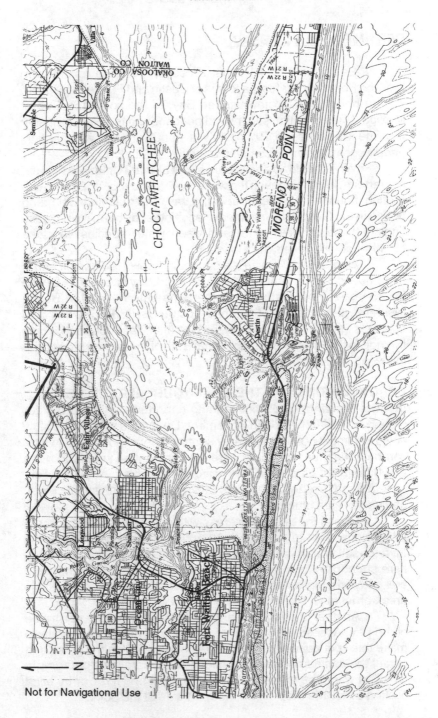

Not for Navigational Use

## DESTIN/FT.WALTON BEACH

East Pass, an inlet that slices Santa Rosa Island from Moreno Point, separates the towns of Destin and Ft. Walton Beach. To the north lies Choctawhatchee Bay, to the south the Gulf of Mexico. Miles of white, sugar sand beaches line the Gulf, arguably the finest beaches in Florida. It's a beautiful area with friendly people, competitive prices, and a family orientation.

Why should an angler care about all that? Unique in Florida, a quarter mile off the beach the water is 40 feet deep. You can catch redfish, flounder, and seatrout in the bay, and dolphin, cobia, and bonito in the Gulf, within minutes of each other by boat. It's not easy finding these shallow water and deep water species so close together anywhere else in Florida.

Captain Joy Dunlap is a nationally known rod builder and is a member of the Emerald Coast Fly Fishers. Joy has lived in Destin for 30 years. Paul Darby is another long time Ft. Walton Beach resident, also known for his fine custom rods. Paul owns and operates Quality Reel Repair at the Shalimar Yacht Basin, the only fly shop in the Ft. Walton Beach area. Both of these men shared the following information with me.

### OPPORTUNITIES FOR THE DO-IT-YOURSELF FLY FISHER

**Inshore Wading**: You'll find wading opportunities in the bay for redfish from March through November. During the winter reds slow down to almost nothing; however seatrout, both spotted and white, can be caught all year. Jacks are also present all year, and often reach double digit sizes. Other species available include ladyfish, sheepshead (a real challenge for the fly fisher!), Spanish mackerel, and sometimes bluefish.

One of the better bay areas with easy access for waders is Elliott Point, east of the SR 98-30 bridge on the north side of the Intracoastal Waterway in Ft. Walton Beach. A huge, lush grass bed here supports a lot seatrout and sometimes reds. Spanish mackerel, ladyfish, big jack crevalle, and bluefish all come through this area sometimes, too.

Another good wading area is White Point, on the north side of the bay. Access is south off of SR 20, and public facilities here make this spot quite popular. Another large and healthy grass bed attract the same species as mentioned in the previous paragraph. One can wade the grass flat looking for trout and reds, or try blind casting along the drop-off on the west side of the point.

**Inshore Boat**: Even anglers with small boats can use them in the bay, being mindful of the weather of course. The same species are available to boaters as to waders. Boaters have more flexibility in where they fish, obviously. Joy says there are few flats here. The fishing tends to be in deeper water. You can sightfish for reds up close to the shoreline, but these tend to be smaller fish.

There are several bayous off of the main bay. In the Ft. Walton Beach area Chico Bayou and Grande Bayou provide good fishing even on the windiest days. You can fish under dock lights at night in these two bayous, too, and expect to find good concentrations of seatrout.

North of Destin are two other bayous, Boggy Bayou and Rocky Bayou. Again, these bodies of water provide good fishing for trout and reds. You'll also run into the occasional striped bass in this area, some of which hit 20 pounds. To the east you will find several others bayous. All invite exploration.

Lastly, at the extreme east end of the bay you'll find an extensive system of creeks and islands where the Choctawhatchee River enters the bay. This pristine area provides excellent fishing all summer long, and being the farthest distance from Destin and Ft. Walton, gets little fishing pressure.

**From the Beach**: Pompano and whiting are the most popular beach fish, although Spanish mackerel, jack crevalle, and bluefish are available during the warmer months. Sinking lines with small crab imitations will take pompano, which can be sight fished, as well as whiting. Clouser minnows will also work for both species.

Near the Coast Guard station on the west side of the pass is a large rock jetty. Adventurous fly fishers can scramble out here and cast off of the rocks. A stripping basket is a necessity!

**Offshore**: Where else in Florida can you catch dolphin from a johnboat? Offshore in Destin is only a long cast from the beach.

The cobia run along this part of the Florida coast is legendary. Cobia reaching triple digit weights cruise off the beaches, following rays, turtles, or just free swimming from March through May and can be sight-fished. You'll need serious tackle- these fish are BIG. Many hundred plus pound fish are caught (on conventional tackle) every year. The only reason a fly fisher hasn't caught one yet is because so few folks fly fish up this way. As Paul Darby put it, "Fly fishing is just exploding onto our fishing scene and lots of folks are getting involved- it's only a matter of time before fly rod world records for cobia are broken."

During the summer you can also catch bonito, big jack

crevalle, amberjacks, kingfish, dolphin, and wahoo within a mile of the beach, especially when the Sargassum weed comes in.

Both Paul and Joy say they and their friends sometimes catch both black and red snapper and grouper on flies, difficult if not impossible to do in other parts of the state. Chum gets the fish up near the surface where they can see and hit the flies. They agree that you had better be ready for a tough fight if you hook a ten pound snapper on a fly. You'd better be properly geared up and ready for a VERY tough fight if you tangle with an 80 or 90 pound cobia or a big amberjack!

## FLIES AND TECHNIQUES

Mr. Darby has very definite opinions about fly selection. He likes the Clouser deep minnow in both chartreuse and white and in gray and white with blue crystal flash. He especially likes this color combination at night. He also likes glass minnow imitations. He often ties these on long shank hooks (Mustad 34011 or equivalent) leaving the front 2/3rds of the shank bare. He then uses these flies for bluefish and Spanish mackerel. Lastly, he likes a shrimp imitation developed by Vance Cook of Pensacola, called the Cook's Critter. Darby prefers this fly to have a tan body and a gray squirrel hair wing.

Capt. Dunlap likes Clouser minnows too, but prefers darker colors, especially in the deeper areas of the bay. Dunlap ties a very simple fly with white Fishair for use offshore.

Darby prefers to find his bay fish in shallower areas so he can see them before casting to them. For this work he uses a floating line. Dunlap does much of his fishing in the bay is in deeper areas. He does a lot of blindcasting with sinking lines.

For the cobia run use big squid flies, or big Deceivers, or other large, light colored patterns. The drill is to cruise slowly along the beach until you spot some fish in the clear water, then position the boat for a good, head-on cast to them.

Offshore fishing is done a couple of different ways. A favorite method involves anchoring near one of the artificial reefs in the area and chumming the fish up to the boat. If possible, lead them far enough away from the reef so that when a big fish takes he can't get back into it.

The other main technique? Cruise along the weed lines which form during the summer looking for fish. When you see some, cast to them!

Any time you see fish on top blasting bait (as jacks,

Spanish, bluefish, bonito or even blackfin or yellowfin tuna all do) get over near them as quickly as possible, drift down onto them, and start flinging hackle at them!

## ACCESS

For Waders: as detailed above.

For Boaters: boat ramps can be found at the following locations-

-on the east side of Choctawhatchee bay, there are ramps at both ends of SR 331.

-on the west side of the bay there is a ramp on the north side of the SR 98 bridge across the Intracoastal Waterway.

-at the north end of Beach Drive in Destin there is a public ramp on Joes Bayou.

-at the east end of Destin Harbor there is a ramp at Sandpiper Cove.

-there is a private ($) ramp at Destin Marina.

-there is a private ($) ramp at East Pass Marina on SR 98.

## FLY SHOPS

-The Destin Fishing Hole, on SR 98 in Destin, (904)837-9043.

-Paul Darby owns Quality Reel Repair, at the Shalimar Yacht Basin off of SR 85 in Shalimar, (904) 651-2991.

## GUIDES

The only guide I could locate in the Destin area was Captain Davis "Catfish" Knight at (904)837-7121. He takes fly fishers out.

## STATE PARKS AND OTHER ATTRACTIONS

-Grayton Beach State Recreation Area is about 15 miles east of Destin, right on the Gulf of Mexico. Camping is available. (904)231-4210.

-Rocky Bayou State Recreation Area is at the north end of Rocky Bayou, about as north as you could get on Choctawhatchee Bay. Camping is available here. (904)897-3222

## ACCOMMODATIONS

There are many motels in this area. The Greater Fort Walton Beach Chamber of Commerce can be reached at (904)244-8191.

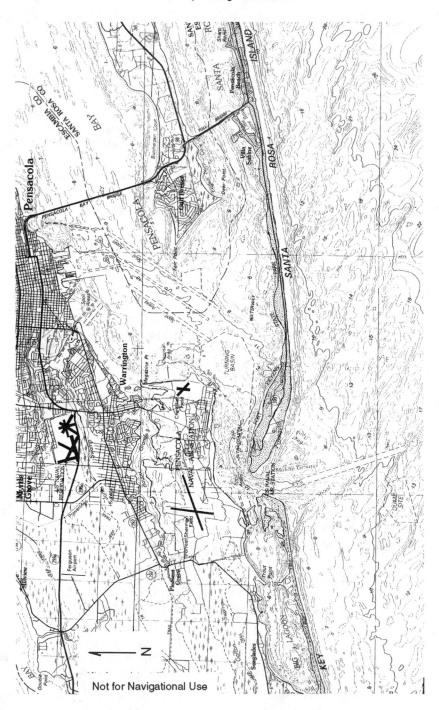

Not for Navigational Use

# PENSACOLA

The last town in our survey of the Florida coast is Pensacola. Last, but certainly not least! With its laid back atmosphere, Pensacola fits most anglers like a comfortable old slipper. There's lots of room for the angler. Pensacola Bay and its branches, Santa Rosa Sound, and Big Lagoon taken together make up an extensive bay system with clear, clean water, healthy grass beds, and abundant fish-seatrout, reds, flounder, jack crevalle, Spanish mackerel, and other species. The Gulf of Mexico beckons those interested in the offshore species.

Like the rest of Florida's panhandle, you'll find fishing best in the summer months. The cobia run starts off the season sometime in April, and fishing continues until October in most years, although sometimes if the weather holds good action can be had until Thanksgiving.

Captain Bob Gray, owner of Gray's Tackle and Guide Service in Pensacola, supplied the information for this section. Bob has lived and fished in this area all his life.

## OPPORTUNITIES FOR DO-IT-YOURSELF FLY FISHERS

**-Inshore Wading:** Fly fishers can wade in heavy grass beds and cast for seatrout, small grouper, Spanish mackerel, and sometimes redfish at Shoreline Park, in Gulf Breeze off SR 98 on the south side of the peninsula. The grass beds extend off of Deer Point to the south and east.

To the south across Santa Rosa Sound is a small island where the Environmental Protection Agency Laboratory is located, in the vicinity of Villa Sabine. Around this island some monster jacks to 30 pounds can be seen during the summer months, slamming into schools of mullet and other baitfish. Bob says gaining access to this area goes only to those bold enough to ask private landowners for permission, and polite enough to have them say yes. I believe seeing a school of big ravenous jacks causing havoc on the surface would give me enough nerve to ask anyone for access!

**-Inshore Boat:** There are many bayous whose finger-like projections extend off of Escambia Bay. These can be fished in almost any weather condition and provide good fishing for spotted seatrout and redfish. Some of them include Bayou Texar, Bayou Chico, and Hoffman's Bayou. Many of these bayous have residential docks where fish gather, especially at night when lights present.

Big Lagoon is another good place to fish, with trout and

reds, Spanish mackerel, and jack crevalle available all summer. Bluefish invade Big Lagoon, too.

Gray's also suggested looking diligently for surface action around the Pensacola Naval Air Station during the summer months, especially that area near the pass. Jacks, bonito, Spanish mackerel, and sometimes even tarpon trap bait here and rip into it. On calm summer mornings this kind of activity is visible from a long way off, and provides extremely exciting angling.

This bay system is a big piece of water. Plan to spend some time poking around and exploring it.

**-From the Beach:** You'll find the same species along the beach here as elsewhere in the Panhandle- pompano, whiting, ladyfish, bluefish, jacks, and Spanish mackerel. Excellent beach access awaits on the east side of the pass in the Gulf Islands National Seashore. At the extreme west end of Santa Rosa Island in the National Seashore the Ft. Pickens Pier and the surrounding vicinity offers some superb angling opportunities. In addition to the typical beach species, king mackerel are sometimes caught from the beach here, and redfish, big, bull redfish, load up in the pass during the fall months. Catching these reds at night is high excitement!

On the west side of the pass excellent beach fishing is available, but only to anglers with boats- there are no roads! But if you visit this thin spit of sand you can fish the beach side or the Big Lagoon side, or fish both sides within a few minutes of each other.

**-Offshore:** Offshore fishing starts in March when the cobia run starts. Big schools of big fish move along the beach. Idle along in the boat looking for fish, then cast to them. Large white and/or pink flies are preferred, with tackle in the 10-11-12 weight range.

Spanish mackerel and bonito are usually found by sighting them working on bait. It's usually best to motor upwind, then drift down on them. You will spook fewer fish this way.

A series of artificial reefs is found two to three miles off the beach. Chumming over these reefs with ground chum or frozen minnows will pull the fish off the reef up to the boat, where they can be fished with flies. You can get king mackerel, bonito, amberjack, and even red snapper this way. You never know what will show up in the chum line, and you can see all of the action.

Lastly, during summer big patches of sargassum weed sometimes blow in. Chicken dolphin are plentiful in these weeds. Cobia like them too. Sometimes you'll find other species around, even sailfish or wahoo. Again, idle along the edge of the weed line looking for fish. When they are spotted, cast to them.

## FLIES AND TECHNIQUES
Captain Gray likes Clouser minnows in red and white with some flash thrown in for much of his inshore work. He also likes the Springer spoon, a spoon-like creation made with sequins and epoxy. He claims this lure is deadly on big seatrout.

Cobia's liking for big pink and white creations has already been noted. Flies for offshore usually are white with some other color like pink, chartreuse, green, or blue thrown in too.

Bobby thinks most fly fishers strip their flies too slow. He likes a fast retrieve, sometimes even going to a two handed strip. He claims to consistently outfish the slow strip crowd this way, so give it a try.

## ACCESS
For waders- much of the access in the Pensacola area on the bay side has already been described. Most of Pensacola Beach is completely accessible to the surf fisherman.

For boaters- Gray thinks there aren't enough ramps in town. Public ramps can be found at the following places-

-both ends of the Three Mile Bridge (SR 98). Use these ramps with caution, as they are shallow.

-at Quietwater Beach, near the SR 319 Causeway that crosses Santa Rosa Sound.

-in Bayou Grande at Navy Point.

-in Bayou Texar.

-at the Rod and Reel Marina west of the pass off of Old Gulf Beach Highway, on the Intracoastal Waterway on Big Lagoon. ($)

-at Shoreline Park in Gulf Breeze. ($)

## FLY SHOPS
Gray's Tackle and Guide Service has two shops-

-13019 Sorrento Road, Pensacola 32507. (904)492-2666.

-207 Gulf Breeze Parkway, Gulf Breeze 32561. (904)934-3141.

## GUIDES
You won't find many fly fishing guides in Pensacola. Bobby Gray is one of the only, if not THE only, one.

## STATE PARKS AND OTHER ATTRACTIONS
Gulf Islands National Seashore, 1801 Gulf Breeze Parkway, Gulf Breeze 32561. (904)934-2600. You can fish here, but no camping is allowed.

-Perdido Key State Recreation Area, c/o Big Lagoon State Recreation Area, 12302 Gulf Beach Highway, Pensacola 32507. (904)492-1595. You can fish here, but no camping is available.
-Big Lagoon State Recreation Area, 12302 Gulf Beach Highway, Pensacola 32507. (904)492-1595. This park is located on Big Lagoon, and you can camp here in addition to the fishing.

## ACCOMMODATIONS
The phone number at the Pensacola Convention and Visitor's Bureau is (904)434-1234.

# Fly Selection for Florida Salt

We all select our flies from combination of knowledge, intuition, and past experience. An examination of Lefty Kreh's book, "Saltwater Fly Patterns", reveals that literally thousands of fly patterns have been devised, all with the same purpose- to entice a fish into striking a fraud made from fur, feathers, or other materials.

Do all these flies work? Most definitely. Does the Florida fly rodder need a barge to carry his fly boxes? Most definitely not. The best advice any fly fisher could give another is to choose those patterns which have proven themselves, ones which inspire confidence and which meets your needs.

What if it's your first visit to Florida? What if you don't have any experience fly fishing in saltwater?

Saltwater fly fishers need flies that float and make a commotion on the surface. Poppers, sliders, and divers fit the bill for this. The size depends on what you're chasing. The smallest surface flies would be about size 4, the largest could be as big as 5/0 for offshore fishes.

Use these surface flies when searching for fish, especially while wading. Poor visibility when wading (due to the low angle of the angler to the water) hampers sightfishing. Try calling the fish by using a popping bug. Surface flies also work well early or late in the day, or in discolored water, for the same reason. Needless to say when fish are crashing bait on top, a popper is a great choice! Poppers are constructed from deer hair, plastic foam, cork, and balsa wood. There's no need to carry all types. Just find the style you like best, and carry several in different sizes.

Many types of seagoing fish eat crabs at every opportunity. Redfish, permit, and bonefish are three that jump to mind. Consider a good crab imitation a must when you observe fish eating these crustaceans. Although crab imitations come in epoxy, deerhair, hot glue, wool, and various other materials, one I devised myself called the Fuzzy Crab is easy to tie and very effective. With a carapace made of furry foam and lead eyes for a fast sink rate, it takes only a few minutes to tie and fish just love it. Again, it's not necessary to carry all the different styles of crab flies, just the one you prefer in a variety of sizes and colors.

Many different minnow imitations exist. You could carry them all, but why? You need large ones and small ones, light colors and dark colors, slow sinkers and fast sinkers. If you have all of this, you have met 90 percent of your needs in Florida salt.

For fishing in deeper water or right on the bottom in shallower areas, the Clouser deep minnow is a must. The deep minnow has lead eyes which make it work somewhat like a jig. Carry Clousers with different weight eyes, to cover different fishing situations, in sizes #4 to #1, in brown and white, tan and white, and chartreuse and white. Lefty Kreh has caught over fifty different species of fish on Clouser minnows. Most of us will never equal his record, but don't go out without these flies.

Grassy areas require a somewhat weedless fly. A pair of reverse-tied flies, one bright and one somber, fill this need. The snapping shrimp pattern and a simple chartreuse and white reverse tie, again from #4 to #1, are excellent choices. I prefer a simple reverse tie to the bendback style, feeling I get a better hookup rate if the hook shank remains straight. Some friends, good fishermen, feel exactly the opposite. Go with what works for you.

Everyone knows Lefty's Deceiver as a minnow imitation, used for everything from freshwater trout to billfish. Carry them in sizes #4 to 3/0, even larger if you fish offshore much, in various combinations of boring brown, grizzly, white, chartreuse, red, and yellow. Large fish often want a decent mouthful, so don't be afraid to tie one on. Have a selection of darker and brighter colors so you can experiment when the fish are spooky or being fussy. Although saltwater fish aren't fussy very often, most anglers prefer being prepared if they are. Some of these flies need weedguards.

Another important pattern is the seaducer which has a heavily hackled body, giving it a very slow sink rate. It's great in shallow water, or when fish are suspended under overhanging structure. It can even be greased with dry fly floatant and used right on top. Some guides like to weight their seaducers with lead eyes. Take these in the same sizes and colors as the deceivers. Again, be sure some have weedguards.

Another style of fly rapidly gaining popularity, especially for bigger species like tarpon and cobia, are the rabbit strip flies. Few materials suggest life like a strip of rabbit fur. There are small versions of these flies, too. The bonefish bunny comes to mind.

Some fish have had special flies designed specifically with them in mind. Tarpon flies come to mind, as do barracuda. Tarpon flies are tied with the wing at the bend of the hook, to cut down on the fouling of the wing around the hook. Cuda flies are tied to imitate needlefish. Bonefish flies tend to be on the small side, tied with a reverse wing, and often weighted to sink in deeper areas where mudding fish are seen.

*Most Florida guides favor the Clouser deep minnow for a wide variety of species.*

231

With a basic selection of flies, anyone going after seatrout, snook, bonefish, tarpon, or any other of Florida's great saltwater gamefish should have the flies and the confidence to fish successfully. Those targeting specific species that have special needs should carry those flies as well. Some of the specialty patterns needed for specific species of fish follow on subsequent pages.

We need a few words about barbless hooks here. I have been fishing barbless hooks exclusively for six years now, certainly long enough to determine their effectiveness. I use Mustad 3407 (a barbed hook) for most of my own flies. Before the hook goes into the vise, it's carefully sharpened and the barb is crushed down with a pair of pliers. Only then does tying begin.

Studies indicate that barbless hooks penetrate better. I cannot say with certainty whether that is true or not. I can say that I have not noticed any difference in the number of fish hooked or lost because of the barbless hooks. Certainly the lack of a barb allows me to unhook the fish I catch much more easily then a barbed hook would. Without the benefit of any hard facts my gut feeling tells me post release mortality is less since the hook causes less damage.

In the time I've been fishing barbless flies I have hooked myself once (in the tip of my right index finger) and my great friend Warren Hinrichs once (in the right forearm). In both cases the hook slid right back out again. This, in and of itself, is enough reason to use hooks without barbs. Barbless hooks make fly fishing so much safer for us!

Different folks sharpen hooks different ways. I do it as follows- use a four inch flat mill file. Luhr-Jensen markets the best one in my opinion. Place the file under the right side of the point at roughly a 45 degree angle to the top of the point and push it back toward the barb. Three or four strokes genarally does the job. Then place the file under the left side of the point again at 45 degrees the other way and again push the file toward the barb. Then lay the file on top of the point and push it back toward the barb. This creates a triangular point. Test it to see if it digs onto your thumb nail. If it doesn't, work on it until it does.

Always remember to press those hook barbs down, and practice catch and release!

## TYING THE FLIES

This section of the book gives directions for tying many of the flies mentioned elsewhere in the book. Some assumptions are made- that the reader knows how to perform basic fly tying techniques, such as starting the thread, attaching lead eyes, tying in hair and feathers, and whip finishing. If you don't know how to do this, get a basic fly tying text. Better, have someone show you how.

Different tiers have differing philosophies on how flies should be tied, on what the end result should look like, on the entire zen of fly tying. My philosophy on fly tying, as in life, is keep it simple. We deal with enough complications every day without making things more difficult for ourselves when we're supposed to be having fun. As long as the fly holds together during use, as long as it does the job it's supposed to do-attracting fish and enticing them to strike- then it has done its job well. If you want to spend an hour tying a fly that could win an award at an art show, that's OK. If you want to tie six flies per hour that might be a little rough around the edges, that's fine too. The important thing is to enjoy it!

Basic materials needed for most flies include the following: -hooks, Mustad 3407 or equivalent, sizes 4 through 3/0;

-thread. Danville's flat waxed nylon is pretty standard among saltwater fly tiers;

-head cement. Clear Sally Hansen's Hard as Nails fingernail polish works as well as anything else, although many tiers are addicted to Whitlock's Flexament;

-lead eyes, 1/100, 1/50, 1/36, and 1/24 ounce;

-a grizzly neck. Economy necks work fine, we're not tying dry flies;

-strung saddle hackle in various colors including white, yellow, red, and brown;

-bucktails in white, chartreuse, yellow, and brown;

-a nice piece of deer body hair, natural color;

-squirrel tails, both natural grey and red squirrel;

-calftails in white, brown, and tan;

-marabou, brown;

-chenile, medium fly tier's in white, brown, orange, and tan;

-medium mylar tinsel;

-crystal flash in pearl and gold or copper; and

-medium mylar tubing, pearl color.

Of course this won't cover everything, but it is a good start. Other materials needed for specific fly patterns will be listed along with the directions for how to tie them.

Let's see how to tie up some patterns.

## Tying in a Double Mono Loop Weedguard

In Florida we have "weeds" in the water in some places. Oftentimes flies are cast against structure, like docks, oysters, or mangrove roots. Weedguards are a simple solution to having the fly fouled with grass, or hanging up all the time, and one of the best types of weed guards for flies is the double mono loop.

Jacksonville fly tier John Bottko says, "The ideal length of your loop should be such that the hook point is protected and neither strand of mono can be pushed to the same side of the hook. You will need to experiment with bare hooks until you find the ideal length of mono for each hook size and style. Once these measurements are determined, save them for future reference."

Tampa tier Jim Stewart uses a clever way to record the correct mono length for any size or style of hook. He bought a yardstick at the local hardware store. Once he determined the correct length of the mono for a particlar hook, he marked the length off on the yardstick, clearly labelled that section of the stick as to the corresponding hook size and style, cut that piece off of the stick, drilled a small hole in the corner of it, and then put it on a bead chain that he keeps with his tying materials. Voila!- permanent reference.

Here's how to make a double mono loop weedguard.

1) Start the tying thread close to the hook eye. Tie in the premeasured and doubled piece of monofilament (hard mono works best) on top of the hook shank. Put two fingers from your left hand (if you're right handed) in the loop and spread it as you wrap the thread toward the bend of the hook to ensure the mono will be tied on evenly on both sides of the hook shank. Wrap the thread all the way back to the bend of the hook.

2) Your loop will now be extending out behind the hook. Take a pair of needle-nosed pliers and crush down the mono at the point of the loop. Now tie your fly.

3) When you've finished with the tie except for the head, pull the crushed point of the mono over the eye of the hook (you'll have to take the hook out of the vise to do this) and tie it into the head as well. Wrap it until it's secure, then whip finish and cement the head. Your weedless fly is ready to fish.

## The Clouser Deep Minnow (Bob Clouser)

Bob Clouser developed his deep minnow for Susquehanna River smallmouth bass. The fly was spectacularly successful on them. Time and experimentation has proved the deep minnow to be spectacularly successful on many other species of fish as well, in both fresh and salt water.

I've taken striped bass, tarpon, snook, seatrout, redfish, black drum, bonefish, jacks, ladyfish, snapper, tripletail, moonfish, Spanish mackerel, landlocked salmon, and many other species with them. Lefty Kreh has taken over fifty different species of fish on Clouser minnows, including permit and king mackerel. It's the fly of choice for about 90 percent of the guides interviewed in this book, and belongs in every saltwater flyfisher's box.

In addition to its fish catching abilities, the deep minnow is easy to tie. This makes it an ideal fly for the beginning tier.

MATERIALS-
Hook: Mustad 3407, size 4-1
Tail: none
Body: none
Wing: bucktail tied reversed. Favorite color combinations include white and chartreuse, white and brown, and white and tan.
Eyes: lead eyes to match size of hook and desired sink rate.

1) After sharpening the hook and squashing down the barb, place hook in vise. Wrap the thread back about halfway down the shank, then wrap it forward again. Stop about 1/4 of the way back from the hook's eye.

2) Tie the lead eyes on top of the shank about 1/4 the distance back from the hook's eye. Coat the wraps with nail polish.

3) Remove the hook from the vise and turn it over so the point is up.

4) Cut a small (about half the diameter of a pencil) bunch of hair from the white bucktail. Pull out the short hairs, then tie the bunch in behind the lead eyes. Coat the wraps with nail polish.

5) Tie in twelve or so strands of crystal flash over the white hair.

6) Cut a small bunch of hair from a dyed bucktail (color your choice). Tie this in over the crystal flash.

7) Taper the head with the thread and whip finish. Coat the head with one or two layers of nail polish.

Versatility is what makes the Clouser minnow such a valuable fly. Its silhouette resembles many baitfish. It can be tied in small sizes for bonefish, large sizes for offshore fish like dolphin, or anything in between. By using small lead eyes and a floating line it can be used on shallow flats. Large lead eyes and sink tip lines or hi-D shooting heads can drop the fly to the twenty foot level, even in currents. It can be crawled along the bottom or ripped through the water.

Fish like it. Try it. You will, too.

## Deerhair Poppers/Sliders/Divers (Hair Bugs)

I love surface lures,especially flyrod surface lures. The crushing strike of a big red on a popper or slider in inches of water is something anyone who enjoys angling should experience.

Sometimes reds will follow hair bugs for several feet before making up their minds. They usually clobber it unless the hook has picked up some floating grass. Watching a huge wake following inches behind your lure will do things to your adrenaline that persons with weak hearts should avoid. Other times reds will strike

out of nowhere. Either way the excitement level is stratospheric.

Other fish blast hair bugs as well. Catching big trout on hair bugs used to be a common occurance until trout were netted into almost oblivion. Even so, I still get one now and then.

You can use hair bugs to get baby tarpon. Although you get awesome strikes, sticking one of these babies when they come up for a bug is really difficult. I believe the pressure wave they push ahead of them moves the bug out of the way of their opening mouth, causing them to miss most of the time. Bring lots of patience.

Charlie Waterman has written reams of material about deerhair bugs in the Everglades' backcountry. Snook crush surface flies, and hair bugs are a popular choice for fly fishers trying to fool the linesiders.

Other fish take them with a vengeance as well. Ladyfish, jack crevalle, bluefish, even such odd catches as pinfish and hardhead catfish have been made by this writer with hair bugs. As long as the water is less than about three feet deep, they'll be effective on most gamefish.

Some fly tiers take tying with deerhair to a lofty art. Steve Bailey and Jim Stewart are two Florida tiers whose creations belong in an art museum more than at the end of a fishing line.

No one will tell you that about my flies. Industrial strength flies for me! But then, I hold that the most important judges of my tying work wear fins.

All of these styles are tied the same way. Once the hair is tied on the trim work determines the look of the finished product. You can cut the hair to form either a popper, a slider, or a diver, depending on which style you prefer.

Materials-

Hook- Mustad 3407 or equivalent, #4-3/0
Tail- tier's choice. Squirrel tail, either grey or red, accented with crystal flash and flanked by a pair of grizzly neck hackles is good.
Body- deer body or elk body hair, color tier's choice.

1) Sharpen the hook, crush down the barb, fix the hook in the vise, and start the tying thread.

2) If you want a mono loop weedguard, tie it in now.

3) Tie in your tail now, using the materials of your choice.

4) Get some coarse deerhair and cut out a good, thick clump. I like a clump thicker than a pencil. Hold the ends and pull out the fluff at the butts, then lie the clump atop the hook. The butts should be facing the hook eye and the ends extending back with the tail.

Wrap the thread loosely around the hair once, then on the second wrap crank down hard. If you're pulling hard enough you'll break the thread once in a while. I hold the hair in place while I do this so I get minimum spin. Although the best tiers do both, I'm a stacker, not a spinner. The hair should flare like crazy. This is good and exactly what you want.

Wrap the thread forward of the tie-in spot, push the hair toward the bend of the hook (use some force), and wrap the thread around the front of the hair two or three turns to lock it into place. You should be getting the idea that this is not a delicate operation.

5) Cut out another clump of deerhair about the same diameter as the first and treat it in a like manner, only this time face the ends of the hair towards the eye of the hook and the butts toward the rear. Again, use serious force to push the whole mass of hair toward the bend of the hook after you tie it in.

6) Continue cutting and tying in and pushing back the hair, alternating which way you face the ends, until you're almost out of room at the hook eye. At this point you should have a gross-looking, fuzzy mass on your hook. Pull the hair out of the way and tie in the weed-weedguard (if used), then whip and cement the head.

7) Take the fuzzball out of the vise and give it a hair cut. Be sure to cut the botton as close to the hook and as cleanly as possible. You want maximum hook gap in your creation. I use a fine-pointed pair of scissors for this, but some folks use a razor blade. Cut it until you get the shape you want. Although I like a blunt popping face, many fine anglers prefer the slider type, and still others want a diver. Trim the hair so as to get what you want.

### The Bolstad Popper/Diver (Sheldon Bolstad)

Deerhair intimidates some tiers, especially if they're just starting. Others, like myself, find what we think is a better mouse-trap. The foam flies of Sheldon Bolstad make producing a fish-catching popper or diver very simple.

You can buy the finished flies or just the heads (my choice)direct from Sheldon. If you buy the unfinished heads you just finish them yourself, any way you want to. Here is one way to finish the fly, whether it's a popper or a diver.

Materials-

-Foam popper or diver head on Mustad 3407, size 1.
-tying thread
-grizzly hackles
-bucktail (color tier's choice)

1) Sharpen the hook, crush down the barb, then place the hook in the vise. The head is already attached. Start the thread immediately behind the head.

2) Tie in one or two pairs of grizzly hackles for the tail.

3) Tie in a clump of bucktail to finish the tail.

4) Tie in a pair of long grizzly hackles and palmer them around the wraps of thread used to tie in the tail. Take them up as close to the back of the foam head, then tie them off. Whip finish and cement. Your fly is finished.

Sheldon Bolstad can be reached at:
3212 E. 52nd Street, Minneapolis, MN 55417

### The Surfin' Wooly (John Bottko)

Jacksonville fly tier, fisherman, and fly shop owner John Bottko likes the beach. He especially likes fly fishing from the beach. He developed this fly to take surf redfish after he found other flies just didn't sink quite fast enough, or present a big enough profile, to interest the fish. It's good anytime you need a bulky, fast sinking fly.

Materials-

-hook, Mustad 34011, size 2/0
-tail, bucktail in center with three hackles on each side and crystal flash on top. Color tier's choice, but white is probably most effective.
-body, Orvis deep water chenille with eight inches of .030 lead wire beneath and Palmered saddle hackle over.
-eyes, hollow plastic doll eyes.

1) Tie in thread, wrap back to bend of hook. Then wrap hook shank with fuse wire.

2) Tie in a clump of bucktail aproximately twice as long as the hookshank in at the bend of the hook. The butts should butt up against the lead wire wrap. Cement the hair into place.

3) Tie in three hackle feathers on either side of the bucktail. They should be splayed inward and the same length as the hair.

4) Tie in the flash on either side of the hackle feathers.

5)Palmer one hackle feather at the base of the tail.

6) Tie in the chenille at the base of the collar, then tie in the hackle feather for Palmering the body. Coat the fuse wire with cement, wrap the thread up to the eye, leaving space to finish the head. Wrap the chenille up to the thread and tie it off. Then Palmer the hackle up to the thread and tie it off. Whip finish and cement.

7) Trim hackle and chenille where the eyes are going to be placed. Apply a dab of Goop to the back of the doll eyes and cement them into place.

Your Surfin' Wooly is ready to fish.

### The Fuzzy Crab (John Kumiski)

Fish like crabs, and every Florida fly fisher should carry some crab imitations. This particular crab pattern is very easy to tie, and uses no buoyant materials. It casts well, and most importantly, is eminently acceptable to the most important judges- the ones with the fins. I call it the Fuzzy Crab- here's how to tie and fish it.

Materials-

Mustad 3407 or equivalent #6-#1
tan calftail
two small grizzly hackles
one large grizzly hackle
lead eyes (1/50 oz. for #6; 1/36 oz. for #4, 1/24th oz. for #2)
brown, tan, olive, or grey Furry Foam, cut to a square shape
tying thread

1) Start the tying thread and tie in the lead eyes behind the eye of the hook.

2) Wind the thread back onto the bend of the hook. Tie in a short piece of calftail, and flank it with the small hackles.

3) Remove the hook from the vise and turn it over (or spin your rotary). Tie in the large hackle such that you can palmer it towards the eye of the hook.

4) Fold the foam to form a triangle. Tie one point of the triangle in under the point of the hook so that it points toward the rear of the fly. The foam should be rolling up the bend of the hook towards the point.

5) Wind the thread to just behind the lead eyes. Palmer the hackle to the thread and tie off. Continue winding the thread to a point just behind the hook eye, leaving enough space to finish the head.

6) Pull the loose end of the foam up to the hook eye and tie it down. It compresses easily and will crush down nicely. Finish the head with a whip finish, and give a couple coats of cement.

7) The foam can be further trimmed with scissors if desired. A round or oval shape works well. Trim some of the hackle off the underside of the fly, leaving just enough sticking out from the sides to suggest legs.

To fish the fuzzy crab-

This is a crab, not a minnow, imitation. When cast, allow it to sink to the bottom. If the cast was accurate to a sighted fish, they'll often spot and gobble it before it hits the bottom. Strips should be kept very short, just enough to hop the fly along the bottom. Experiment with it in shallow water to get the right action.

When the fish takes it, they'll usually hold on for a few seconds due to the nature of the body material. This gives the angler adequate time to detect the strike and set the hook. Although I've had jarring strikes while fishing it, usually the take is gentle.

Tie up a couple of crabs for your next saltwater outing.

## The Rattlin' Minnow (Tom Jindra)

Although at first glance this fly looks like it's tied on a keel hook, it's actually a reverse tie on a 2X long shank hook. The design is clever. The fly incorporates a plastic rattle like those used in plastic worms, adding the element of sound. It has become one of my favorite subsurface minnow imitations for situations with low light or dirty water .

Lead eyes can be added if desired. I carry it unweighted, and also with 1/100th ounce and 1/50th ounce lead eyes. This makes it much more versatile. The unweighted versions can be used in skinny water or over thick grass, and the weighted models can be used in deeper water in channels, around oysters, over potholes, and other similar locations.

Although my favorite color combination is chartreuse over white, the color is the tier's choice. Use whatever shades suit your needs best. Here's how to tie it.

MATERIALS

Hook- Mustad 34011, 2X long, #2
Body- hollow braided Mylar tubing, color tier's choice, stuffed with a plastic worm rattle
Wing- bucktail or other hair, color(s) tier's choice
Lead eyes- 1/100th or 1/50th ounce (optional)

1) Sharpen the hook and crush down the barb, place in vice. If using lead eyes, tie them on top of the hook about 1/4 inch behind the hook eye.

2) Wrap the thread to the bend of the hook and down the bend a little way. Measure a length of the mylar tubing against the hook shank.

Cut off a little more than you'll need. Extend the mylar slightly behind where the thread stops and tie it in. The end of the tubing extending past the thread will unravel, making a sort of a tail.

3) Wrap the thread up the shank of the hook to a point behind the lead eyes (if you're using them) or to a point about 1/3 inch behind the hook's eye. Let the bobbin hang there while you prepare the rattle.

4) I use the rattles manufactured by Woodies Rattlers (14235 Winterset Dr, Orlando 32812). These are plastic and can be trimmed and filed somewhat. I like to get the point and sharp angles off of them with the file. I think it helps the fly's body last longer. After tapering it down a little, insert the rattle into the mylar tubing. Then tie off the open end of the tube with the thread. Coat the tube and hook shank with a coat of epoxy. Let the epoxy set until dry.

5) After the body dries take the fly out of the vice, turn it over, and put it back in. The wing is tied inverted, going up over the hook point. I usually tie in a small clump of white bucktail, then a small clump of crystal flash, then a small clump of chartreuse bucktail. Use whatever colors you like best. After the wing is tied in, whip finish and cement the head and the fly is ready to fish.

## The Seaducer (Homer Rhodes)

I do not know how this very effective pattern developed. My copy of J. Edson Leonard's FLIES contains this quote by Homer Rhodes:

"My favorite all-year fly is my Shrimp Fly that I developed nineteen years ago after taking my first bonefish. These flies have a yellow, barred rock, and white stiff neck feather (rooster) in each wing with a heavy salt and pepper yellow and white hackle."

The color plate in the book shows a dressing identical to that of the fly now called the Seaducer. Leonard's book was published in 1950. It seems pretty obvious that the pattern has been around for awhile, by more than one name.

The Seaducer works best in shallow water. Not only do the hackles greatly slow its descent, they also provide a measure of protection against grass fouling the hook. The feathers function as a weedguard. As mentioned earlier, some guides like this pattern tied with lead eyes to give it a jigging action.

The fly will take all of Florida's saltwater gamefish, excepting perhaps permit. I have not tried it on bonefish myself, but after rereading Homer Rhodes' description, I think I'll tie some up in #4 and #6 and try it on my next trip to the Keys.

There are many good color combinations for this fly. Like most lures, every angler has his own favorite color or combination of colors. Experiment to see which ones you like best. Be sure to carry both light and dark flies in different sizes.

Here is how to tie it.

MATERIALS

Hook- Mustad 3407 or equivalent
Wing- three or four pairs of neck or saddle hackles, tied in at bend of hook. Accent with crystal flash or flashabou.
Hackle- large neck hackles in complimentary or contrasting color wound palmer from bend of hook to head of fly.

1) Sharpen hook and press down barb, then affix in vise. Wrap thread to bend of hook.

2) Choose three or four pairs of matching hackles, color(s) your

choice. They should all be about the same length. Tie these in at the bend of the hook. I find it much easier to keep these lying correctly if I soak the butts in my mouth first, then tie them in. Coat the wrappings with nail polish, then tie in the flash.

3) Tie in a pair of large neck hackles at right angles to the hook shank and pointing away from you by wrapping the thread over the butts in an "X" pattern a few times. Coat the wrappings with nail polish.

4) Wrap the thread part of the way toward the eye of the hook, then wind the neck hackles around the hook palmer style. The fly will hold up better if you wrap the thread over the feathers a few times as you wind them. When you get to the hackle tips, tie off the first pair and tie in another pair. Repeat this step as many times as it takes (usually three or four) to get to the eye of the hook.

5) Once you run out of space in which to wrap more feathers, tie off the last pair of hackles, build up a bit of a head, whip finish and cement.

Your Seaducer is now finished and ready to fish.

*This Everglades tarpon fell for a yellow and grizzly Seaducer.*

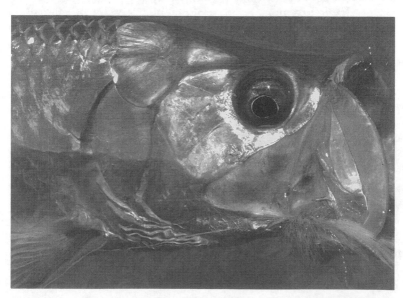

## Lefty's Deceiver (Lefty Kreh)

Of all the flies developed for use in salt water, this one more than any other is the universal baitfish imitation. Anyone examining any flyfisher's fly box will probably find this fly in various sizes and color combinations. We all use it!

The Deceiver may be tied as an imitator or an attractor fly. The length can be anything between two and fourteen inches. Color combinations could be anything from natural minnow colors to dayglow pink and green. The fly is not a specific pattern, but a method of tying.

When dressing this fly, remember that maintaining the minnow profile is important. For this, the wing must have enough bulk, usually six or eight saddle or neck hackles, and the collar must extend well past the bend of the hook.

Although the wing is normally tied with hackle feathers, marabou or synthetics like fishair could be substituted. Certainly by using synthetic materials a fly with a length in excess of twelve inches can be tied, making it useful even for large pelagic species like billfish.

Bucktail is normally used for the collar, often accented with flashabou or crystal flash. Marabou is also used as a substitute for bucktail in the collar. In addition to the collar, cheeks of various materials can be tied in, as can be herl as a topping. Don't make the dressing of the fly too full or it may not sink.

The fly I've described here is the "classic" Deceiver. Remember, feel free to substitute materials as suits your needs.

Materials-

HOOK- Mustad 3407 or equivalent
WING- three or four pairs of matched saddle or neck hackles tied in at bend of hook. Colors are tier's choice. The photo shows three pairs of white hackles topped by a pair of grizzly hackles.
COLLAR- Bucktail extending back well past the bend of the hook.
BODY- optional. The fly shown here lacks a body.

1. Sharpen the hook, mash the barb, and place it into the vise. Wind on the tying thread and wrap it to the bend of the hook.

2. Match three or four pairs of hackles (neck or saddle) and tie them in at the bend of the hook. Wetting the butts with saliva first will make tying them in easier. "Matching" in this case means by length, not by color. Colors may be freely mixed. Putting some cement on the wraps will insure the feathers remain in place.

3. Wind the thread to a point about one-third of the way behind the eye of the hook. Cut some bucktail of sufficient length to reach well past the bend of the hook and tie it in. I like to tie in three small bunches of bucktail- one on each side and one on top of the hook. Before tying in the final top bunch I tie in my flash.

4. If cheeks are desired, tie them in after the collar. A topping of peacock herl is another another nice touch. Whip finish and cement the head. If eyes are desired, wait for the cement to dry and paint them on. After the paint dries, cement the head again. The fly is now finished.

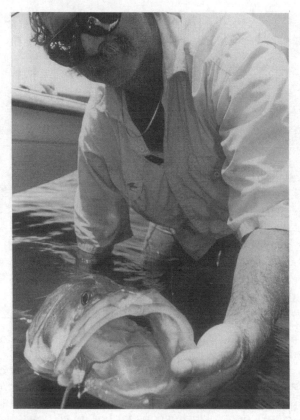

*A snook like this one can obviously take a large fly. Be sure to carry some!*

## Rabbit Strip Flies

Dave Whitlock likely had his hand in the development of this fly, originally designed to take largemouth bass. Certainly Whitlock has produced several different, related patterns, all of which have proved effective on largemouths.

Tarpon bunnies become more popular on Florida's flats every year. In addition to tarpon, cobia, snook, and redfish also find them to their liking. Few nonliving items suggest life more than a wet strip of rabbit skin sliding seductively through the water.

The fly can be tied weighted with lead eyes or bead chain, or left unweighted. Again, this depends on the angler's needs. With lead eyes tied on the top of the hook shank, the hook point will ride up. Equipped with a double mono loop weedguard, the fly like this

could be fished exactly like a plastic worm. Design the fly to fit your own particular needs.

This particular rabbit strip pattern is my own version. Feel free to substitute materials or add others (like flash) to get the effect you want. Just don't forget the rabbit strip!

Here's general instructions for how to tie one.

HOOK- tier's choice. Mustad 3407 is still a good all around hook.
TAIL- Rabbit skin with fur, length and color tier's choice. Purple, olive, brown, and black are all good.
WING- Marabou fibers, color tier's choice.
HACKLE- wide, webby neck hackles tied Palmer style. Again, the color is the tier's choice.
EYES- lead or bead chain, if desired.

1) Wrap the thread onto the hook. If eyes are desired, tie them on behind the eye of the hook, leaving sufficient room to finish the head. If the hook point is to ride down, tie the eyes under the hook. If the hook point is to ride up, tie the eyes on top of the hook. If a mono weedguard is desired (not shown), tie the mono in now.

2) Wind the thread to the bend of the hook. Leave the bobbin

hanging, and turn your attention to the fur strip. Cut it to the desired length. Keep in mind that a long soggy strip of rabbit skin is not the most aerodynamic creation ever devised- it can be difficult to cast. Taper one end of the strip to a point with the scissors, then tie the point on at the bend of the hook. If the fly is to ride hook point down, the fur should point up, and vice versa.

3) Dab the wraps with cement. Cut of two or three bunches of marabou fibers and tie them in just in front of where the strip is attached. Then tie in two long webby neck hackles in front of the marabou butts, and dab with cement.

4) Wind the thread up to the eyes (or near the hook eye if no eyes are used). Wrap the hackles up to this point and tie them off. Whip the head and cement and your leech is ready to catch fish.

### The Snapping Shrimp (Chico Fernandez)

Bonefish eat lots of different kinds of foods. Crabs, minnows, various types of marine worms, assorted molluscs, and all kinds of shrimp are greedily crushed and swallowed by hungry bones. One kind of shrimp that the bonefish particularly relishes ithe snapping shrimp. The fly that imitates it bears the same name.

Snapping shrimp are strange-looking little creatures. Small (a two incher is a big one) and brown, they bear a LARGE claw which can be as much as a third as long as the entire body. They can snap the claw shut to make an audible click. It's never happened to me, but I understand they can give a mean pinch with this appendage as well. The claw is tipped with bright orange- an important feature in the fly.

The snapping shrimp pattern was developed by Chico Fernandez to imitate this important bonefish food. Chico, knowing about that orange tip on the claw, added an orange tag to the fly to help fool the spooky bonefish.

Certain design features are found in most bonefish flies. They tend to be small, mostly tied on #6, #4, or #2 hooks. Smaller flies are generally used in shallow water for waking or tailing fish, where the larger patterns are used in deeper water or in muds. The wing is usually tied in a reverse style to help keep the hook point from fouling in the grass. If necessary, lead wire can be added to the body to sink them faster in deeper water. Lead eyes provide the same result.

Finally, the snapping shrimp pattern works on fish other than bonefish. I carry it in my winter redfish fly box, knowing that small dark flies often work better for cold water reds. Captain Rodney Smith of Satellite Beach tells me that he has great success off the beach on both pompano and whiting with this pattern. The orange tag imitates the egg sac found on sand fleas. Don't be afraid to try it on other species.

Hook- Mustad 3407 or equivalent, #2-6
Tag- medium orange chenille
Body- medium tan chenille
Wing- tan calftail with a grizzly saddle hackle tip on either side.

1) Sharpen the hook, press down the barb, and affix the hook in the vise. Wrap on the thread and wind it back to the bend.

2) Tie in a piece of orange chenille. Wrap the thread forward about 1/4 inch, then wrap the chenille forward two wraps. Tie it off, tie in the tan chenille, and wrap the thread up near the hook eye. Wrap the tan chenille up to the thread and tie it off. Be sure to leave room for the wing and the head.

3) Take the hook out of the vise and flip it over, then insert it back

into the vise. Cut off a clump of calftail about half the diameter of a pencil and pull out all the short hairs. When tying this in, the tips should extend past the point of the hook about 1/2". Slap some cement on the wraps to help hold the thing together. Pick two small grizzly hackles the same length as the wing. Match them up, wet the butts with some saliva, then tie them in too. The hackles should lie on either side of the hair wing.

4) All that remains is to touch some cement to the butts of the hackles, whip the head, and cement it. Your snapping shrimp is now ready to do battle.

## The Braided Cuda Fly

This is a fly that would give your average freshwater trout fishermen nightmares, or perhaps fits of hysteria. It looks like Bo Derek's hairstyle in the movie "10". But to barracuda it evidently bears some resemblance to a needlefish, and they love to eat the things. Here's how to tie one.

HOOK- Mustad 3407 (or equivalent), size 1-1/0.
TAIL- Ultra Hair or Fishair, color(s) tier's choice, four to eight inches long, braided. Choose bright, fluorescent colors for these.

BODY-Thirty pond monofilament, wrapped over the tying thread, wrapped over the butts of the tail material.
HEAD- Nylon thread, a complementing or contrasting color to the tail.

1) Sharpen the hook and crush down the barb, then affix it in the vise. Start the tying thread, then immediately lay a piece of 30 pound mono about 15 inches long on top of the hook shank. Wrap the tying thread over it back to the bend of the hook. The mono should extend out beyond the hook point, and will be used later.

2) Tie in the tail material at the bend of the hook. The butts should extend up to about 1/8 of the way behind the hook eye, leaving just enough room to tie off the head. Carefully wrap the thread over the tail material back up to near the eye of the hook. Coat these wraps with head cement.

3) Wrap the mono in tight spirals toward the eye of the hook. When it reaches the point where the body ends, tie it off. Make a smoothly tapered head, then whip finish and cement. Your fly body is finished, but the tails still needs work.

4) Separate the strands of the tail into three more or less even bunches. Don't get too worked up about this as the cuda aren't that fussy and once one eats it it will be finished anyway. These are definitely one fish flies. Braid the material, starting from the bend of the hook until you have an inch or two left unbraided at the end. Use monofilament to make a small uni-knot on the end of the braid, then coat it with head cement. This will hold the braid and keep it from coming out. Once the cement dries, the fly is ready to fish.

Before fishing this fly haywire twist a four inch section of thin single strand wire to the eye of the hook. Use an Albright special to attach a piece of 30 pound mono to the other end of the wire. You can tie a loop in the end of the mono and loop to loop it to the end of your leader, or simply blood knot it to the leader.

This fly has to be stripped FAST to entice strikes. Lots of fishermen will stick the rod under their armpit and use both hands to strip in order to get more speed. So this winter when the bonefishing is off and big cuda cruise the Keys flats soaking up sunshine, try throwing one of these strange looking flies at them.

*The upper tarpon fly here is a marabou version of the classic Cockroach.*

## The Cockroach Tarpon Streamer

Ask any ten fly fishermen what their favorite fly is and you're likely to get ten different answers. Ask any ten tarpon fishermen to name their top five flies though, and it is very likely you will hear "Cockroach" ten times. In saltwater fly tying, a field filled with innovation and experimentation, the Cockroach is as close to being a standard pattern as you are likely to find.

This pattern is used as a generic example of how to tie any tarpon pattern. Tarpon flies in general are simple to tie. While this particular fly uses a collar of squirrel tail, some tiers prefer Palmered hackle. Others like marabou. Still others combine materials used on the collar. Some people substitute a rabbit strip for the tail hackles, as in the Apte 2 tarpon streamer. Tie them how you like them!

Let's take a look at how to tie a Cockroach.

Materials:

HOOK- Mustad 3407 or equivalent, size 1/0 to 5/0. The hook shown is a Billy Pate tarpon hook by Wright/ McGill, size 3/0.
THREAD- the pattern calls for black. Many fishermen prefer bright orange tying thread though, because it makes the fly easier for them to see while it is in the water. Danville's flat waxed nylon works

wonderfully for all tarpon flies, and comes in a wide variety of colors.
WING- four pairs of matched grizzly neck hackles splayed out-
wards. Neck hackles will usually work better than saddles due to
their wider profile.

COLLAR- natural gray squirrel tail. Again, many tiers use different
material for the collar. Although the original recipe calls for grey
squirrel, some use red squirrel, others bucktail. You can use what
you like, but remember that there is something about squirrel tail
that fish find very attractive. Your Cockroach will be ready to fish as
soon as the cement dries.

1) Before putting the hook in the vise, get the file and sharpen it well.
Then put the hook in the vise and start the tying thread back near
the bend of the hook.

2) Find four pairs of matching grizzly hackles. Arrange the butts so
that four hackles on each side will splay apart after they've been tied
in. Wet the butts with saliva and tie them in at the bend of the hook,
then cement the wraps with head cement.

3) Take the squirrel tail and cut off a hank of hair about one third less
than the diameter of a pencil. Strip out all of the short underhairs.
Place the hair over the wraps holding the hackles, arranging it so
that it is evenly distributed around the shank of the hook, then tie it
in. Cement the wraps.

4) Use the tying thread to build up a tapered head, leaving bare
metal at the front of the shank. Then whip finish and cement. For
anglers who prefer to snell their flies to the shock tippet, this clean
space on the front of the hook is very important.

The fly is finished and ready to be attached to a shock
leader. The fly with leader attached is then kept in a tarpon box to
await use.

# LAST WORD

Florida has such incredible potential as a fishing destination, it's been sad to see the fisheries abuses that have occured over the past decade. Although snook and redfish populations are in good shape, seatrout populations in many parts of the state are in pitiable condition due to years of overfishing. The net ban should help a lot, but much more remains to be done.

Join the Florida Conservation Association, or the Florida League of Anglers, or the Federation of Fly Fishers, or your local fly fishing club, or all of these organizations. Recreational anglers are too disorganized to have anything near the political clout they deserve. Mark Sosin told me that at the congressional hearings on the Magnuson Act reauthorization he was the ONLY representative of 17 million recreational anglers. How many representatives from the commercial fishing industry were there? A heck of a lot more than one, I'm sure.

Consider the next generation of fly fishers and conservationists, too. Take a kid fishing. It could be your child, or a relative, or a neighbor, or your fishing club could hold a fishing day for kids. Children need to see the majesty of nature for themselves, and fishing is as good a way as any for them to learn about and become involved in preserving our tremendous natural heritage. Younger kids can fish with bait, and will want to learn about fly fishing as they get older. My two sons both tie flies (although they're pretty rough!) already. As I write this Alex is four, and Maxx is six. Maxx has caught fish on my fly rod (I cast, he retrieves). He tells me, "All I have to do is learn to cast and I'll be a six year old fly fisherman!"

Finally, remember courtesy and etiquette while out on the water. Treat other fishermen the way you'd like to be treated. And best of luck to you as you flyrod in Florida salt.

# APPENDIX
## Commercial Fly Tiers

The following people tie and sell flies for use in Florida saltwater. Many are excellent sources of information about fishing.

Ken Bay
145 N. Halifax Avenue, #106
Daytona Beach, FL 32118
(904)239-7164
Saltwater and freshwater flies, made to order.

Sheldon Bolstad
3212 East 52nd Street
Minneapolis, MN 55417
(612)722-5804
Sheldon produces unique foam poppers and divers, originally designed for smallmouth bass, which are very effective on several species of Florida saltwater fish.

Joe Branham
3903 Bend Drive
Valdosta, GA 31602
(912)247-4702
Joe's specialties include epoxy flies, destination selections, all types of saltwater flies. Joe's fly designs have been featured in most of the major saltwater fly fishing magazines.

Mike Eaddy
3740 NW 61st Place
Gainesville, FL 32653
(904)372-2967
Mike's work is highly recommended.

Terry Friedrich
3440 Royal Oak Drive
Titusville, FL 32780
(407)269-9808
Terry ties commercially for many shops. Additionally, he is extremely knowledgeable about surf fishing with fly tackle at the Canaveral National Seashore.

Charlie Heartwell
25 Panorama Way
Beverly, WV 26253
(304)636-6272
Charlie ties all kinds of flies, from trout to billfish. His work is highly recommended.

Steve Kilpatrick
7117 SW Archer Road #2203
Gainesville, FL 32608
(904)378-5069
In addition to flies, Steve also produces custom fly tying benches and accessories.

David L. Rabe
817 Riverside Drive
Milford, OH 45150
(513)831-2484
David ties both freshwater and saltwater flies, custom or traditional.

Jim Stewart
1104 S. Dunbar Avenue
Tampa, FL 33629
(813)287-2761
Jim ties the most unbelievably well done hair bugs (he calls them hair plugs!) that you will ever see. He has a minimum order and a long waiting list.

John O. Thompson
2457 Tree Ridge Lane
Orlando, FL 32817
(407)657-4737
John ties a wide variety of saltwater flies, including foam poppers and sliders. He also makes the highest quality wooden custom tying benches, lead eye painters, fly drying racks, tarpon boxes, leader stretchers, and other tying and fishing accessories.

## FLY TACKLE MANUFACTURERS AND SUPPLIERS

Get all of these catalogs and spend some money! Failure for a company to be listed here results more from an error on my part than any other reason.

Abel Reels
165 Aviador Street
Camarillo, CA 93010
(805)484-8789

The Bass Pond
PO Box 82
Littleton, CO
800-327-5014
Bass Pond has a huge selection of fly tying materials.

Cabela's
812 13th Avenue
Sydney, Nebraska
800-237-4444
Cabela's has everything for the fly fisher.

Cortland Line Company, Inc.
3736 Kellogg Road
PO Box 5588
Cortland, NY 13045-5588
(607)756-2851

Feather Craft Co., Inc.
PO Box 19904
St. Louis, MO 19904
800-659-1707
Fly fishing outfitters, fly tying and rod building supplies.

Fenwick
5242 Argosy Avenue
Huntington Beach, CA 92648
(714)897-1066

Fin-Nor Corp.
2021 SW 31st Avenue
Hallandale, FL 33009-2031
(305)966-5507
Makers of fine fly (and other) reels and fishing accessories.

Fisher Graphite and Fiberglass Fishing Rods and Blanks
PO Box 3147
Carson City, NV 89702
(702)246-5220

G. Loomis Saltwater Fly Rods
1359 Downriver Drive
Woodland, WA
800-662-8818

Islander Reels
6771 Kirkpatrick Crescent
Saanichton, BC Canada V8M IZ8
(604)544-1440

Kaufmann's Streamborn
PO Box 23032
Portland, OR 97281-3032
(503)639-6400
Outfitters, trips, flies, and tackle.

L.L. Bean, Inc.
Freeport, ME 04033
800-221-4221
Bean has everything for the fly fisher.

Lamson USA
PO Box 469
Redmond, WA 98073
(206)881-0733
Manufacturers of the Lamson fly reels.

McKenzie Fly Tackle Co., Inc.
1272 River Road
Eugene, OR 97404
(503)689-8371
Manufacturers of artificial flies.

O. Mustad and Son (USA) Inc.
PO Box 838
Auburn, NY13201
(315)253-2793
Manufacturers of fish hooks.

Offshore Angler, Inc.
1935 South Campbell
Springfield. MO 65898
(417)887-1915
They have a good line of saltwater fly fishing tackle.

Orvis, Inc.
Historic Rt. 7A
PO Box 798
Manchester, VT 05254-0798
800-548-9548
Orvis has everything for the fly fisherman.

Penn Fishing Tackle Mfg. Co.
3028 W. Hunting Park Ave.
Philadelphia, PA 19132
(215)229-9415
Penn makes a full line of quality fly (and other) rods and reels.

Plano Molding Company
Plano, IL 60545-1601
(708)552-3111
Plano makes tackle boxes. You need some to carry those flies!

Redington Fly Rods, Inc.
2324 SE Indian Street
Stuart, FL 34997
(407)220-8108
Redington makes a rod unconditionally guaranteed for 25 years.

Ross Reels
One Ponderosa Court
Montrose, CO 81401
(303)249-1212

Sage Fly Rods
8500 NE Day Road
Bainbridge Island, WA 98110
800-533-3004

Scott Hand Crafted High Performance Fly Rods
89 Monroe Center
Grand Rapids, MI 49503
(616)456-5103

Seamaster Fly Reels
16115 SW 117th Avenue Suite A-8
Miami, FL 33177-2408
(305)253-2408

Shakespeare Fishing Tackle Division
3801 Westmore Drive
Columbia, SC 29223
(803)754-7000
Shakespeare makes two lines of fly rods as well as the venerable
Pflueger Medalist fly reels.

St. Croix of Park Falls Limited
PO Box 279
Park Falls, WI 54552
(715)762-3226
St. Croix carries several lines of fine fly rods.

STH Reels
PO Box 816
Marathon, FL 33050
800-232-1359
STH manufactures the popular STH cassette fly reels.

3M/Scientific Anglers
3M Center, Building 223-4NE
St. Paul, MN 55144-1000
800-525-6290
Makers of Scientific Anglers fly lines and System fly reels.

Umpqua Feather Merchants
PO Box 700
Glide, OR 97443
800-322-3218
Suppliers of fishing flies and leaders.

Teeny Saltwater Fly Lines
Teeny Nymph Co.
PO Box 989
Gresham, OR 97030
(503)667-6602

Thomas and Thomas Rodmakers, Inc.
2 Avenue A
Turners Falls, MA 01376
(413)863-9692

R.L. Winston Rod Co.
Drawer T
Twin Bridges, MT 59754
(406)684-5674

World Wide Sportsman, Inc.
PO Box 787
Islamorada, FL 33036
(305)664-4615
Outfitters, tackle, and trips around the world.

## The Federation of Fly Fishers and its Florida Affiliates

The Federation's motto is "Conserving- Restoring- Educating through Fly Fishing". Their long term goal is, and I quote: "The Federation of Fly Fishers will be a world leader for fly fishing for all species in all waters."

The Federation offers a lot of member benefits for very reasonable yearly dues. If you are interested enough in fly fishing to have read this book, you will benefit from belonging to the FFF. The address: Federation of Fly Fishers, PO Box 1595, Bozeman, MT 59771. Their phone number is 1-800-618-0808.

The Federation has many fly rod clubs as affiliates in the state of Florida. If you're in town on the night they have their meetings, stop in. You can meet many of the members and maybe get an invitation to fish with them! Their addresses are listed below. Local fly shops can often put you in touch with one of the members.

Backcountry Fly Fishers
PO Box 584
Naples, FL 33939

Backcountry Flyfishing Association of Altamonte Springs
PO Box 150442
Altamonte Springs, FL 32715

Backcountry Fly Fishing Association of Brevard County
PO Box 524
Melbourne, FL 32902

Emerald Coast Flyrodders
PO Box 1131
Ft. Walton Beach, FL 32549

First Coast Fly Fishers
PO Box 56696
Jacksonville, FL 32223

Fly Fishers of Northwest Florida
PO Box 10151
Pensacola, FL 32524-0151

North Florida Fly Fishers
PO Box 7044
Gainesville, FL 32605

Southwest Florida Fly Fishers
1349 Sunrise Drive
Ft. Myers, FL 33903

St. Andrews Fly Fishers
PO Box 20133
Panama City, FL 32407

Suncoast Fly Fishers
PO Box 9794
Tampa, FL 33674

Tampa Bay Fly Fishing Club
8702 N. Rome Ave.
Tampa, FL 33604

Treasure Coast Fly Rod Club
521 North 2nd St.
Ft. Pierce, FL 34984

## The Florida Conservation Association (FCA)

The FCA was instrumental (along with Florida Sportsman magazine) in generating the popular support which led to the passage of Amendment 3, the ban on entanglement nets in state waters. The FCA has been at the forefront of legislative fisheries conservation in Florida for at least a decade now. Friends don't let friends fish without belonging to FCA!

Anyone interested in fisheries conservation in Florida owes it to themselves to join FCA. At 25 bucks a year, it's a cheap investment in your fishing future. Not only that, you'll receive six issues of the award-winning TIDE magazine a year and other benefits. Tell them Kumiski sent you.

Florida Conservation Association
1890 Semoran Boulevard
Suite 237
Winter Park, FL 32792
(407) 672-2058

## The International Game Fish Association (IGFA)

The IGFA keeps track of all the world records caught on all the different types of tackle, both all-tackle and line class world records. If you have any interest in setting any world records, belonging to IGFA is a MUST. Their annual World Record Game Fishes book is worth the cost of membership in itself.
The International Game Fish Association
1301 East Atlantic Boulevard
Pompano Beach, FL 33060
Phone (305) 941-3474

## The Florida League of Anglers (FLA)

The FLA is another group active in fisheries conservation. They publish a monthly newsletter that keeps members abreast of the latest fisheries news from around the state.
Florida League of Anglers
PO Box 1109
Sanibel, FL 33957-1109

## Where To Purchase Nautical Charts

Anyone going boating in Florida needs National Oceanic and Atmospheric Administration (NOAA) nautical charts. Most marinas and many fly shops carry them, but anyone towing a boat down from out-of-state may want to have them in hand first. All the NOAA charts can be purchased through the mail or over the telephone from:

NOAA
National Ocean Service
6501 Lafayette Drive
Riverdale, MD 20737-1199
(301)436-6990

# INDEX

accessories, 20
Alafia River, 190
alligators, 39
Anastasia State Park, 112
anchors, 34
Angler's Image, 184, 188
angling techniques, 41
Anna Maria Island, 190
Apalachee Bay, 206
Aucilla River, 207

backing, 13
Backcountry Fly Shop, 135
Bahia Honda Key (and State Park), 159, 164
Baker, Capt. Lee, 148
Banana River, 121, 127
Banana River Manatee Refuge, 121
barracuda, 66
Bathtub Beach, 138
Bayou Chico, 225
Bayou Texar, 225
Bayport, 197
Bear Lake Canoe Trail, 152
Big Lagoon, 225
Big Lagoon State Recreation Area, 228
Big Manatee River 190
Big Mud Creek, 137
Big Pine Key, 164
Bimini twist, 13
Bird Tower, 207
Biscayne Bay, 146
Biscayne National Park, 147
black drum, 68
Blacks Rock, 207
Blind Pass, 191
blind-casting, 49
bluefish, 69
boats, 31
Boca Chica, 165
Boca Grande, 181
Boggy Bayou, 221

Bolin, Capt. Frank, 114
Bolstad poppers/divers, 240
bonefish, 70
bonito, 75
Bottko, John, 110, 241
Bradenton, 186, 190
Braided Cuda Fly, 225
Busciglio, Capt. Tommy, 161

C-11 canal, 142
C-13 canal, 142
C-14 canal, 142
Caloosahatchee River, 181
Canaveral National Seashore, 116
canoes, 34
Cape Sable, 152
Cape San Blas, 212
"Captain Blood", 218
Captain Harry's Fishing Supply, 198
Captain Joe's Ultimate Angler, 218
Captiva Island, 177
Cardenas', Jeffrey, Saltwater Angler, 167
Carlisle's Tackle, 170
Carysfort Reef, 170
Casa Cola Creek, 112
Cayo Costa State Park, 184
Cedar Key, 202
Cero mackerel, 81
Charlie Richter's Fly Shop, 148
Chico Bayou, 221
Chittum, H.T. & Co., 157
Choctawhatchee Bay, 220
Choctawhatchee River, 221
chumming, 51
Clam Pass, 174
Clapboard Creek, 108
Clearwater Pass, 191
Clouser Deep Minnow, 236
Cobbs Rock, 207
cobia, 76, 108
Cockroach Bay, 191
Cockroach tarpon streamer, 257
Cocoa, 127

Cogburn's Clothing Company, 218
Collier-Seminole State Park, 175
Constable, Capt. Butch, 140
Content Keys, 159, 165
Coogler's Beech, 197
Crystal River, 196
cuda fly, 255
Cutcheons, Capt. Marshall, 167

Darby, Paul, 223
Daytona Beach, 116
Deceiver, 249
Deep Point, 225
deerhair bugs (flies), 237
Destin, 220
Destin Fishing Hole, 223
Dollar Bay, 173
dolphin, 77
Dortch, Capt. Buddy, 218
double surgeon's knot, 28
double surgeon's loop, 24
Dunedin, 190
Dunedin Pass, 191
Dunlap, Capt. Joy, 220
Dupre, Capt. Jim, 204

East Bay, 215
East Coast Outdoors, 114
East Creek, 112
East Flats, 206
East Pass, 220
Economy Tackle, 188
Elbow Reef, 156
electric motors, 34
Elliott Key, 147
Elliot Point, 220
Ersch, Capt. Eric 125, 129
Escambia Bay, 225
Everglades Angler, 170, 175
Everglades City, 169
Everglades National Park, 151, 169, 170

Fairbanks, Capt. J.R., 144
Fecher, Capt. Ray, 167
fighting fish, techniques, 64

files, hook sharpening, 20
first aid, 39
Fishing Unlimited, 184
Flamingo, 151
flies-
    selection, 229
    tying, 233
    materials, 233
    weedguards, 235
Florida Bay, 151
Florida Keys Outfitters, 158
flounder, 108
Fly Fisherman, The, 124
Fly Shop of Fort Lauderdale, 144
Fornabio, Capt. Charlie, 135
Fort DeSoto Park, 190
Fort Island Gulf Beach, 191, 196
Fort Lauderdale, 142
Fort Pickens Pier, 226
Fort Pierce Inlet, 137
Fort Walton Beach, 220
Fuzzy Crab, 243

Gasparilla Island, 181; State
    Recreation Area, 184
Gentile, Capt. Gregg, 140
Geroy, Capt. Todd, 175
Gordon Pass, 173
Grand Lagoon, 215
Grande Bayou, 220
Grassy Key, 159
Gray, Capt. Bobby, 227
Gray's Tackle & Guide Service, 227
Greenan, Capt. Pete, 184, 186
Guana River State Park, 108, 110
Guerin, Capt. Mike, 167
guides, 35
Guinta, Capt. John, 213
Gulf Islands Natioanl Seashore, 226, 227
Gulf of Mexico, 177, 190, 197, 206, 212, 215, 220

hair bugs, (flies), 237
Half Hitch Tackle, 218
Hampton, Capt. Billy, 200

Harry Goode's, 129
Harry Harris Park, 155
Harris, Capt. Ken, 167
Hawkins, Capt. Paul, 193
hazards to fishermen, 37
Hillsborough River, 190
Hinrichs, Warren, 108
Hobe Sound National Wildlife
        Refuge, 138
Hoffman's Bayou, 225
Hofmeister, Capt. Scott, 140
Holliday, Capt. Mike, 140
Homosassa, 196
Honeymoon Island, 190, 193
hooks,
        barbless, 232
        sharpening, 232
House of Refuge, 138
Huff, Capt. Steve, 161
Hufnagle knot, 26
Hurricane Pass, 191
Hutchison Island, 137

inproved clinch knot, 21
Indian River, 121,127, 132, 133
insects, biting and stinging, 37
Intracoastal Waterway, 112, 116,
        117, 142, 173, 220
Islamorada, 155

Jack crevalle, 78
Jacksonville, 108
John's Guns & Fly Fishing, 209
Johns Pass, 191
Johnson Bay, 173
jonboats, 33

Kantner, Capt. Steve, 144
Kee (Keewaydin) Island, 174
Key Biscayne, 146, 147
Key Largo, 155, 156
Key West, 164
king mackerel, 81
knots-
        Albright special, 25
        Bimini twist, 22

double surgeon's, 28
double surgeon's loop, 24
haywire twist, 25
Hufnagle, 26
improved clinch, 20
snelling a hook, 28
uni-knot, 20
Kokomon's Tackle Outlet, 184
Kumiski, Capt. John, 124


LMR Fly Shop, 142
ladyfish, 80
Lake Worth, 142
leader stretchers, 17
leaders, 14-
        fluorocarbon, 15
        formulas, 15
        pretied, 15
        wire, 17
Lefty's Deceiver, 249
Lehr's Economy Tackle, 179
Leisure Time Fly Shop, 200
Lido Key, 186
lightning, 38
line-to-leader connections, 14
lines, 12
Little Duck Key, 159
Little Manatee River, 190, 193
Little Mud Creek, 137
Little Talbot Island State Park, 109
Locke, Capt. Tommy, 184
Locklear, Capt. Mike, 200
Long, Capt. Jim, 200
Long Key State Park, 155, 159
Long Point Park, 132
Longboat Pass, 186
Lower Keys, 164

mackerel, 81
Mangrove Outfitters, 170, 175
Marathon, 155
Marquardt's Marine, 213
Mason's Creek, 197

Matanzas Inlet, 112
Matheson Hammock, 146
McNichols, Capt. Joe, 170
Melbourne, 127
Merritt Island, 127; National Wildlife
      Refuge, 123, 125
Mexico Beach, 212
Miami, 146
Middle Keys, 159
Miller, Capt. Bill, 193
Missouri Key, 159, 164
Mosquito Lagoon, 116, 121
Moss, Capt. Ray, 184
motors, electric, 34
Moultrie Creek, 112
Mr. CB's Bait & Tackle, 186
Mullet Key, 190
Myakka River, 181

Naeve, Capt. Brandon, 188
nail knot,14
Naples, 173
Nassau Sound, 109
New Smyrna Beach, 116
North Bay, 215

Oak Hill, 121
O'Bannon, Capt. Phil, 184
Old Pass, 215

Pallot, Capt. Flip, 150
Palm Beaches, 142
Palm Coast, 112
Panama City, 215
Parsons, Capt. Terry, 135
Pass-a-Grille, 191
Pass Buoy #24, 207
Peace River, 181
Pellicer Creek, 112
Pennekamp, John, State Park, 157
Pensacola, 225
permit, 84
Pierce, Capt. Tom, 135, 167
Pine Island (Homosassa), 197
Pine Island Sound, 177, 181
Pinellas Point, 190

Playalinda Beach, 124
pliers, 20
Point Crisp, 186
Point O'Rocks, 186
Ponce Inlet, 116
Port Canaveral, 122, 128
Port Orange, 116
Port St. Joe, 211
Puopolo, Capt. Glenn, 175
pushpoles, 34

Quality Reel Repair, 223
quick release clip, anchor, 34
Quick Reference Guide, 101
Quilligan, Capt. Denis, 193

rabbit strip flies, 251
Ragland, Capt. Nat, 161
Rattlin' Minnow fly, 244
Rebeck, Capt. Ron, 119
redfish, 86, 108
reels, 11
Rehr, Capt. Mike, 179, 184
Rock Garden, 207
Rocky Bayou, 220
rods, 10
Rookery Bay, 173

Saddlebunch Keys, 165
St. Andrew's-
      Bay, 215
      Pass, 215
      State Park, 216, 218
St. John's River, 109
St. Joseph-
      Bay, 211, 215
      Peninsula State Park, 216
St. Lucie-
      Inlet, 137, 138
      River, 137, 138
St. Marks, 206-
      River, 206
      National Wildlife Ref., 206
St. Martin's Aquatic Preserve, 196
St. Petersburg, 190
Salt Creek, 112

Saltwater Angler, 167
Salty Feather Fly Shop, 110
San Carlos Bay, 177
Sanibel Island, 177
Santa Rosa-
        Island, 220
        Sound, 225
Sarasota, 186
Satellite Beach, 124
Schmidt, Capt. Mark, 167
Sea Boots Outfitters, 167
Seaducer Fly, 247
searching, techniques for, 42
seatrout, 87, 108
Sebastian-
        Inlet, 132
        River, 132
Seven Mile Bridge, 164
Shalimar Yacht Basin, 223
Shallow Water Outfitters, 184
sharks, 39, 89
Shell Island, 216
shock tippets, 16
Shoreline Park, 225
Siesta Key, 186
sightfishing, 44
Simpson Creek, 108
Sister's Creek, 108
Smith, Capt. Joe III, 218
Smith, Capt. Rodney, 125, 129, 135
snapper, 92
Snapping Shrimp Fly, 253
snook, 92
Southern Angler, 139
Space Coast, 121
Spanish Harbor, 165-
        Bridge, 165
        Channel, 165
Spanish mackerel, 81
Sporting Classics, 193
Spruce Creek, 116
Stagg, Capt. Bruce, 157
Stickney Point, 186
stingrays, 38
String, Capt. Ray, 188
stripping baskets, 20

Stuart, 137
sunburn, 37
Surfin' Wooly Fly, 241

Tackle Box, The, 204
Tallahassee, 206
Tampa, 190
tarpon, 94
Tarpon Belly Keys, 165
Tarpon Fly, Cockroach, 257
Taylor, Capt. Ben, 157
teasers, 50
techniques, fishing, 41
Ten Thousand Islands, 169
Thousand Islands, 127
Titusville, 121
Tolomato River, 112
Towers K, S, O, 207
tripletail, 98
Tropical Outfitters, 139
Trosset, Capt. Bob, 167
tuna, 99

Underwood, John, 206
Upper Keys, 155

Vaughn, Capt. Michael, 167
Venice, 186

Wabasso Bait & Tackle, 135
waders & wading gear, 30
wading, 52
Wakulla Beach, 206
Ware, Capt. Mike, 218
Weber, Capt. Jim, 148
weedguards, 235
Weedon Island, 190, 193
West Bay, 215
West Flats, 206
Whale Key, 186
White Key, 186
White Point, 220
Williams, Capt. Bruce, 220
World Class Angler, 161
World Wide Sportsman, 157
Zwick's Channel, 187

# Come On Down and Enjoy Exceptional Angling with Captain John Kumiski!

Some of Florida's finest saltwater fishing occurs in the Indian River Lagoon system. Consisting of the Mosquito Lagoon, the Indian River, the Banana River, and various feeder streams, the 156 long mile estuary offers anglers a wealth of opportunities. Trophy redfish, seatrout, snook, tarpon, jack crevalle, and many other species of fish challenge the angler seeking a variety of action.

It's a four season fishery, too. While chill winds blast the northern part of the country, fishermen in Florida sometimes enjoy the hottest fishing of the year. Summer months provide some incredible angling action to those willing to face the heat. Spring and fall are often the most exciting times of all to fish, with large-scale baitfish migrations putting hungry predators on the prowl.

Capt. John provides only custom trips. Pick your species (within season) and how you would like to fish. Fly, spin, or plug, bring your favorite outfit along or he'll supply tackle for you. We also supply lunch (full day trips only) and all licenses. Fish from a skiff, or a canoe, or wade, or combine different methods on one trip.

He even offers a unique trip by canoe into the Banana River Manatee Sanctuary to those in good physical condition. Since motors of any kind are prohibited in the refuge, it receives a lot less fishing pressure than other nearby waters. Although fishing can be spectacular here, this trip is only for those in good physical condition who like to paddle!

Another custom trip John offers is a completely outfitted backcountry fishing/camping trip in Everglades National Park. You can leave out of either Chokoloskee or Flamingo, and many different options are available. Call for more information.

Of course, John provides instruction to those who request it. A full-time science teacher for many years, John combines his knowledge of fishing with his skills as an instructor to provide the finest outdoor learning experiences. He holds an FFF Fly Casting Instructor certification.

In addition to the fishing, Florida's wildlife helps to provide an extraordinary aesthetic experience. Wading birds commonly observed include snowy egrets, reddish egrets, great blue herons, white and glossy ibis, and roseate spoonbills. We see dolphins on almost every trip, and often see manatees, too. One creature sometimes observed who has a little more sinister reputation is the American Alligator.

So come fishing with Captain John. He'll do everything we can to show you the most enjoyable angling experience ever. Of course children are welcome, too!

For more information write us at P.O. Box 940153, Maitland, FL 32794-0153, or call/fax at (407) 834-2954, or E-mail at CIS 73742,100. We look forward to fishing with you!

## TRIP OPTIONS:

| What and Where | Tackle | Time of Year |
|---|---|---|
| Sight-fishing for REDFISH-<br>-Mosquito Lagoon<br>-Indian River (also snook and baby tarpon in summer)<br>-Banana River (also snook and baby tarpon in summer) | Fly, spin, plug | ALL |
| Baby Tarpon, Sebastian River | Fly, spin, plug | Summer |
| Port Canaveral Smorgasbord<br>-day, many different species available<br>-under lights at night | Fly, spin, plug | Summer, fall |
| Cape Canaveral<br>Jacks, Spanish mackerel,<br>  cobia, tripletail | Fly, spin, plug | Summer, fall |
| Indian River Power Station<br>ladyfish, crevalle, sometimes<br>  snook and baby tarpon | Fly, spin, plug | Late fall, winter,<br>early spring |
| Banana River Manatee Refuge<br>Redfish, seatrout<br>Black Drum<br>snook, baby tarpon, crevalle, | Fly ONLY | All year<br>all year<br>winter<br>summer |

This trip is by canoe- for those in good physical condition ONLY.

Everglades National Park- by special arrangement ONLY.

**INCLUDED** in the fee of $300.00 per day (most trips):

-boat (Dolphin Backcountry 16', or MonArk 14', or Old Town Tripper canoe)
-Licenses
-tackle, lures, flies, bait, etc.
-lunch

3/4 day and 1/2 day trips also available.

**ANGLERS should bring a hat, polarized sunglasses, and sunscreen.**

Anglers wishing to bring their own tackle should consult the follwing list:

Fly Tackle

9' rod, 8 or 9 weight, w/ matching reel containing a MINIMUM of 100 yards of Dacron backing and a floating weight forward line.
Flies- Bring the following flies if you'd rather use your own.
-Clouser deep minnow, size 2, chartreuse & white
-Clouser deep minnow w/ small eyes, brown, #4 (winter)
-popper or hair bug, #2-1/0, color irrelevant
-seaducers, red & white and yellow & grizzly, #2 or 1
-Deceivers in your favorite colors, size 2 and UP! Off the beaches the cobia and jacks hit really big flies!
-crab pattern, Merkin or fuzzy crab, #2 or 1, brown, gray, or olive
-Any other saltwater favorites you may have.

Spinning Tackle

6-7' rod with matching reel with 150 yards MINIMUM of new 8-12 pound test.

Equivalent type of plug tackle.

## About the Author

**JOHN A. KUMISKI** is a U.S. Coast Guard licensed captain and inshore fishing guide. His award-winning writing and photography appear regularly in Saltwater Fly Fishing, American Angler, Florida Sportsman, Tide, the FFF Quill, and other outdoor publications. He is the author of Flyrodding Florida Salt- How and Where to Catch Saltwater Fish on Flies in the Sunshine State, Saltwater Fly Fishing, and Fishing the Everglades- A Complete Guide for the Small Boater.

Some of the organizations he belongs to include the Florida Guides Association, the Florida Conservation Association, the International Game Fish Association, the Federation of Fly Fishers, the Florida League of Anglers, the Florida Outdoor Writers Association, the South Eastern Outdoor Press Association, and the Outdoor Writers Association of America. He holds a flycasting instructor certification from the FFF, and is a two term past president of the Backcountry Flyfishing Association of Altamonte Springs.

# Resource Catalog- INFORMATION!
## from Argonaut Publishing Company

## FLYRODDING FLORIDA SALT- How and Where to Catch Fish on Flies in the Sunshine State by Captain John Kumiski

Do you like fumbling around when fishing new areas, trying to fit all the pieces together so you can find and catch fish? This book contains everything you need to fly fish successfully almost anywhere along the lengthy Florida coastline. The book is divided into three main sections:

-the first solves the problem of "how-to" by explaining what tackle to use, which techniques to try, and what types of fish you can expect to catch;

-the second solves the "where-to" problem by featuring interviews with dozens of Florida's top fly fishing guides. In these pages they reveal their favorite spots and how to fish them, including many of their closely guarded secrets;

-the third solves the "with what?" problem, and features detailed instructions on how to tie up a selection of flies guaranteed to work in most Florida waters.

The appendix features a list of commercial fly tiers, complete with names, addresses, phone numbers, and specialties. Also included is a list of fly tackle manufacturers and suppliers, and a list of FFF affiliated fly fishing clubs in Florida, as well as many other conservation groups.

*"The best part of Flyrodding Florida Salt is the extensive where-to-go section that blankets the coast by area with not only tips on specific fishing spots, but areas for wading, boat fishing, best flies and techniques, access, local fly shops, guides, and other attractions and accommodations. For any saltwater fly rodder living in Florida or going there sometime, this practical guide is a must-read."*
**-C. Boyd Pfeiffer**

**Before YOU visit the Sunshine State, GET THIS BOOK!!!**

JK-03..............................................................................$27.97

## FISHING THE EVERGLADES- A COMPLETE GUIDE FOR THE SMALL BOATER by John A. Kumiski

A sprawling wilderness area with marine habitat consisting largely of shallow salt water and mangrove forests, newcomers often find the Everglades intimidating. Hidden within the mazes of flats, bays, creeks, channels, and mangrove islands lie the feeding areas of the gamefish for which the Everglades are famous- snook and tarpon, redfish and seatrout, sharks, snapper, sheepshead, and many others. How can these fish be found? What techniques are used to take them?

Boats are the vehicles for exploring the Everglades. Small boats. Hand powered and motor driven craft both have their place here. An enterprising angler with a small boat, some time, and a sense of adventure can learn to fish successfully in the park. How? **Fishing the Everglades- A Complete Guide for the Small Boater** is a resource by John A. Kumiski which explains the secrets of finding and catching fish in Everglades National Park. The book discusses such vital topics as tackle selection (both fly and conventional), effective lures and natural baits, knots and rigging, tactics and techniques, and boating and camping in the park. Further, the book is a complete trip planning guide, whether the intention is a day trip or a two week long expedition.

If you're even thinking of visiting the Everglades, you need this book!

JK-01...............................................................................$12.95

## AN IMPORTANT NEW BOOK ON SALTWATER FLY FISHING!!!

**Saltwater Fly Fishing- Tackle and Techniques for Fly Fishing Coastal Bays, Inshore and Offshore** by **Captain John A. Kumiski** is a valuable new guide for coastal flyrodders of all backgrounds that delivers a delightful blend of inshore and offshore fly rod how-to. From light rods for seatrout, school stripers, bluefish, weakfish, snook, bonefish, and redfish to powerhouse tackle designed for taming huge tarpon and yellowfin tuna, it's all here in one easy-to-read collection of tips, tricks, and techniques that will please fly fishermen everywhere. Tackle, rigging, and casting tips are quickly followed by in-depth chapters on flats and inshore fishing that includes proven methods used by fly fishing guides.

Over two dozen of the best fly patterns are included with detailed tying instructions and background on where, when, and how to best fish them. Close up photos show exactly how these flies are tied.

A generous selection of photos and illustrations show how to rig fly tackle, leaders, and tippets for all types of saltwater fly fishing, how to cast effectively, and how to read the water to find more fish.

**Saltwater Fly Fishing** is published by the Fisherman Library. If you want to know more about fishing saltwater with the long rod, you need this book! Write or call and order your copy today!

JK-02..................................................................................$18.95

### The Indian River Flats Fishing Guide- Oak Hill to St. Lucie Inlet by **Martin Smithson**

Do you feel like you don't know where to start when you're fishing a new area? Do you want to fish (and catch) in the extensive Indian River system?

Marty Smithson has assembled a series of over 60 aerial photographs of the entire Indian River Lagoon system, giving a bird's eye view of all the hot spots. Several well known Indian River guides, including Mark Nichols of DOA Lures, Captain Gregg Gentile, Captain Terry Parsons, Captain Bill Rogers, and Captain Frank Catino share favorite fishing locations and techniques. Location maps show the locations of grass beds and one chapter tells how to protect those grass beds while fishing. There's plenty of how-to information included, too, and revealing, easy to read information on the biology of trout, snook, redfish, and tarpon.

If you ever fish in the Indian River Lagoon, this book is a must-have for your library. Published by Fishsonian Publications.

MS-01.................................................................................$14.95

### A FISHERMAN'S GUIDE TO MARTIN & ST. LUCIE COUNTIES by **Robin Smillie**

The St. Lucie River has the BEST snook fishing in Florida. It also has plenty of big tarpon, jack crevalle, and seatrout. But if you want to fish there successfully, you need to know where to go!

Robin Smillie pinpoints the best places to fish, almost to the point of telling exactly where to put your bait. A Fisherman's Guide has maps and directions to many secret honey holes, bridges, piers, boat ramps, canals and locks, beach access, and the inlets. It also contains information on species identification, fishing tips, best baits, rigs, and tackle, some information on local history, and a discussion of which tides are the best ones to fish and why.

For anyone visiting this area, this book is the next best thing to chartering with Captain Gregg Gentile. Highly recommended.

RS-01.................................................................................$11.95

## FISHING IN THE FLORIDA KEYS AND FLAMINGO
by **Stu Apte**

Fishing the Florida Keys is **the** classic where-to book on light tackle fishing in the Florida Keys. If you're thinking of going there, you need it, and that's that. Does Stu have the qualifications to write a book like this? He lived in the Keys for years and was one of the most sought-after professional guides, fishing such other legends as Al McClane and Joe Brooks. He's also held 44 different world records.

This little gem contains tips from Stu on light tackle fishing, offshore fishing, backcountry know-how, and charts which clearly show where the best fishing spots are. It belongs in every Florida angler's library.

SA-01.................................................................................$6.95

## THE COMPLETE GUIDE TO FLORIDA KEYS FISHING-
## BOOK 1, INSHORE FISHING
## BOOK 2, OFFSHORE FISHING
by **Robert Lewis Knecht**

Mr. Knecht has created what may become a modern classic on fishing in the Keys. Knecht owns Key Largo Bait and Tackle (the famous Yellow Bait Shop). After years of answering the same questions over and over and over again, he got smart and wrote this amusing and extremely informative book.

The inshore book covers bridge, creek, and dock fishing; Aida and Coleman lantern repair; lobstering and shrimping in the Keys; rigging live baits; and how to throw a cast net. Captain Mark

Krowka, an IGFA world record holder, also wrote a chapter on flats fishing in Biscayne Bay, Key Largo, and Flamingo. Knecht's bizarre sense of humor makes the book a genuine pleasure to read. Highly recommended.

RK-01.................................................................................$7.95

The offshore book covers terminal tackle for offshore fishing; fishing patch reefs; reef fishing; deep water fishing; trolling; drifting; catching and rigging live bait; and shark fishing. Again, it's a very amusing and very informative book.

RK-02.................................................................................$9.95

## THE FLORIDA ATLAS AND GAZETTEER
from **DeLorme Mapping**

Are you tired of getting lost trying to find those out-of-the way fishing spots? The Florida Atlas and Gazetteer solves your problem! Containing detailed road maps of the entire state, this book is an invaluable resource when finding your way from point A to point B on Florida's highway system is your highest priority.

DL-FL...............................................................................$16.95

## COASTAL LORAN & GPS COORDINATES
by **Captain Rodney and Susie Stebbins**

Here at last is the book fishermen, divers, boaters, and all who navigate the nation's waters have been looking for! For fishing and diving this is the electronic navigator's bible. Fifteen years in the making, this book lists thousands of accurate and seperate LO-RAN-C and GPS coordinates for the entire U.S. seaboard, Great Lakes, Gulf of Mexico, Florida Keys, Dry Tortugas and the Caribbean along with the Islands from the Bahamas to the Virgins, including Puerto Rico. If you own a LORAN-C or GPS then you need Coastal Loran & GPS Coordinates!

S-LGC..............................................................................$29.95

**CAMPSITE TO KITCHEN- Tastes and Traditions from America's Great Outdoors.** Produced by the **Outdoor Writers Association of America**

Campsite to Kitchen teems with the bounty of the great outdoors as it guides you through memorable and savory recipes. Nationally recognized outdoor writers light the fires of hunting and fishing camps with stories of days gone by and traditions that will outlive us all.

Sample Crappie Croquettes, Quail on the Half Shell, Cooter Soup, and Old Fashioned Persimmon Pudding, to name just a few of the tempting recipes shared by these experts.

Set your sights on good times, and take your family on a fun filled adventure from Campsite to Kitchen.

WC-09...............................................................................$15.95

## FLORIDA SPORTSMAN FISHING CHARTS

Florida Sportsman Fishing Charts reveal hotspots learned over the years by the fishing experts at *Florida Sportsman* Magazine, clearly marked on a copy of a NOAA chart. They hold nothing back, giving you hundreds of locations and vital information on seasons, methods, and baits. Quite simply, these charts will help you catch more fish. Each chart is coated and comes in a protective plastic zip-top envelope. Highly recommended.

FS-699 Stuart/Ft. Pierce
FS-700 Ft. Lauderdale/Palm Beach
FS-701 Greater Miami
FS-702 Upper Keys and Florida Bay
FS-703 Lower Keys and Key West
FS-704 Flamingo, Everglades National Park
FS-705 Ten Thousand Islands
FS-707 Greater Tampa/St. Pete

Each Florida Sportsman chart...............................................$6.95

## SPECIAL REPORTS

Special Reports provide the detailed how-to and where-to information you need in order to step into a new area or situation and fish confidently and successfully.
Special Reports-- $6.00 each, or three for $14.00

-How to Find and Catch Bonefish on Long Key...................SR-LK
-How to Find and Catch Bonefish at Pennekamp State Park..SR-KL
-Fishing Keys Bridges.........................................................SR-KB
-How to Find and Catch Fish at Flamingo, Everglades National Park..................................................................................SR-FF
-Day Trips for Canoeing Anglers from Flamingo, Everglades National Park..................................................................SR-CF
-How to Find and Catch Backcountry Snook from Flamingo, Everglades National Park...............................................SR-FS
-Fishing The Cape Sable Area, Everglades National Park...SR-CS
-Fishing Chatham Bend, Everglades National Park............SR-CB
-Fishing Lostman's River, Everglades National Park...........SR-LR
-How to Find and Catch Redfish in Nassau Sound..............SR-NS
-Fishing for Redfish in Jacksonville's Backcountry..............SR-JR
-How to Find and Catch Redfish at the Merritt Island National Wildlife Refuge................................................................SR-MI
-Fishing at Ponce Inlet and New Smyrna Beach, Canaveral National Seashore........................................................SR-NS
-Fishing the Banana River Manatee Refuge.......................SR-MR
-Tactics for Sebastian River Tarpon....................................SR-SR
-How to Find and Catch Fish in Bull Bay, Charlotte Harbor...SR-CH
-Fishing Captiva Pass and Redfish Pass...........................SR-CP
-How to Find and Catch Pine Island Redfish.......................SR-PI
-Fishing at Cayo Costa State Park......................................SR-CC
-Constructing Saltwater Fly Rod Leader Systems...............SR-LS
-Practical Fly Selection for Florida's Saltwater....................SR-SF
-Getting Started in Saltwater Fly Fishing............................SR-GS
-A Primer for Waders........................................................SR-PW
-How to Increase Your Ability to See Fish...........................SR-HS
-How to Fight Fish Successfully with Light Tackle................SR-FF
-Practical Tips for Redfish on the Surface...........................SR-RT
-Fly Fishing for Jack Crevalle...........................................SR-JC
-Orlando as a Fishing Destination......................................SR-OF
-Getting Started in Tying Flies for Saltwater.......................SR-FT
-Improve Your Fishing Photography...................................SR-FP

**Sawyer Solutions:**
### A Practical Guide to OUTDOOR PROTECTION

Enjoying the outdoors begins with knowing how to be there safely. <u>Sawyer Solutions: A Practical Guide to Outdoor Protection</u> gives you straightforward answers to questions about prevention and treatment of threats to outdoor peace of mind. Reviewing the information and safety suggestions in this guide will surely enhance your outdoor experience.

Full of prevention and treatment tips plus background information on bites, stings, and skin care, this little book belongs in every outdoor lover's library.

SS-01 .................................................................................$9.99

**Headstart Fishing Handbook**
by **W. Horace Carter** and **Bud Andrews**

This all-new, comprehensive primer for beginning anglers and their parents contains 440 pages of lessons, techniques, and advice. Pulitzer Prize winning journalist W. Horace Carter teamed up with big bass world champion Bud Andrews to produce this guidebook to family outdoor adventures. The <u>Headstart Fishing Handbook</u> teaches today's kids to enjoy fishing tomorrow!

HC-01 ...............................................................................$16.95

---

### OUR GUARANTEE-

Our business is built on service. We want you to be 100% satisfied. If a book doesn't meet your expectations, return it to us for a refund. Please follow the directions below.

### RETURNS POLICY

You may return any book provided it is in the same condition in which it was sent to you. Please enclose a copy of your invoice/receipt and a brief explanation for the return. Sorry, no returns on Special Reports.

### SEND AN ARGONAUT PUBLISHING COMPANY GIFT CERTIFICATE!

An Argonaut Publishing gift certificate is a quick and convenient gift for that special person who loves fishing. To order, just enclose a check, money order, or bank card number with expiration date. Mark "Gift Certificate" on the order form, along with the recipient's name and address and the amount. We'll send them a certificate, a card, and a current copy of our catalog.

---